is book is to be returned on or before

N or

WOMEN
AT THE
PODIUM

WOMEN
AT THE
PODIUM

MEMORABLE SPEECHES
IN HISTORY

SELECTED AND INTRODUCED BY

S. MICHELE NIX

HARPER RESOURCE
An Imprint of HarperCollins*Publishers*

Grateful acknowledgment is made to reprint the following:

Dolores Ibárruri. From *Dolores Ibárurri: Speeches & Articles 1936–1938.* © 1938. Reprinted by permission of Lawrence & Wisehart, Ltd.

Margaret Thatcher. Reprinted by permission of Margaret Thatcher.

Elizabeth II. Reprinted by permission of Elizabeth II. Buckingham Palace, London.

Gloria Steinem. Reprinted by permission of Gloria Steinem.

Dorothy Thompson. © 1937 by Dorothy Thompson. Reprinted by permission of McIntosh & Otis, Inc.

Clare Boothe Luce. Reprinted by permission of the Henry Luce Foundation, Inc.

Katharine Graham. Reprinted by permission of Katharine Graham.

Ayn Rand. Reprinted by permission of the Executor, Estate of Ayn Rand. © 1982 by Leonard Peikoff, Executor, Estate of Ayn Rand. All rights reserved.

Benazir Bhutto. Reprinted by permission of Benazir Bhutto.

Diana, Princess of Wales. Reprinted by permission of The British Royal Family. Buckingham Palace, London.

HarperCollins books may be purchased for educational, business, or sales promotional use. For information please write: Special Markets Department, HarperCollins Publishers Inc., 10 East 53rd Street, New York, NY 10022.

FIRST EDITION

Printed on acid-free paper.

Designed by Michael Mendelsohn at MM Design 2000, Inc.

Library of Congress Cataloging-in-Publication Data has been applied for.

ISBN 0-380-80286-4

00 01 02 03 04 RRD 10 9 8 7 6 5 4 3 2 1

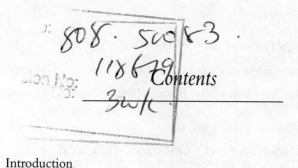

Contents

Introduction   1

PART 1
TO ARMS AND ARMISTICE

Boadicea Summons Her Soldiers to Battle (61)   11

Bloody Mary Inveighs Against Wyatt's Rebellion (1554)   13

Queen Elizabeth I Braces Her Troops for the   17
  Spanish Armada (1588)

Anna Dickinson Thunders for the Union Cause (1863)   19

Emmeline Pankhurst Recruits for the Great War (1914)   23

Helen Keller Calls for a Strike Against War (1916)   26

Dolores Ibárruri Inflames the Spanish Civil War (1936)   33

Madame Sun Yat-sen Accepts the International   36
  Stalin Peace Prize (1951)

Golda Meir Appeals for Reconciliation (1957)   41

Margaret Thatcher Marshalls Support for the   44
  Falklands War (1982)

PART 2
PLEDGES OF ALLEGIANCE AND PATRIOTISM

Empress Theodora Stands Her Ground (532)   53

Queen Elizabeth I Delivers a Reproof   55
  to Her Parliament (1566)

Frances Wright Defines Patriotism (1828)   59

Princess Elizabeth Makes a Vow to the British Empire (1947)   63

Margaret Thatcher Hails a New Britain (1982)   67

PART 3

TRIBUTES AND COMMEMORATIONS

Julia Ward Howe Praises Poet Oliver Wendell Holmes (1879)   73

Mary Lease Extols the Virtues of Kansas (1893)   77

Voltairine de Cleyre Memorializes the   83
Haymarket Martyrs (1900)

Jane Addams Salutes George Washington (1903)   87

Queen Elizabeth II Remembers the Year that Was (1992)   93

PART 4

SPEECHES ON SOCIAL JUSTICE

Maria Stewart Calls for the Upliftment of Her Race (1832)   99

Angelina Grimké Speaks Above the Shouts of an   106
Angry Mob (1838)

Frances Harper Advocates Liberty for Slaves (1857)   113

Zitkala-sä Speaks to the History of Native Americans (1896)   117

Mother Jones Exhorts the Miner to His Duty (1902)   124

Margaret Chase Smith Denounces McCarthyism (1950)   128

PART 5

SPEECHES ON WOMEN'S RIGHTS

Elizabeth Cady Stanton Keynotes the First Women's   137
Rights Convention (1848)

Sojourner Truth Asks a Pointed Question (1851)   143

Abby Kelley Foster Blasts Passivity and Laziness (1851)   146

Lucy Stone Speaks as a Disappointed Woman (1855)   153

Sojourner Truth Keeps Things Stirring (1867)   157

Elizabeth Cady Stanton Sees the Male Element as a   160
Destructive Force (1868)

Susan B. Anthony Defines "Citizenship" Under the   164
Constitution (1872)

Frances Willard Makes a Plea for "Home Protection" (1876)   167

Belva Lockwood Calls Forth History (undated)   171

Emmeline Pankhurst Exhorts British Women to Be   177
Militant (1912)

Jeannette Rankin Urges a "Small Measure of Democracy"   180
for Women (1918)

Hillary Rodham Clinton Honors the First Women's Rights   186
Convention (1998)

PART 6

SPEECHES TO THE COURT

Hortensia Speaks Before the Roman Tribunal (42 B.C.)   201

Emma Goldman Addresses Her Jury (1917)   204

Elizabeth Gurley Flynn Disputes the Smith Act (1953)   211

PART 7

DECLARATIONS OF THE FOURTH ESTATE

Dorothy Thompson Chides Hitler's Definition of a Free   219
Press (1937)

Clare Boothe Luce Takes the American Press to Task (1960)   226

Katharine Graham Gives a Vigilant Press Its Due During   238
Watergate (1974)

PART 8
POLITICAL SPEECHES

Anna Howard Shaw Parodies Emotionalism in Politics (1913) — 251

Lady Astor Reflects on Women in Politics (1922) — 254

Clare Boothe Luce Delivers Her "G.I. Joe and G.I. Jim" Speech (1944) — 261

Eleanor Roosevelt Defends the United Nations (1952) — 270

Barbara Jordan Argues for the Impeachment of Richard Nixon (1974) — 276

Margaret Thatcher Takes Up the Leadership of Her Party (1975) — 282

Shirley Chisholm Says Vote for the Individual, Not the Party (1978) — 287

Jeane Kirkpatrick Excoriates the San Francisco Democrats (1984) — 294

PART 9
COMMENCEMENTS

Gloria Steinem Defines a New Kind of Humanism (1971) — 303

Ayn Rand Makes the Case for Philosophy (1974) — 315

Barbara Bush Triumphs at Wellesley (1990) — 324

Madeleine Albright Speaks to the Nationalist Impulse (1994) — 329

PART 10
RELIGIOUS SPEECHES

Mary Baker Eddy Preaches the Doctrine of Christian Science (1895) — 339

Maude Royden Preaches to the Newly Enfranchised (1920)   345

Elizabeth Dole Finds Lessons in the Story of Esther (1987)   350

Benazir Bhutto Labels Discrimination and Intolerance   360
as Betrayers of Islam (1995)

PART 11
FAREWELLS AND TRANSITIONS

Elizabeth Woodville Grey Entrusts Her Son to the   367
Archbishop of Canterbury (1483)

Lady Jane Grey Speaks from the Gallows (1554)   370

Queen Elizabeth I Presents Her Golden Speech (1601)   372

Maria Stewart Bids Farewell to the Podium (1833)   377

Kate Richards O'Hare Gives the Farewell Address of a   382
Socialist (1919)

Princess Diana Seeks a More Private Life (1993)   386

Select Bibliography   389

Acknowledgments   395

Index   397

Introduction

A great speech reaches far beyond the podium. It rouses its audience. It lingers in the mind. Sometimes it shakes the welcoming hand of history, which is how it finds it way into anthologies such as this. The speeches presented here belong to some of history's most influential women: royals and revolutionists, suffragists and social reformers, legends of politics and the press. Some of these speeches changed the course of events by swaying people to battle or to the vote; some framed the debate on our most important social and political issues; some are treasures of wit and poetry that the mind can take in as art; but all bear witness to the vast contributions women have made to oratory. With mindful words, Margaret Thatcher calmed a country at war. With impassioned voice, Elizabeth I called her soldiers to it. Sojourner Truth asked the question: "And ain't I a woman?"

For centuries, women fought just to be heard. "Speak softly and carry a big lipstick" is one of history's long-running themes that a woman should not speak in public. Women did, of course, but not in great numbers and often at great risk. History tells us of Hortensia and a few other women who bravely spoke during ancient times and a few learned women of the Renaissance, who delivered Latin orations to intimate audiences or spoke to the public through writings. There is Elizabeth I, who left us the recorded and commanding orations of a self-assured ruler. We know of Deborah Sampson, who, disguised as a man, fought during the Revolutionary War and later spoke publicly in defense of her actions. We know of exceptions, in other words: women who defied convention to be heard above societies that, for much of history, denied them the platforms that led to public expression—the pulpit, the bench, the political soapbox—even the basics of citizenship, education, and work. It wasn't until the nineteenth century, with trails first blazed by Frances Wright, Maria Stewart, and the Grimké sisters, and on their heels Susan B. Anthony and Elizabeth Cady Stanton, that women began to take to the podium in number, shocking society and, with even greater audacity, demanding their rights.

By the twentieth century, women could make public speeches without apology, usually without fear, though there was still the lingering sense of novelty, and, well into the mid century, the question of decorum: "A woman's place in public is to sit beside her husband, be silent, and be sure her hat is on straight," Bess Truman said. But as generations of Lady Astors, Clare Boothe Luces, and Barbara Jordans entered politics; as Golda Meir, Margaret Thatcher, and Benazir Bhutto assumed the bully pulpit, women were no longer driven away from the podium but, at last, invited to it.

That's a brief history of a long struggle—during which, many speeches by women went unrecorded. Others sit unearthed and unappreciated in archives, untranslated for Western consumption, excerpted in the odd biography or, in some speech anthologies, limited to the albeit important but narrow category of women's rights. In this first-ever collection of speeches by women throughout history, my aim is to broaden the categories of selection, as best possible, and showcase the many moving, eloquent, and sometimes controversial words of women that have spirited audiences, inspired action, or defined the great occasions of history.

A speech is meant to be heard not read. But as we will find many speeches read like great literature, thrilling the mind's eye in ways that place the speaker before us. "In the recorded orations," wrote poet and lecturer Julia Ward Howe in 1900, "the flying word is made to remain, the fleeting impression reproduces itself; we live for the moment the life of days long vanished."

To read these speeches is to find ourselves standing in the great Byzantine palace hall as Empress Theodora, despite news of an approaching rebel force, resolves never to leave her home; kneeling at Whitehall as the Virgin Queen delivers her last major speech to the realm; listening with the crowd at Franklin Hall as Maria Stewart urges her race to rise above servitude; and peering over the shoulder of Madame Sun Yat-sen as she decries "American aggression."

We hear the whispers of "Don't let her speak!" aimed at Sojourner Truth and the cheers bestowed Jane Addams as she honors George Washington. We imagine the austere face of Margaret Chase Smith as she denounces McCarthyism and the outstretched hand of Golda Meir as she pleads for peace. We're on the march with Susan B. Anthony and on the hustings with Lady Astor.

The moments are vivid, as Boadicea stirs for battle from an open field in ancient Britain; as Lady Jane Grey readies for death on the gallows; as Princess Diana returns the stare of cameras and asks for "a more private life." We see slavery through the descriptive speech of Frances Harper; the Haymarket Riot through the eyes of Voltairine de Cleyre; the Spanish Civil War through the battlecry of Dolores Ibárruri; and Watergate through the determined words of Barbara Jordan and Katharine Graham.

But why restrict ourselves to the role of observer? As Anna Dickinson, we can shake our fists in the air as we recruit for the Civil War; as Angelina Grimké, we can duck rum bottles as we defy a proslavery mob; as Maude Royden, we can hear our voice bounce off stained glass as we preach from the pulpit; and as Dorothy Thompson, we can pound the lectern as we rail against Hitler.

Some of our speakers take on heated issues still in debate:

Clare Boothe Luce critiques the American press; Eleanor Roosevelt defends the United Nations; Madeleine Albright warns of the dark side of nationalism. Still other speakers wheedle their audiences with humor and wit, as we see in Anna Howard Shaw's parody of the political convention, Julia Ward Howe's tribute to poet Oliver Wendell Holmes, and Barbara Bush's commencement address at Wellesley.

There are many oratorical styles represented in this collection—everything from the homespun to the direct to the high falutin', everything from the quietly spoken to the spirited, speeches said with arms waving, feet stomping, and crowds cheering. And yet, in a book that sweeps across generations, that draws from every point of power and privilege, no one style necessarily trumps another. Each speech found here is compelling, stirring, or eloquent for its own reason. Sojourner Truth's speeches are rustic but dropped jaws with deadpan honesty. Princess Diana's speech is a simple press statement, devoid of flourish, but packed with emotion and made powerful looking back from a tragedy. Mary Lease's salute to Kansas is grandiloquent—yet vivid and forceful and extolled by her nineteenth-century audience as "the finest piece of word painting we have ever seen."

When it comes to delivery, some speakers pull from the gut, others from the heart, and others from the moment at hand. It was the resolve of Empress Theodora in crisis that made her speech sing: "May I never be deprived of this purple robe, and may I never see the day when those who meet me do not call me empress." It was the sheer nerve of anarchist Emma Goldman that silenced a courtroom: "Gentlemen of the jury, most of you, I take it, are believers in the teachings of Jesus Christ. Bear in mind that he was put to death by those who considered his views as being against the law." It was the unshaken assurances of Margaret Thatcher that steadied Britain at war: "Let us, then, draw together in the name, not of jingoism, but of justice."

There's no getting around it, however: Oratory is a learned art. Or as Emerson famously said: "All the great speakers were bad speakers at first." Even the great orator Demosthenes, at one time despondent that he was losing audiences to "drunken sots, mariners, and illiterate fellows," realized the need for practice. So did Elizabeth I, who wrote out many of her speeches—revising, rehearsing, memorizing—before addressing her Parliament. Anna Howard Shaw sermonized alone to the trees, until laws allowed her into the ministry. Maude Royden, also a preacher but first a suffragist, perfected her skill as an outdoor speaker, which meant, she said: "You must stand up in a chair on a street corner in London and say to two children and a dog, 'People of England!' And, oh, I do assure you that is a difficult thing to do."

In her first attempts at speechmaking, Eleanor Roosevelt broke in midspeech in a fit of giggles, until she learned to control her nerves. And Margaret Thatcher, deemed shrill by the press, took voice lessons to lower her pitch.

Still, the women in this book offered their audiences more than just well-delivered speeches. Within this collection we see the powerful force of well-chosen words. Each speech here has a message, clearly conveyed. Some of these speeches shine with imagery, repetition, and cadence. Some draw eloquence from language that is simple and direct.

Many speeches here are trenchant, argued with emotionally charged words. We see this in Clare Booth Luce's "G.I. Joe and G.I. Jim" speech, as she assails the "unheroic Roosevelt Decade: a decade of confusion and conflict that ended in war"; Margaret Thatcher's attack of the Labour Party—politicians, she said, "trying to prove their Socialist virility by relentlessly nationalizing one industry after another"; and Jeane Kirkpatrick's Republican keynote, as she skillfully disarms "the blame America first crowd." Luce biographer Wilfred Sheed believes Clare's early training in politics left an indelible mark, "so that the various other things you can do with rhetoric besides sneering, brow-beating, and sounding noble had to come later" and that her career as an orator might have benefited from "saner origins." Perhaps so, but I say bless those origins, and her talent, for they combined to make a punchy, effective, and accomplished speaker.

Luce suffered for her choice of words, however. When push came to rhetorical shove, she was "The Candor Kid." Margaret Thatcher, for her outspokenness, swatted the barb of "Attila the Hen" and, courtesy of the Soviet Press, earned the moniker the "Iron Lady," which she used to skillful advantage. "I stand before you tonight," she said at a 1976 gala, "in my red chiffon evening gown, my face softly made up, my fair hair gently waved . . . the Iron Lady of the Western World! Me? A Cold War warrior? Well, yes—if that is how they wish to interpret my defense of values and freedoms fundamental to our way of life."

That's one of Thatcher's more memorable quotes. Great speakers often leave us humming a tune of lines and phrases. Think of Churchill's "blood, toil, sweat and tears," Martin Luther King Jr.'s "I Have a Dream," Thatcher's stern retort: "The lady's not for turning." Here, we find Queen Elizabeth I's "I have the heart and stomach of a king" speech; again, Sojourner Truth's "Ain't I a Woman?"; Dolores Ibárruri's "They shall not pass!"; Thatcher's "Falklands Factor"; and Queen Elizabeth II's "*annus horribilus*," among others.

Today's term for the memorable phrase is "soundbite"—the line of speech captured on a ten-second media newsclip. Many speech enthusiasts lament the beating eloquence takes in the electronic age. And yet the breadth of media has exposed contemporary leaders to audiences vastly larger than any Demosthenes ever could have imagined. That's the paradox: as the art declines, the audience grows. Still, even though "plainspeak" has replaced a grander style, every generation seems to mourn the erosion of rhetoric, of public debate, of speechmaking. Modern oratory endears itself to history with age.

Many leaders aspire to have their speeches "endeared"—their words remembered in history books—analyzed as brilliant and Lincolnesque. Others, if their gaze is where it should be, focus on their audiences in the here and now. In either case, we see a greater reliance on speechwriters.

Speechwriting is a craft as old as oratory itself: Seneca helped Nero. Alexander Hamilton helped George Washington. Elizabeth Cady Stanton helped Susan B. Anthony. Theodore Sorenson helped John F. Kennedy craft some of history's finest and most celebrated speeches, and Peggy Noonan did the same for Ronald Reagan. Speechwriters today help leaders meet the need for fresh material in the face of a dizzying multiplication of media and recycled broadcasts. What makes these collaborations work as they should? Good speakers will involve themselves in the speechwriting process and make the words their own: "Speechwriting was for me," wrote Margaret Thatcher, "an important political activity. As one of my speechwriters said, 'No one writes speeches for Mrs. Thatcher: they write speeches with Mrs. Thatcher.' Every written word goes through the mincing machine of my criticism before it gets into a speech."

And that is how it should be—because in the end, speakers alone shoulder the speech. They stand unaccompanied on stage with nothing but the spoken word as art. And though some speakers fritter away those moments—reflexing at the podium with pedantic prose, hollow delivery, rhetorical flourishes with no heft—others sway us with words that are meaningful and relevant, and delivered with ringing conviction.

The women in this book understood the power of oratory. They used it to cast down enemies, turn wars, blaze opportunities, honor the lost, and lighten moments. They used it to shape the political and moral forces that define us. From the podium, they swashbuckled. And no matter what their chosen subject, they were unfailingly witty, insightful, articulate, controversial, inspiring, or moving about it.

My hope is that you will marvel as much as I have these achievements. After all, it's easy to see where this proud beginning has led—to a century where the novelty of a woman speaking in public has worn off and the demands for her leadership have never been greater.

PART 1

TO ARMS

AND

ARMISTICE

Boadicea Summons
Her Soldiers to Battle

" . . . we must conquer or die."

Trenchant, charismatic, memorialized in British history books, Boadicea was queen of the Iceni, a tribe that lived in ancient Britain in the time of Roman Emperor Nero. Widowed in the year 60, Boadicea was flogged and her daughters raped when she protested the seizure of her lands and wealth by a local Roman governor—but she gained vengeance in one of the bloodiest battles of Britain.

The Roman general, Suetonius Paullinus, was away in the north attacking the Druids when the dreadful news came; the queen's men had slaughtered nearly 70,000 Romans. Paullinus returned, readying for attack on an open plain that would pit his army of scarcely 10,000 soldiers against Boadicea's 100,000 rebels. It was the year 61, and the Britons, heady with their previous victory, brought their wives and children to witness the carnage, placing them in wagons at the field's border.

With her two daughters by her side, the queen—tall, with long fair hair, harsh voice, and spear in hand—rode by chariot among her troops to speak to the souls of her men.

It will not be the first time, Britons, that you have been victorious under the conduct of your queen. For my part, I come not here as one descended of royal blood, not to fight for empire or riches, but as one of the common people, to avenge the loss of their liberty, the wrongs of myself and the outrages of my children.

The wickedness of the Romans is at its height, and the gods have already begun to punish them, so that instead of being able to withstand the attack of a victorious army, the very shouts of so many thousands will put them to flight. And, if you, Britons, would but consider the number of our forces, or the motives of the war, you will see that in this battle we must conquer or die.

Is it not much better to fall honorably in defense of liberty, than be again exposed to the outrages of the Romans? This is a woman's resolve. As for you men, you may, if you please, live and be slaves.

The queen's disorganized rebels were no match for Paullinus's skilled army. The Britons scattered and fled, only to be hemmed in by their own wagons. As the massacre ensued, Boadicea, distraught by defeat and the prospect of capture, poisoned herself.

Bloody Mary
Inveighs Against Wyatt's Rebellion

" . . . fear them not; for I assure you, I fear them nothing at all."

Here is Mary I—calm, deliberate, and refusing to blink as Sir Thomas Wyatt and his rebels take positions near the outskirts of London. The first woman to rule England in her own right, the only surviving child of King Henry VIII and Catherine of Aragon, Mary (1516–1558) suffered heartbreak when her father sought divorce from Catherine and chose to "quit Rome." Young Mary was forever separated from her mother and forced to acknowledge her illegitimacy and renounce Catholicism.

In 1553, at age thirty-seven, she assumed the crown of England after the death of her half-brother, Edward VI, and an unsuccessful attempt to put Lady Jane Grey on the throne—but her proposed marriage to twenty-six-year-old Philip of Spain and the prospect of a Spanish alliance left the nation uneasy and provoked Wyatt into action. This speech, delivered on February 1, 1554, and reconstructed by sixteenth-century historian John Foxe, reveals the resolute queen at Guildhall, assuaging all fears of her marriage and exhorting her subjects to "pluck up" their hearts and "stand fast against these rebels," which they did; Wyatt's insurrection was crushed, and Mary married Philip II on July 25, 1554.

Unfortunately, Mary's reign, which began with the restoration of papal supremacy and laws against heresy, brought three years of religious persecution. Rebels were hanged and heretics burned at the stake, a cruelty that gave rise to her now-famous sobriquet "Bloody Mary." Meanwhile, husband Philip, quickly estranged, drew England into war between Spain and France in 1557. Mary lost Calais and the favor of her people and was lonely, ill, and childless—and dead in less than a year. Enter the reign of Gloriana, Elizabeth I.

———•◦•———

I am come unto you in mine own person, to tell you that, which already you see and know; that is, how traitorously and rebelliously a number of Kentishmen have assembled themselves against both us and you. Their pretense (as they said at the first) was for a marriage determined for us: To the which, and to all the articles thereof, ye have been made privy. But since, we have caused certain of our privy council to go again unto them, and to demand the cause of this their rebellion; and it appeared then unto our said council, that the matter of the marriage seemed to be but a Spanish cloak to cover their pretended purpose against our religion; for that they arrogantly and traitorously demanded to have the governance of our person, the keeping of the Tower, and the placing of our councillors.

Now, loving subjects, what I am, ye right well know. I am your queen, to whom at my coronation, when I was wedded to the realm and laws of the same (the spousal ring whereof I have on my finger, which never hitherto was, or hereafter shall be left off), you promised your allegiance and obedience unto me. And that I am the right and true inheritor of the crown of this realm of England, I take all Christendom to witness. My father, as ye all know, possessed the same regal state, which now rightly is descended unto me: and to him always ye showed yourselves most faithful and loving subjects; and therefore I doubt not, but ye will show yourselves such likewise to me, and that ye will not suffer a vile traitor to have the order and governance of our person, and to occupy our estate, especially being so vile a traitor as Wyatt is; who most certainly, as he hath abused mine ignorant subjects which be on his side, so doth he intend and purpose the destruction of you, and spoil of your goods. And I say to you, on the word of a prince, I cannot tell how naturally the mother loveth the child, for I was never the mother of any; but certainly, if a prince and governor may as naturally and earnestly love her subjects, as the mother doth love the child, then assure yourselves, that I, being your lady and mistress, do as earnestly and tenderly love and favor you. And I, thus loving you, cannot but think that ye as heartily and faithfully love me; and then I doubt not but we shall give these rebels a short and speedy overthrow.

As concerning the marriage, ye shall understand, that I enterprised not the doing thereof without advice, and that by the advice of all our privy council, who so considered and weighed the great commodities that might ensue thereof, that they not only thought it very honorable, but also expedient, both for the wealth of the realm, and also of you our subjects. And as touching myself, I assure you, I am not so bent to my will, neither so precise nor affectionate, that either for mine own pleasure I would choose where I lust, or that I am so desirous, as needs I would have one. For God, I thank him, to whom be the praise therefore, I have hitherto lived a virgin, and doubt nothing, but with God's grace, I am able so to live still. But if, as my progenitors have done before, it may please God that I might leave some fruit of my body behind me, to be your governor, I trust you would not only rejoice thereat, but also I know it would be to your great comfort. And certainly, if I either did think or know, that this marriage were to the hurt of any of you my commons, or to the impeachment of any part or parcel of the royal state of this realm of England, I would never consent thereunto, neither would I ever marry while I lived. And on the word of a queen, I promise you, that if it shall not probably appear to all the nobility and commons in the high court of parliament, that this marriage shall be for the high benefit and commodity of the whole realm, then will I abstain from marriage while I live.

And now, good subjects, pluck up your hearts, and, like true men, stand fast against these rebels, both our enemies and yours, and fear them not; for I assure you, I fear them nothing at all. . . .

Queen Elizabeth I
Braces Her Troops for the Spanish Armada

". . . I have the heart and stomach of a king . . ."

As the Spanish Armada of 130 tall ships sailed for England in 1588, readying to wield the Catholic sword against Protestantism, Queen Elizabeth I (1533–1603)—determined to "rule as well as reign"—traveled to Tilbury by barge to review and embolden her troops.

On August 9, the indomitable queen, mounted on a grand white warhorse, delivered this speech as her officers repeated her words amid thousands of kneeling soldiers. Though she had "the body of a weak and feeble woman," she told them, she herself would take up arms against tyrants, as any king would do. The warrior queen would have to wait; still at Tilbury, she learned that her navy and its auxiliaries (and convenient bad weather) had denied success to Philip II, who was both the Armada's leader and one of Elizabeth's many rejected suitors.

My loving people, we have been persuaded by some that are careful of our safety, to take heed how we commit ourselves to armed multitudes, for fear of treachery. But I assure you, I do not desire to distrust my faithful and loving people.

Let tyrants fear; I have always so behaved myself that, under God, I have placed my chiefest strength and safeguard in the loyal hearts and good will of my subjects. And therefore I am come amongst you at this time, not as for my recreation or sport, but being resolved, in the midst and heat of the battle, to live or die amongst you all; to lay down, for my God, and for my kingdom, and for my people, my honor and my blood, even the dust.

I know I have the body of a weak and feeble woman, but I have the heart and stomach of a king, and of a king of England, too, and think foul scorn that Parma or Spain or any Prince of Europe should dare to invade the borders of my realm, to which, rather than any dishonor should grow me, I myself will take up arms. I myself will be your general, judge and rewarder of every one of your virtues in the field.

I know already for your forwardness that you have deserved rewards and crowns, and we do assure you, in the word of a Prince, they shall be duly paid you. In the mean, my lieutenant general shall be in my stead, than whom never prince commanded a more noble and worthy subject; not doubting by your obedience to my general, by your concord in the camp and by your valor in the field, we shall shortly have a famous victory over these enemies of my God, of my kingdom and of my people.

Anna Dickinson
Thunders for the Union Cause

"You have not liberty!—gain it."

By the time Anna Dickinson (1842–1932) was thirteen she had experienced the thrill of her first published article; by eighteen, the excitement of her first publicly delivered address; by twenty-two, the trepidation of her first public assault—a curl was shot off her head in mid-speech.

"If the word 'slave' is not in the Constitution, the *idea* is," she said at an anti-slavery meeting in 1860. She was forceful and eloquent—and, compared to others on the platform, the mere sprig of youth. Abolitionist William Lloyd Garrison, who had published her first article, dubbed Dickinson "The Girl Orator" and invited her to deliver a speech on "The National Crisis," which effectively launched her career as a speaker on behalf of abolition and Republican politics—and, after the war, on women's suffrage and temperance. Five thousand people gathered in New York in 1863 to cheer the "the Joan of Arc of the abolition movement," and the following year, it was the House of Representatives that gushed, with a speaking invitation signed by more than one hundred members.

On July 6, 1863, young "Joan" joined abolitionist Frederick Douglass on the rostrum when she gave this recruitment speech in National Hall, Philadelphia. The Secretary of War had recently granted African Americans the right to fight, and enlistment was fast becoming the byname for patriotism. Here, as was her style, Dickinson "waves the bloody shirt"—wrapping her appeal around the high drama of slavery's worst moments.

———•—•———

True, through the past we have advocated the use of the black man. For what end? To save ourselves. We wanted them as shields, as barriers, as walls of defense. We would not even say to them, fight beside us. We would put them in the front—their brains contracted, their souls dwarfed, their manhood stunted—mass them together; let them die! That will cover and protect us. Now we hear the voice of the people, solemn and sorrowful, saying, "We have wronged you enough; you have suffered enough; we ask no more at your hands; we stand aside, and let you fight for your own manhood, your future, your race." Anglo-Africans, we need you; yet it is not because of this need that I ask you to go into the ranks of the regiments forming to fight in this war. My cheeks would crimson with shame, while my lips put the request that could be answered, "Your soldiers? Why don't you give us the same bounty, and the same pay as the rest?" I have no reply to that. But for yourselves; because, after ages of watching and agony, your day is breaking; because your hour is come; because you hold the hammer which, upheld or failing, decides your destiny for woe or weal; because you have reached the point from which you must sink, generation after generation, century after century, into deeper depths, into more absolute degradation; or mount to the heights of glory and fame.

The cause needs you. This is not our war, not a war for territory; not a war for martial power, for mere victory; it is a war of the races, of the ages; the Stars and Stripes is the people's flag of the world; the world must be gathered under its folds, the black man beside the white.

Thirteen dollars a month and bounty are good; liberty is better. Ten dollars a month and no bounty is bad, slavery is worse. The two alternatives are before you; you make your own future. The "to-be" will, in a little while, do you justice. Soldiers will be proud to welcome as comrades, as brothers, the black men of Port Hudson and Milliken's Bend. Congress, next winter, will look out through the fog and mist of Washington, and will see how, when Pennsylvania was invaded and Philadelphia threatened, while white men haggled over bounty and double pay to defend their own city, their own homes, with the tread of armed rebels almost heard in their streets; black men, without bounty, without pay, without rights or the promise of any, rushed to the beleaguered capital, and were first in their offers of life or of death. Congress will say, "These men are soldiers; we will pay them as such; these men are marvels of loyalty, self-sacrifice, courage; we will give them a chance of promotion." History will write; "Behold the unselfish heroes; the eager martyrs of this war."

You hesitate because you have not all. Your brothers and sisters of the South cry out, "Come to help us, we have nothing." Father! you hesitate to send your boy to death; the slave father turns his face of dumb entreaty to you, to save his boy from the death in life; the bondage that crushes soul and body together. Shall your son go to his aid? Mother! you look with pride at the manly face and figure, growing and strengthening beside you! He is yours; your own. God gave him to you. From the lacerated hearts, the wrung souls, of other mothers, comes the wail, "My child, my child; give me back my child!" The slavemaster heeds not; the Government is tardy; mother! the prayer comes to you; will you falter?

Young man, rejoicing in the hope, the courage, the will, the thews and muscles of young manhood; the red glare of this war falls on the faces and figures of other young men, distorted with suffering, writhing in agony, wrenching their manacles and chains, shouting with despairing voices to you for help—shall it be withheld?

The slaves will be freed—with or without you. The conscience and heart of the people have decreed that. Xerxes scourging the Hellespont, Canute commanding the waves to roll back, are but types of that folly which stands up and says to this majestic wave of public opinion, "Thus far." The black man will be a citizen only by stamping his right to it in blood. Now or never! You have not homes!—gain them. You have not liberty!—gain it. You have not a flag!—gain it. You have not a country!—be written down in history as the race who made one for themselves, and saved one for another.

Emmeline Pankhurst
Recruits for the Great War

"There are women today who never thought to envy men their manhood . . ."

British suffragist Emmeline Pankhurst (1858–1928) led the Women's Social and Political Union from 1903 until the outbreak of World War I. "Deeds not words" compelled the women; they smashed windows, disrupted meetings, and chained themselves to the homes of important men. Arrest was a "noble sacrifice" for the publicity of their causes.

As for "true violence," "male violence": "War is not women's way!" Pankhurst said. "To the women of this Union human life is sacred!" Yet news of the "German Peril" (and personal memories of the Franco-Prussian war) stirred her patriotic loyalties. On November 30, 1914, at Kingsway Hall, London, she delivered this droll but pointed exhortation.

W e women are the weaker sex. (*Laughter.*) We have been told that our hands are full with our domestic concerns and our maternal duties. In times of peace we have a good deal to say on that, but in times of war we are compelled to take men at their word. Men say to us, "Leave the fighting to us. It does not become women to fight. We protect women. We fight

for you. We shield you from the difficulties and ills of life."
Well, this is a testing time for men and women, too. We take
you, gentlemen, at your word. We say it is the duty of men to
do their best to redeem their pledges to women. We have not
been allowed to prepare ourselves for self-defense because we
are women. ("*Hear, hear.*")

During the last few days I have been thanking God I was
not a superior person (*laughter*), and that I had not a facile
pen or a great sense of saturnine humor so that I must
indulge in something parallel to Nero's fiddling while Rome
burned. I cannot find words strong enough to condemn the
people who at this moment are haggling with imperfect
knowledge over diplomacy and what led to the war, and who
is to blame for it. I will tell you who is to blame if things are
not as they ought to be. It is you enfranchised men. It is the
Bernard Shaws and all the rest of them. (*Cheers and laughter.*)
They say the science of government is only suited to the
male sex. Then when you face a great national peril and your
very existence as a nation is at stake, they begin to argue in
newspaper columns in order that our enemy may quote them
on the walls of Belgium. If we have rulers who are wrong-
doers, it is the fault of the people who made them rulers.
When the war is over will be the time to settle these questions of diplomacy. Here we are in war. Our honor, our reputation, our very existence are at stake. It is a time for people
either to criticize helpfully or to hold their tongues. If we
women, with our grievances against men, can hold our
tongues, I think other people might do so. (*Cheers.*) If
there are mistakes, the right and proper thing to do if you
love your country is to try to get things put right quietly
by influence. . . .

The views I have always held I still hold. Nothing is more
horrible than wars of aggression. But I believe that, whatever

faults we have had in the past, now we are engaged in a right-eous war. Much as I love peace, I believe there are times when it is right to fight. And I say to young men: There are women today who never thought to envy men their manhood, but who would, at least for this purpose, be glad to be men. (*Cheers.*)

Helen Keller
Calls for a Strike Against War

"What a price to pay for an abstraction—the lives of millions of young men."

Left blind and deaf from scarlet fever when she was nineteen months old, Helen Keller (1880–1968) had felt "a phantom living in a no-world" until, at age seven, her teacher and later lifelong friend, Anne Sullivan, taught her to communicate through manual sign language. Three years later, she could read, write, and speak, and by the time she graduated from Radcliffe College in 1904, she was a worldwide celebrity and the author of two autobiographical books. At first the public platform was, she said, "a pillory where I stood cold, riveted, trembling, voiceless," but after learning to articulate and modulate her voice, she relaxed into a distinguished lecture career that would last for more than five decades.

In 1916, the thirty-five-year-old Keller was already one of the most popular figures of the Socialist movement, although she saw herself more as a social reformer than a revolutionist—an advocate of the deaf and blind, a champion of women's suffrage and of labor. But war was the ultimate oppression, she believed, supported by "consciousless governments and corporations," and, in this speech, delivered to a packed audience at New York's Carnegie Hall on January 5, 1916, she unleashes one of her most famous attacks against the paragons of war and capitalism—and her patronizing critics. The invective, defiant to its last word, pitches against preparedness arguments and urges workers to "straighten up and fold" their arms—to strike against war.

The United States declared war against Germany in 1917. Though Keller stayed loyal to her politics, she rarely spoke publicly for socialism after 1922, when she decided to devote her time fully to the American Foundation for the Blind.

T o begin with, I have a word to say to my good friends, the editors, and others who are moved to pity me. Some people are grieved because they imagine I am in the hands of unscrupulous persons who lead me astray and persuade me to espouse unpopular causes and make me the mouthpiece of their propaganda.

Now, let it be understood once and for all that I do not want their pity; I would not change places with one of them. I know what I am talking about. My sources of information are as good and reliable as anybody else's. I have papers and magazines from England, France, Germany and Austria that I can read myself. Not all the editors I have met can do that. Quite a number of them have to take their French and German secondhand.

No, I will not disparage the editors. They are an overworked, misunderstood class. Let them remember, though, that if I cannot see the fire at the end of their cigarettes, neither can they thread a needle in the dark. All I ask, gentlemen, is a fair field and no favor. I have entered the fight against preparedness and against the economic system under which we live. It is to be a fight to the finish, and I ask no quarter.

The future of the world rests in the hands of America. The future of America rests on the backs of 80 million working men and women and their children. We are facing a grave national crisis in our national life. The few who profit from the labor of the masses want to organize the workers into an army which will protect the interests of the capitalists. You are urged to add to the heavy burdens you already bear the burden of a larger army and many additional warships.

It is in your power to refuse to carry the artillery and the dreadnoughts and to shake off some of the burdens, too, such as limousines, steam yachts and country estates. You do not need to make a great noise about it. With the silence and dignity of creators you can end wars and the system of selfishness and exploitation that causes wars. All you need to do to bring about this stupendous revolution is to straighten up and fold your arms.

We are not prepared to defend our country. Even if we were as helpless as Congressman Gardner says we are, we have no enemies foolhardy enough to attempt to invade the United States. The talk about attack from Germany and Japan is absurd. Germany has its hands full and will be busy with its own affairs for some generations after the European war is over.

With full control of the Atlantic Ocean and the Mediterranean Sea, the allies failed to land enough men to defeat the Turks at Gallipoli; and then they failed again to land an army at Salonica in time to check the Bulgarian invasion of Serbia. The conquest of America by water is a nightmare confined exclusively to ignorant persons and members of the Navy League.

Yet, everywhere, we hear fear advanced as argument for armament. It reminds me of a fable I read. A certain man found a horseshoe. His neighbor began to weep and wail because, as he justly pointed out, the man who found the horseshoe might someday find a horse. Having found the shoe, he might shoe him. The neighbor's child might some day go so near the horse's heel as to be kicked, and die. Undoubtedly the two families would quarrel and fight, and several valuable lives would be lost through the finding of the horseshoe.

You know the last war we had we quite accidentally picked up some islands in the Pacific Ocean which may some day be the cause of a quarrel between ourselves and Japan. I'd rather drop those islands right now and forget about them than go to war to keep them. Wouldn't you?

Congress is not preparing to defend the people of the United States. It is planning to protect the capital of American speculators and investors in Mexico, South America, China and the Philippine Islands. Incidentally this preparation will benefit the manufacturers of munitions and war machines.

Until recently there were uses in the United States for the money taken from the workers. But American labor is exploited almost to the limit now, and our national resources have all been appropriated. Still the profits keep piling up new capital. Our flourishing industry in implements of murder is filling the vaults of New York's banks with gold. And a dollar that is not being used to make a slave of some human being is not fulfilling its purpose in the capitalistic scheme. That dollar must be invested, in South America, Mexico, China, or the Philippines. . . .

Every modern war has had its root in exploitation. The Civil War was fought to decide whether the slaveholders of the South or the capitalists of the North should exploit the West. The Spanish-American War decided that the United States should exploit Cuba and the Philippines. The South African War decided that the British should exploit the diamond mines. The Russo-Japanese War decided that Japan should exploit Korea. The present war is to decide who shall exploit the Balkans, Turkey, Persia, Egypt, India, China, Africa. And we are whetting our sword to scare the victors into sharing the spoils with us. Now, the workers are not interested in the spoils; they will not get any of them anyway.

The preparedness propagandists have still another object, and a very important one. They want to give the people something to think about besides their own unhappy condition. They know the cost of living is high, wages are low, employment is uncertain and will be much more so when the European call for munitions stops. No matter how hard and incessantly the people work, they often cannot afford the comforts of life; many cannot obtain the necessities.

Every few days we are given a new war scare to lend realism to their propaganda. They have had us on the verge of war over the *Lusitania*, the *Gulflight*, the *Ancona*, and now they want the workingmen to become excited over the sinking of the *Persia*. The workingman has no interest in any of these ships. The Germans might sink every vessel on the Atlantic Ocean and the Mediterranean Sea, and kill Americans with every one—the American workingman would still have no reason to go to war.

All the machinery of the system has been set in motion. Above the complaint and din of the protest from the workers is heard the voice of authority.

"Friends," it says, "fellow workmen, patriots; your country is in danger! There are foes on all sides of us. There is nothing between us and our enemies except the Pacific Ocean and the Atlantic Ocean. Look at what has happened to Belgium. Consider the fate of Serbia. Will you murmur about low wages when your country, your very liberties, are in jeopardy? What are the miseries you endure compared to the humiliation of having a victorious German army sail up the East River? Quit your whining, get busy and prepare to defend your firesides and your flag. Get an army, get a navy; be ready to meet the invaders like the loyal-hearted freemen you are."

Will the workers walk into this trap? Will they be fooled again? I am afraid so. The people have always been amenable to oratory of this sort. . . . They know that honest sweat, persistent toil and years of struggle bring them nothing worth holding on to, worth fighting for. Yet deep down in their foolish hearts they believe they have a country. Oh blind vanity of slaves!

The clever ones, up in the high places know how childish and silly the workers are. They know that if the government dresses them up in khaki and gives them a rifle and starts them off with a brass band and waving banners, they will go forth to fight valiantly for their own enemies. What a price to pay for an abstraction—the lives of millions of young men; other millions crippled and blinded for life; existence made hideous for still more millions of human beings; the achievement and inheritance of generations swept away in a moment—and nobody better off for all the misery!

The workers have no liberties of their own; they are not free when they are compelled to work twelve or ten or eight hours a day. They are not free when they are ill paid for their exhausting toil. They are not free when their children must labor in mines, mills and factories or starve, and when their women may be driven by poverty to lives of shame. They are not free when they are clubbed and imprisoned because they go on strike for a raise of wages and for the elemental justice that is their right as human beings. . . .

The kind of preparedness the workers want is reorganization and reconstruction of their whole life, such as has never been attempted by statesmen or governments. The Germans found out years ago that they could not raise good soldiers in the slums so they abolished the slums. They saw to it that all the people had at least a few of the essentials of civilization—decent lodging, clean streets, wholesome if scanty food, proper medical care and proper safeguards for the workers in their occupations. That is only a small part of what should be done, but what wonders that one step toward the right sort of preparedness has wrought for Germany! For eighteen months it has kept itself free from invasion while carrying on an extended war of conquest, and its armies are still pressing on with unabated vigor. It is your business to force these reforms on the administration.

Let there be no more talk about what a government can or

cannot do. All these things have been done by all the belligerent nations in the hurly-burly of war. Every fundamentalist industry has been managed better by the governments than by private corporations.

It is your duty to insist upon still more radical measures. It is your business to see that no child is employed in an industrial establishment or mine or store, and that no worker is needlessly exposed to accident or disease. It is your business to make them give you clean cities, free from smoke, dirt and congestion. It is your business to see that this kind of preparedness is carried into every department of the nation, until every one has a chance to be well born, well nourished, rightly educated, intelligent and serviceable to the country at all times.

Strike against all ordinances and laws and institutions that continue the slaughter of peace and the butcheries of war. Strike against war, for without you, no battles can be fought. Strike against manufacturing shrapnel and gas bombs and all other tools of murder. Strike against preparedness that means death and misery to millions of human beings.

Be not dumb, obedient slaves in an army of destruction. Be heroes in an army of construction.

Dolores Ibárruri
Inflames the Spanish Civil War

"Fascism shall not pass!"

On July 18, 1936, writer, orator, and politician Dolores Ibárruri (1895–1989) thundered over the airwaves of Spain: "It is better to die on one's feet than to live on one's knees! *No pasarán!*" "They shall not pass!" would echo for the three-year duration of the Spanish Civil War.

Daughter of a Basque miner, a servant before joining the Socialist Party in 1917, Ibárruri became a journalist, writing under the pseudonym "La Pasionaria" (the passion flower). As the first Communist groups in Spain began to organize, she joined the party in 1920, and in 1936, was elected to Parliament, scarcely five months before the war began.

On August 23, 1936, one hundred thousand people swelled the bleachers of Mestal Stadium in Valencia to cheer as Ibárruri inveighed against fascism. "Listen" as she fills her speech with a litany of impassioned phrases. And "lean in" as she grows weak from exhaustion and barely gets out her last few words.

———— •◦• ————

Comrades, people of Valencia! . . .
I have come to you in these tragic and gloomy hours, when the fate of Spain and especially the future of the working

masses is being decided. I have come to you, my mouth filled with the acrid taste of gunpowder, my mind filled with the impressions of the difficulties facing our comrades who are fighting on the summits and slopes of the Guadarramas, who realize the importance of our struggle and who are prepared to die rather than fall into the clutches of fascism. I have come to you from the field of battle, from that great fight which is assuming the character of a heroic epic, for we entered battle armed only with enthusiasm, self-sacrifice and supreme devotion to the cause of the people in order to fight an enemy furnished with all the means of warfare, which he has stolen from the people. . . .

If, when entering the firing line to fight the enemy who is threatening our national liberty, we have such enthusiasm in the rear, then I say to you, the working people of Valencia, what I said when I saw the weapons in the hands of the militia, when I saw the rifles in the hands of the troops loyal to the government: Fascism shall not pass!

Fascism shall not pass because the wall of bodies with which we have barred its way is today strengthened by weapons of defense we have captured from the enemy—a cowardly enemy, because he has not the ideals which lead us into battle. The enemy therefore has no dash and impetuosity, whereas we are borne on the wings of our ideals, of our love, not for the Spain which is dying together with the enemy, but for the Spain we want to have—a democratic Spain.

When we speak of Spain, we mean not only the name; we mean a democratic Spain, not the Spain which is clinging to her old traditions; we mean a Spain which will give the peasants land, which will socialize industry under the control of the workers, which will introduce social insurance so that the worker may not be condemned to a homeless old age; we mean a Spain which will completely and comprehensively, and in a revolutionary spirit, solve the economic problems that lie at the foundation of all revolutions. (*Loud and prolonged applause.*)

On all fronts communists, anarchists, socialists and republicans are fighting shoulder to shoulder. We have also been joined by nonparty people from town and country, because they too have realized what a victory for fascism would mean to Spain.

The struggle, started within the frontiers of our country, is already assuming an international character, because the working people of the whole world know that if fascism were to triumph in Spain, every democratic country in the world would be confronted with the fascist danger. The working people have realized this, as is borne out by the messages of solidarity we are constantly receiving from all parts of the world. International fascism, too, has realized the significance of the struggle of the Spanish people against the enemies who have violated their oath of loyalty to the country and to the country's flag. These violators of their vows have broken their promises and have rebelled vile alliance with seditionary priests and debauched sons of the aristocracy, and are committing endless crimes in all the inhabited places through which they pass. One needs the brush of Goya . . . to depict the horrors and revolting crimes committed by these elements led by arrogant fascist generals who have long ago revealed who they are and what they are capable of.

Dante's Inferno is but a pale reflection of what happens in places through which these modern vandals pass. The slaughtered children and old people, the raped and hacked bodies of women, the demolished monuments of art. . . . Wherever they pass they sow death and desolation. And what is taking place in the districts captured by the fascists would have taken place all over Spain, if they had not been opposed by a people inspired by faith in its own strength. . . .

We shall very soon achieve victory and return to our children.

Madame Sun Yat-sen
Accepts the International Stalin Peace Prize

*"I accept this prize in the name of one-fourth
of mankind . . ."*

Born in Shanghai, educated in the United States, Soong Ching
Ling (1890–1981) became a leading figure of the People's Republic of China and died as its honorary head of state. Wife of Sun
Yat-sen, father of the Chinese Republic, she broke with Nationalists soon after her husband's death when his successor, Chiang Kai-shek, led a slaughter of Chinese Communists in 1927—the
same year he married Soong's younger sister, May Ling.

Awarded the International Stalin Peace Prize in 1951,
Soong delivered this acceptance speech on September 18 in
Beijing. She had a backdrop for her remarks: the Korean War
was in its second year and General Douglas MacArthur was
musing "old soldiers never die . . ." after being fired by Truman
for insubordination.

In her speech, she was outspoken but softspoken—blasting
"American aggression" as friends fell silent to hear her in the
capital city's grand Huairentang Hall. The "joy expressed at the
dismissal of the warmonger MacArthur" was an indication, she
says, that the American people want peace, though, she argues,
their government does not.

The United Nations–backed campaign ended on July 27,
1953.

Mr. Chairman, Fellow Partisans of Peace:
I will remember tonight and hold it dear not only for what it means to me personally, but also for the honor it accords the Chinese people. One does not work for peace singlehandedly, but rather expresses the desires and hopes of the masses of people and acts jointly with them. Thus, I accept this International Stalin Peace Prize in the name of my countrymen, who in the past one hundred years, and especially in the last thirty, have seen their land and their neighbors' repeatedly ravaged by war. I accept this prize in the name of a people who since October 1, 1949, have tasted the joy of liberation, national unity and unprecedented organization for peaceful construction. I accept this prize in the name of one-fourth of mankind, who, as a result of their experiences, have in firm determination joined the ranks of the partisans for world peace.

The Chinese people have given ample evidence of their stand. Over 223 million signatures were affixed to the Stockholm Appeal. This was exceeded by the 344,053,057 people . . . who have signified that they want a peace pact between the five great powers, and 339,903,092 people . . . who voted against the U.S. rearmament of Japan. But even if this is not convincing enough, you have only to witness the herculean accomplishments of the Chinese people in reconstructing our nation. These symbolize without question how we treasure peace. If in a few short years we could emancipate the land for hundreds of millions of peasants, stimulate agricultural production to the point of self-sufficiency and beyond; if we could achieve in industry and trade the conditions for complete rehabilitation and further development; if we could simultaneously undertake gigantic, fundamental public construction projects, just imagine what we could do with a period of prolonged world tranquility! Such a future would hold no limits for New China!

Because we wholeheartedly want such a future, the Chinese people have also given ample evidence of their courage in protecting peace. Along with their Korean comrades-in-arms, the Chinese Volunteers have shown that, for this high purpose, we are ready to shed our blood. No greater demonstration could be made in the name of peace. It is at the same time a demonstration of our unwilling perseverance in the face of imperialist aggression and our unequivocal intention to beat it back whenever it threatens our people's domain.

In the momentous struggle of building up our land, resisting American aggression, aiding Korea and protecting our homes, it is quite obvious to the Chinese people who stands constantly by our side and upon whose warm solicitude we can always count. It is with good reason that our farmers and workers call their Soviet friends "Big Brother," and look to Stalin as the greatest leader of all the peace forces. . . .

This unbreakable unity is based on our mutual appreciation for people's rule and peace. It is like a new star which has risen in the heavens and which shines with the brightness of the first magnitude. For this is a historical alignment that has changed the whole course of world relationships. . . .

While this is the bright area of the world in which we live, there is another side from which emanates gloom and cynicism, from which sounds forth a constant barrage that war is inevitable. The unwanted and unreasonable leadership of the United States keeps this group of lands in tow. There appropriations for the people's welfare and culture are slashed to a pittance, while those for war preparations reach unheard of figures. This causes glee among the chiefs of a favored few corporations as they have a feast of profits. But it taxes the people until they are grim-faced and frustrated. There also a mockery is made of democracy. The people's leaders are jailed merely for having an idea in their heads, and those who sincerely utter the word "peace" are treated as common criminals. At the same time, the people are kept divided and impotent by planned hate campaigns, especially in the United States where they result in the legal murder of Willie McGees because they are people of color.

But there is a limit to the people's patience and even in this hysterical, foreboding sector, the penetrating rays of peace and sanity valiantly struggle to throw back the darkness. For all of their repression, in their own bailiwicks, the warmongers are not having everything the way they want it. The U.S. banker-generals may be able to snap their whips and have governments jump, but when it comes to whipping the people into line for their war plans, that is another question. The people balk. . . . They want peace.

The recent French and Italian elections indicate that truth cannot be spelled with a dollar mark. The U.S.-backed governments and their fascist cohorts used gerrymandering, vote rigging, threats and actual violence. But in spite of these, the electorate in those two countries cast large and most significant votes for the parties which stand for people's rule and peace.

In Spain, over one million workers went out on strike against hunger caused by Franco oppression and unofficial inclusion in the Atlantic Pact for war. Once more the cities of heroic Spain have echoed with the cry, "Death to fascism!" In Japan and Western Germany, the people have evidenced their refusal to be cannon fodder in U.S. plans for world conquest. In England, the wave of protests mounts. The people voice their indignation at government officials displaying truckling subservience as junior partners to the United States. In the colonial and semicolonial lands, there is a deep stirring. It signifies that the oppressed see the direct connection between their independence struggles and world peace, recognize that the threat to one is a threat to the other.

We can see that in the United States itself, although not fully organized, the people express their discontent with the

Wall Street clique. We saw the joy expressed at the dismissal of the warmonger MacArthur. We witnessed the support they gave the calls for peace in Korea—Johnson's resolution in the Senate and Y. A. Malik's speech at the United Nations. This support developed spontaneously, despite news blackout and distortion in the so-called free press. Radio commentators, news columnists, public opinion polls, notwithstanding their monopoly control, are forced to admit that the people want the war in Korea ended. Churchmen, professors, workers, the epic American Peace Congress with 5,000 delegates—all further report that the people in the United States want overall peace, the same as do men and women throughout the entire world. As the casualty figure in Korea mounts, as more of their youngsters are pressed into uniform and spread all over Europe and Asia, American mothers, fathers, and wives are frantic with anxiety. . . .

However, the agents of destruction have no ear for the word "peace" as they rush pell-mell to rearm. They have stepped up the instigation of fascism at home to stifle any resistance. They have twisted their youth into fascist beasts and unleashed them overseas. . . . They are out to pulverize the idea of people's rule, to ruthlessly censor from all minds the people's struggle to live as human beings can and should live, cooperatively and at peace. This is their morbid purpose, their fanatical frenzy.

But J. V. Stalin has told us that at this time war is not inevitable. We can still avert this terrible catastrophe if the people take the task of protecting peace into their own hands. . . . If the world's common men and women, the ones who bear the sufferings of war, unite in demanding sincere negotiation in place of force to settle differences, then there will be no war. This endorsement and action can materialize by obtaining the widest consideration for the World Peace Council program, by obtaining . . . a peace pact among the five great powers. . . .

We must carry the struggle to that point of achievement.

Golda Meir
Appeals for Reconciliation

*"The deserts of the Middle East are in need of
water, not bombers."*

"God knows what this girl may be able to do," Golda Meir's father
said after hearing his daughter fire from the soapbox. Self-assured,
stubborn, idealistic, an active member of the Zionist movement,
young "Goldie" would rise to fame as politician, diplomat and, by
1969, Israel's fourth prime minister. She would become "our
Golda"—the "Mother Courage" who struggled to wage peace
between Arab and Jew, which deadlocked with the founding of
the Jewish state in the mid-twentieth century. "Someday when
peace comes, we may forgive the Arabs for having killed our
sons," she said, in a now oft-quoted line, "but it will be harder for
us to forgive them for having forced us to kill their sons."

The deadlock was ten years old when Meir (1898–1978),
then Israel's foreign minister, delivered this speech. Speaking
before the United Nations General Assembly on October 7,
1957, she stunned listeners by concluding a formal statement with
this extemporaneous appeal to Arab nations. Using direct, simple
language (recounting "our greatest grief"), Goldie was back on
the soapbox—this time with less fire but olive branch waving.

M r. President, from this rostrum I should like to address a solemn appeal to the Arab states of the Middle East: Israel is approaching her tenth anniversary. You did not want it to be born. You fought against the decision in the United Nations. You then attacked us by military force. We have all been witnesses to sorrow, destruction and the spilling of blood and tears. Yet Israel is here, growing, developing, progressing. It has gained many friends and their number is steadily increasing.

We are an old tenacious people and, as our history has proved, not easily destroyed. Like you, we have regained our national independence, and as with you, so with us, nothing will cause us to give it up. . . .

In light of these facts, what is the use or realism or the justice of policies and attitudes based on the fiction that Israel is not here, or will somehow disappear? Would it not be better for all to build a future for the Middle East based on cooperation? Israel will exist and flourish even without peace, but surely a future of peace would be better both for Israel and for her neighbors.

The Arab world with its ten sovereignties and three million square miles can well afford to accommodate itself to peaceful cooperation with Israel. Does hate for Israel and the aspiration for its destruction make one child in your countries happier? Does it convert one hovel into a house? Does culture thrive on the soil of hatred? We have not the slightest doubt that eventually there will be peace and cooperation between us. This is a historic necessity for both peoples. We are prepared; we are anxious to bring it about now.

Mr. President, I should also like to address myself to all delegates in this Assembly and especially to the powers directly involved in the problems of the Middle East. The deserts of the Middle East are in need of water, not bombers. The tens of millions of its inhabitants are craving for the means to live and not for the implements of death. I ask all of you—old members of the United Nations and the new—use your influence not to deepen the abyss of misunderstanding, but to bridge it.

And I wish to conclude with a word of deepest appreciation to those countries, member states of the United Nations, who ten years ago helped to lay the foundations for Israel's statehood and whose continued understanding, assistance and friendship have enabled us to weather the storms which have beset our path.

Many of these are countries without direct interest of any kind in our area. But their appreciation of the moral, the social, the historic and religious factors involved led them to profoundly held convictions which they have maintained with staunchness and with courage. Their friendship and their help will never be forgotten by the people of Israel and the Jewish people as a whole. . . .

In celebrating the tenth anniversary of Israel's independence, we look back on a decade of struggle, of achievement in some areas, of failure in others. But by and large it has justified a thousandfold the vision of those who saw in the reestablishment of Israel's nationhood a historic act of reparation and of statesmanship. Our greatest grief has been the lack of progress toward peace with our Arab neighbors. It is our profoundest hope that the coming period may make a decisive forward step in this regard, to the inestimable benefit of all the people of the Middle East and perhaps the entire world.

Margaret Thatcher
Marshalls Support for the Falklands War

"Let us, then, draw together in the name, not of jingoism, but of justice."

When Argentine forces invaded the Falkland Islands in April 1982, Margaret Thatcher (b. 1925) weighed the difficulties of a military response. "But when you are at war," she later wrote in her memoirs, "you cannot allow the difficulties to dominate your thinking: you have to set out with an iron will to overcome them. And anyway what was the alternative? That a common or garden dictator should rule over the Queen's subjects and prevail by fraud and violence? Not while I was prime minister." She dispatched a task force to retake the islands.

Iron will was not something Britain's first female prime minister—the longest serving British prime minister of the twentieth century—went lacking. The Iron Lady, so-called by the Soviet press in 1976, earned her long tenure (1979–1990) at No. 10 Downing with a steadfastly conservative philosophical resolve. "The lady's not for turning," was her famous phrase in 1980.

At a Conservative Women's Conference in London on May 26, 1982, Thatcher was resolute, never reckoning, as she spoke of Britain's honor as a nation, its just cause against aggression, amid the intensity of the Falklands War. Her parting lines are from Shakespeare's *King John*—always powerful when uttered by a patriot.

. . . In a series of measured and progressive steps, over the past weeks, our forces have tightened their grip on the Falkland Islands. They have retaken South Georgia. Gradually they have denied fresh supplies to the Argentine garrison. Finally, by the successful amphibious landing at San Carlos Bay in the early hours of Friday morning, they have placed themselves in a position to retake the islands and reverse the illegal Argentine invasion.

By the skill of our pilots, our sailors and those manning Rapier missile batteries onshore, they have inflicted heavy losses on the Argentine Air Force—over fifty fixed-wing aircraft have been destroyed.

There have, of course, been tragic losses. You will have heard of the further attacks on our task force. HMS *Coventry* came under repeated air attack yesterday evening and later sank. One of our Merchant Marine ships, the *Atlantic Conveyor*, supporting the task force, was also damaged and had to be abandoned. We do not yet know the number of casualties but our hearts go out to all those who had men in these ships.

Despite these grievous losses, our resolve is not weakened. We know the reality of war. . . .

It was eight weeks ago today that information reached us that the Argentine Fleet was sailing towards the Falklands. Eight thousand miles away. . . . At that stage there were only two ways of trying to stop it—through President Reagan, whose appeal to Argentina was rebuffed, and the United Nations, whose plea was also rejected.

There were those who said we should have accepted the Argentine invasion as a *fait accompli*. But whenever the rule of force as distinct from the rule of law is seen to succeed, the world moves a step closer to anarchy.

The older generation of this country, and generations before them, have made sacrifices so that we could be a free society and belong to a community of nations which seeks to resolve disputes by civilized means. Today it falls to us to bear the same responsibility.

What has happened since that day, eight weeks ago, is a matter of history—the history of a nation which rose instinctively to the needs of the occasion.

For decades, the peoples of those islands had enjoyed peace—with freedom, with justice, with democracy. That peace was shattered by a wanton act of armed aggression by Argentina in blatant violation of international law. And everything that has happened since has stemmed from that invasion by the military dictatorship of Argentina. We want that peace restored. But we want it with the same freedom, justice and democracy that the islanders previously enjoyed.

For seven weeks we sought a peaceful solution by diplomatic means: through the good offices of our close friend and ally, the United States; through the unremitting efforts of the secretary-general of the United Nations. . . . We worked tirelessly for a peaceful solution. But when there is no response of substance from the other side, there comes a point when it is no longer possible to trust the good faith of those with whom one is negotiating.

Playing for time is not working for a peaceful solution. Wasting time is not willing a peaceful solution. It is simply leaving the aggressor with the fruits of his aggression.

It would be a betrayal of our fighting men and of the islanders if we continued merely to talk, when talk alone was getting nowhere.

And so, seven weeks to the day after the invasion, we

moved to recover by force what was taken from us by force. It cannot be said too often: we are the victims; they are the aggressors. As always, we came to military action reluctantly. But when territory which has been British for almost a hundred and fifty years is seized and occupied; when not only British land, but British citizens are in the power of an aggressor, then we have to restore our rights and the rights of the Falkland Islanders.

There have been a handful of questioning voices raised here at home. I would like to answer them. It has been suggested that the size of the Falkland Islands and the comparatively small number of its inhabitants—some eighteen hundred men, women and children—should somehow affect our reaction to what has happened to them.

To those—not many—who speak lightly of a few islanders beyond the seas and who ask the question, "Are they worth fighting for?" let me say this: right and wrong are not measured by a head count of those to whom that wrong has been done. That would not be principle but expediency. And the Falklanders, remember, are not strangers. They are our own people. As the Prime Minister of New Zealand, Bob Muldoon put it in his usual straightforward way, "With the Falkland Islanders, it is family."

When their land was invaded and their homes overrun, they naturally turned to us for help, and we, their fellow citizens, eight thousand miles away in our much larger island, could not and did not beg to be excused. We sent our men and our ships with all speed, hoping against hope that we would not have to use them in battle but prepared to do so if all attempts at a peaceful solution failed. When those attempts failed, we could not sail by on the other side.

And let me add this. If we, the British, were to shrug our shoulders at what has happened in the South Atlantic and acquiesce in the illegal seizure of those faraway islands, it would be a clear signal to those with similar designs on the territory of others to follow in the footsteps of aggression.

Surely we, of all people, have learned the lesson of history: that to appease an aggressor is to invite aggression elsewhere, and on an ever-increasing scale.

Other voices—only a few—have accused us of clinging to colonialism or even imperialism. Let me remind those who advance that argument that the British have a record second to none of leading colony after colony to freedom and independence. We cling not to colonialism but self-determination.

Still others—again only a few—say we must not put at risk our investments and interests in Latin America; that trade and commerce are too important to us to put in jeopardy some of the valuable markets of the world.

But what would the Falklanders, under the heel of the invader, say to that? What kind of people would we be if, enjoying the birthright of freedom ourselves, we abandoned British citizens for the sake of commercial gain?

Now we are present in strength on the Falkland Islands. Our purpose is to repossess them. We shall carry on until that purpose is accomplished.

When the invader has left, there will be much to do—rebuilding, restoring homes and farms, and, above all, renewing the confidence of the people in their future. Their wishes will need time to crystallize and, of course, will depend in some measure on what we and others are prepared to do to develop the untapped resources and safeguard the Islands' future.

Madam Chairman, our cause is just. It is the cause of freedom and the rule of law. It is the cause of support for the weak against aggression by the strong.

Let us, then, draw together in the name, not of jingoism, but of justice. And let our nation, as it has so often in the past, remind itself and the world:

Nought shall make us rue,
If England to herself do rest but true.

PART 2

PLEDGES

OF

ALLEGIANCE

AND

PATRIOTISM

Empress Theodora
Stands Her Ground

". . . the royal purple is the noblest shroud."

On January 18 of the year 532, Byzantine Emperor Justinian stood morose as his generals predicted certain defeat against the rebel Hypatius. Gloom hung in the palace hall as his advisers urged him to flee. A swift warship stood ready to sail to Heraclea, on the southern shore of the Black Sea, his last chance, they told him, to save himself and his wife, Empress Theodora.

Escape? The strong-willed empress had heard enough. She rose from her throne and, with this brief but forceful declaration, shamed her husband and his men into action. Hypatius and the rebels were soon dead.

———

My lords, the present occasion is too serious to allow me to follow the convention that a woman should not speak in a man's council. Those whose interests are threatened by extreme danger should think only of the wisest course of action, not of conventions.

In my opinion, in the present crisis if ever, flight is not the right course, even if it should bring us to safety. It is impossible for a person, having been born into this world, not to die, but for one who has reigned it is intolerable to be a fugitive. May I never be deprived of this purple robe, and may I never see the day when those who meet me do not call me empress.

If you wish to save yourself, my lord, there is no difficulty. We are rich, over there is the sea, and yonder are the ships. Yet reflect for a moment whether, once you have escaped to a place of security, you would not gladly exchange such safety for death. As for me, I agree with the adage that the royal purple is the noblest shroud.

Queen Elizabeth I
Delivers a Reproof to Her Parliament

*"I will never break the word of a prince, spoken
in a public place, for my honor's sake."*

Vain, truculent, willful, and majestic, Queen Elizabeth I wanted an end to her Parliament's vexing questions of marriage and succession. "My lords, do whatever you wish," she said to a deputation of the upper house. "As for me, I shall do no otherwise than pleases me. Your bills can have no force without my assent and authority." Yet her nobles could not be assuaged; nor could her "troublesome Commons"—who threatened to withhold a subsidy to their spinster queen unless she named either a husband or a successor.

Elizabeth seethed. They never would have treated her father, Henry VIII, this way, she insisted. Her wrath in need of venting, she summoned thirty representatives from each house to Whitehall on November 5, 1566. Her harangue, delivered in a loud, declarative voice, focused pointedly at the Commons and bishops (the *Domini Doctores*, who had been the principal agitators in the House of Lords).

No one should challenge her love for her kingdom, she scolds. To name a successor would invite conspiracy, she warns, and with it bring "some peril unto you and certain danger unto me."

In the end, Elizabeth heeled her delegates with assurances, however unconvincing, to resolve the matter when "convenient."

——◆·◆——

Was I not born in the realm? Were my parents born **. . .** in any foreign country? Is there any cause I should alienate myself from being careful over this country? Is not my kingdom here? Whom have I oppressed? Whom have I enriched to other's harm? What turmoil have I made in this Commonwealth that I should be suspected to have no regard to the same? How have I governed since my reign? I will be tried by envy itself. I need not to use many words, for my deeds do try me.

Well the matter whereof as I am informed they would have made their petition, consisteth in two points—in my marriage and the limitation of success of the Crown, wherein my marriage was first placed, as for manners' sake. I did send them answer by my Council that I would marry although of my own disposition I was not inclined thereunto. But that was not accepted nor credited, although spoken by their Prince. And yet I used so many words that I could say no more: and were it not now I had spoken those words, I would never speak them again. I will never break the world of a prince, spoken in a public place, for my honor's sake. And therefore I say again, I will marry as soon as I can conveniently, if God take not him away with whom I mind to marry, or myself, or else some other great let happen. I can say no more, except the party were present. And I hope to have children. Otherwise I would never marry.

A strange order of petitioners that will make a request and cannot be otherwise ascertained by their Prince's word, and yet will not believe it when it is spoken! But they, I think, that moveth the same will be as ready to mislike him with whom I shall marry, as they are now to move it. And then it will appear they nothing meant it. I thought they would have been rather ready to have given me thanks than to have made any new request for the same. There have been some that ere this have said to me they never required more than that they once might hear me say I would marry. Well, there was never so great a treason but might be covered under as fair a pretense.

The second point was the limitation of the succession of the crown: wherein was nothing said for my safety but only for themselves. A strange thing that the foot should direct the head in so weighty a cause; which cause hath been so diligently weighed by us, for that it toucheth us more than them. I am sure there was not one of them that ever was a second person, as I have been, and have tasted of the practices against my sister—who I would to God were alive again. I had great occasions to hearken to their motions, of whom some of them are of the Common House, but when friends fall out, truth doth appear according to the old proverb, and were it not for my honor their knavery should be known. There were no occasion in me that time I stood in danger of my life, my sister so incensed against me: I did differ from her in religion and I was sought for divers ways. So shall my successor never be. . . .

It is said, I am no divine. Indeed, I studied nothing else but divinity till I came to the crown; and then I gave myself to the study of that which was meet for government, and am not ignorant of stories wherein appeareth what hath fallen out for ambition of kingdoms—as in Spain, Naples, Portugal, and at home; and what cocking hath been between the father and the son for the same. You would have a limitation of succession. Truly, if reason did not subdue will in me, I would cause you to deal in it, so pleasant a thing it should be unto me. But I stay it for your benefit. For if you should have liberty to treat of it, there be so many competitors—some kinfolks, some servants, and some tenants; some would speak for their master, and some for their mistress, and every man for his friend—that it would be an occasion of a greater charge than a subsidy. And if my will did not yield to reason, it should be that thing I would gladliest desire to see you deal in.

Well, there hath been error: I say not errors, for there were too many in the proceeding in this matter. But we will not judge that these attempts were done of any hatred to our person, but even for lack of good foresight. I do not marvel, though *Domini Doctores* with you, my Lords, did so use themselves therein, since after my brother's death they openly preached and set forth that my sister and I were bastards. Well, I wish not the death of any man, but only this I desire: that they which have been the practicers herein may before their deaths repent the same, and show some open confession of their fault, whereby the scabbed sheep may be known from the whole.

As for mine own part, I care not for death; for all men are mortal. And though I be a woman, yet I have as good a courage, answerable to my place, as ever my father had. I am your anointed Queen. I will never be by violence constrained to do anything. I thank God I am endued with such qualities that if I were turned out of the realm in my petticoat, I were able to live in any place in Christendom.

Your petition is to deal with the limitation of the succession. At this present it is not convenient; nor never shall be without some peril unto you and certain danger unto me. But were it not for your peril, at this time I would give place, notwithstanding my danger. Your perils are sundry ways; for some may be touched, who resteth now in such terms with us as is not meet to be disclosed, either in the Common House or in the Upper House. But as soon as there may be a convenient time, and that it may be done with least peril unto you—although never without great danger unto me—I will deal therein for your safety, and offer it unto you as your Prince and head, without request; for it is monstrous that the feet should direct the head.

And therefore this is my mind and answer. . . .

Frances Wright
Defines Patriotism

"Patriotism, in the exclusive meaning, is surely not made for America."

Born in Dundee, Scotland, Frances Wright (1795–1852) was an orphan at age two and an heiress to her grandfather's considerable fortune. Her 1821 book, *Views of Society and Manners in America,* documented her first visit to America and so captured the attention of the French military general Marquis de Lafayette that, in 1824, he invited Wright and her sister to accompany him to the United States for a return trip.

Wright stayed in America and founded Nashoba, a colony for free blacks in Tennessee (which failed three years later), then moved to New Harmony, Indiana, a cooperative colony established by her friend and social reformer Robert Dale Owen. It was there that Wright became the first woman in America to gain fame as a public speaker. Her speeches promoted abolition, religion, education, and equal rights for women, and drew the repeated wrath of angry mobs. But, yes, her critics admitted, though they pelted her with stones, "The Priestess of Beelzebub" had a gift for oratory.

This is Wright's famous Independence Day address, delivered at New Harmony on July 4, 1828—a speech forceful in its appeal, eloquent in its use of repeated phrases, and powerful in its message: the universal and true meaning of patriotism.

From the era which dates the national existence of the American people dates also a mighty step in the march of human knowledge. And it is consistent with that principle in our conformation which leads us to rejoice in the good which befalls our species, and to sorrow for the evil, that our hearts should expand on this day—on this day, which calls to memory the conquest achieved by knowledge over ignorance, willing cooperation over blind obedience, opinion over prejudice, new ways over old ways, when, fifty-two years ago, America declared her national independence, and associated it with her republic federation. Reasonable is it to rejoice on this day, and useful to reflect thereon; so that we rejoice for the real, and not any imaginary, good; and reflect on the positive advantages obtained, and on those which it is ours farther to acquire.

Dating, as we justly may, a new era in the history of man from the Fourth of July, 1776, it would be well—that is, it would be useful—if on each anniversary we examined the progress made by our species in just knowledge and just practice. Each Fourth of July would then stand as a tidemark in the flood of time by which to ascertain the advance of the human intellect, by which to note the rise and fall of each successive error, the discovery of each important truth, the gradual melioration in our public institutions, social arrangements, and, above all, in our moral feelings and mental views. . . .

In continental Europe, of late years, the words "patriotism" and "patriot" have been used in a more enlarged sense than it is usual here to attribute to them, or than is attached to them in Great Britain. Since the political struggles of France, Italy, Spain, and Greece, the word "patriotism" has been employed, throughout continental Europe, to express a love of the public good; a preference for the interests of the many to those of the few; a desire for the emancipation of the human race from the thrall of despotism, religious and civil: in short, patriotism there is used rather to express the interest felt in the human race in general than that felt for any country, or inhabitants of a country, in particular. And "patriot," in like manner, is employed to signify a lover of human liberty and human improvement rather than a mere lover of the country in which he lives, or the tribe to which he belongs.

Used in this sense, patriotism is a virtue, and a patriot a virtuous man. With such an interpretation, a patriot is a useful member of society, capable of enlarging all minds and bettering all hearts with which he comes in contact; a useful member of the human family, capable of establishing fundamental principles and of merging his own interests, those of his associates, and those of his nation in the interests of the human race. Laurels and statues are vain things, and mischievous as they are childish; but could we imagine them of use, on *such* a patriot alone could they be with any reason bestowed. . . .

If such a patriotism as we have last considered should seem likely to obtain in any country, it should be certainly in this. In this which is truly the home of all nations and in the veins of whose citizens flows the blood of every people on the globe. Patriotism, in the exclusive meaning, is surely not made for America. Mischievous everywhere, it were here both mischievous and absurd. The very origin of the people is opposed to it. The institutions, in their principle, militate against it. The day we are celebrating protests against it.

It is for Americans, more especially, to nourish a nobler sentiment; one more consistent with their origin, and more conducive to their future improvement. It is for them more especially to know why they love their country; and to *feel* that they love it, not because it *is* their country, but because it is the palladium of human liberty—the favored scene of human improvement. It is for them, more especially, to examine their institutions; and to *feel* that they honor them because they are based on just principles. It is for them, more especially, to examine their institutions, because they have the means of improving them; to examine their laws, because at will they can alter them. It is for them to lay aside luxury whose wealth is in industry; idle parade whose strength is in knowledge; ambitious distinctions whose principle is equality. It is for them not to rest, satisfied with words, who can seize upon things; and to remember that equality means, not the mere equality of political rights, however valuable, but equality of instruction and equality in virtue; and that liberty means, not the mere voting at elections, but the free and fearless exercise of the mental faculties and that self-possession which springs out of well-reasoned opinions and consistent practice. It is for them to honor principles rather than men—to commemorate events rather than days; when they rejoice, to know for what they rejoice, and to rejoice only for what has brought and what brings peace and happiness to men.

The event we commemorate this day has procured much of both, and shall procure in the onward course of human improvement more than we can now conceive of. For this—for the good obtained and yet in store for our race—let us rejoice! But let us rejoice as men, not as children—as human beings rather than as Americans—as reasoning beings, not as ignorants. So shall we rejoice to good purpose and in good feeling; so shall we improve the victory once on this day achieved, until all mankind hold with us the Jubilee of Independence.

Princess Elizabeth
Makes a Vow to the British Empire

"God help me to make good my vow . . ."

Princess Elizabeth (b. 1926) was ten years old when her uncle, Edward VIII of England, broadcast his now-famous farewell to the Commonwealth. "I have found it impossible to carry the heavy burden of responsibility . . ." he said, "without the help and support of the woman I love." The woman was Wallis Simpson, the American divorcée deemed unacceptable by Britain's religious and political establishment.

The high drama in the House of Windsor unfolded in 1936, known to history as the Year of Three Kings—the turbulent period marked by the death of Elizabeth's grandfather, George V, the abdication of her uncle, and the accession of her father, George VI. The young princess, as heir presumptive, spent the next several years "readying for destiny," which came at age twenty-five when her father died from lung cancer in 1952. Elizabeth, by then married to the Duke of Edinburgh, was the mother of two children, Charles and Anne. "A fair and youthful figure," Winston Churchill said, "princess, wife, and mother, is heir to all our traditions and glories."

Five years earlier, on April 21, 1947, a still future queen marked her twenty-first birthday with this speech, broadcast by radio while on tour of South Africa. Unlike her uncle's "renunciation of responsibility," as the family saw it, Elizabeth's speech is a pledge to the Empire—a vow, as she declares here, of life-long service to the realm. More than a quarter of the world's population watched her formalize this vow in 1953, when her coronation as Queen Elizabeth II was televised live from West-minster Abbey.

O n my twenty-first birthday, I welcome the opportunity to speak to all the peoples of the British Commonwealth and Empire, wherever they live, whatever race they come from, and whatever language they speak. Let me begin by saying "thank you" to all the thousands of kind people who have sent me messages of goodwill. This is a happy day for me; but it is also one that brings serious thoughts, thoughts of life looming ahead with all its challenges and with all its opportunity. At such a time it is a great help to know that there are multitudes of friends all round the world who are thinking of me and who wish me well. I am grateful and I am deeply moved.

As I speak to you today from Cape Town, I am six thousand miles from the country where I was born. But I am certainly not six thousand miles from home. Everywhere I have traveled in these lovely lands of South Africa and Rhodesia, my parents, my sister, and I have been taken to the heart of their people and made to feel that we are just as much at home here as if we had lived among them all our lives. That is the great privilege belonging to our place in the worldwide Commonwealth—that there are homes ready to welcome us in every continent of earth. Before I am much older, I hope I shall come to know many of them.

Although there is none of my father's subjects from the old-est to the youngest whom I do not wish to greet, I am thinking especially today of all the young men and women who were born about the same time as myself and have grown up like me in the terrible and glorious years of the Second World War. Will you, the youth of the British family of nations, let me speak on my birthday as your representative? Now that we are coming to manhood and womanhood, it is surely a great joy to us all to think that we shall be able to take some of the burden off the shoulders of our elders who have fought and worked and suffered to protect our childhood.

We must not be daunted by the anxieties and hardships that the war has left behind for every nation of our Commonwealth. We know that these things are the price we cheerfully undertook to pay for the high honor of standing alone, seven years ago, in defense of the liberty of the world. Let us say with Rupert Brooke "Now, God be thanked Who has matched us with His hour."

I am sure that you will see our difficulties, in the light that I see them, as the great opportunity for you and me. Most of you have read in the history books the proud saying of William Pitt that England had saved herself by her exertions and would save Europe by her example. But in our time we may say that the British Empire has saved the world first, and has now to save itself after the battle is won. I think that is an even finer thing than was done in the days of Pitt; and it is for us, who have grown up in these years of danger and glory, to see that it is accomplished in the long years of peace that we all hope stretch ahead.

If we all go forward together with an unwavering faith, a high courage, and a quiet heart, we shall be able to make of this ancient Commonwealth, which we all love so dearly, an even grander thing—more free, more prosperous, more happy, and a more powerful influence for good in the world—than it has been in the greatest days of our forefathers.

To accomplish that we must give nothing less than the whole of ourselves. There is a motto which has been borne by many of my ancestors—a noble motto, "I serve." Those words were an inspiration to many bygone heirs to the throne when they made their knightly dedication as they came to manhood. I cannot do quite as they did.

But through the inventions of science I can do what was not possible for any of them. I can make my solemn act of dedication with a whole Empire listening. I should like to make that dedication now. It is very simple. I declare before you all that my whole life whether it be long or short shall be devoted to your service and the service of our great imperial family to which we all belong. But I shall not have strength to carry out this resolution alone unless you join in it with me, as I now invite you to do: I know that your support will be unfailingly given. God help me to make good my vow, and God bless all of you who are willing to share in it.

Margaret Thatcher
Hails a New Britain

*"We know we can do it—we haven't lost the
ability. That is the Falklands Factor."*

Margaret Thatcher made this stirring declamation at a Conservative rally in Cheltenham on July 3, 1982, three weeks after
white flags flew over the Argentine command in the Falklands.
The speech is one of her finest—and most famous—and signaled a new spirit in Britain, emboldened by victory in the
South Atlantic.

Typical of the Thatcher style, the speech is declarative,
steeped in the words of an unabashed nationalist: The Right
Honorable Lady saw a nation that could achieve anything in
peace, having proved itself in war. Britains agreed; the "Falklands
Factor" transformed her party's political prospects and led to the
prime minister's landslide reelection in 1983.

———◦•◦———

Today we meet in the aftermath of the Falkands Battle. Our
country has won a great victory and we are entitled to be
proud. This nation had the resolution to do what it knew had to
be done—to do what it knew was right.

We fought to show that aggression does not pay, and that
the robber cannot be allowed to get away with his swag. We

fought with the support of so many throughout the world: the Security Council, the Commonwealth, the European Community, and the United States. Yet we also fought alone—for we fought for our own people.

Now that it is all over, things cannot be the same again, for we have learned something about ourselves—a lesson which we desperately needed to learn. When we started out, there were the waverers and the faint hearts: the people who thought that Britain could no longer seize the initiative for herself; the people who thought we could no longer do the great things which we once did; and those who believed that our decline was irreversible—that we could never again be what we were. There were those who would not admit it—even perhaps some here today—people who would have strenuously denied the suggestion but—in their heart of hearts—they too had their secret fears that it was true: that Britain was no longer the nation that had built an Empire and ruled a quarter of the world.

Well, they were wrong. The lesson of the Falklands is that Britain has not changed and that this nation still has those sterling qualities which shine through our history. This generation can match their fathers and grandfathers in ability, in courage, and in resolution. We have not changed. When the demands of war and the dangers to our own people call us to arms—then we British are as we have always been—competent, courageous, and resolute.

When called to arms—ah, that's the problem. It took the battle in the South Atlantic for the shipyards to adapt ships way ahead of time; for dockyards to refit merchantmen and cruise liners, to fix helicopter platforms, to convert hospital ships—all faster than was thought possible; it took the demands of war for every stop to be pulled out and every man and woman to do their best.

British people had to be threatened by foreign soldiers and

British territory invaded and then—why then—the response was incomparable. Yet why does it need a war to bring out our qualities and reassert our pride? Why do we have to be invaded before we throw aside our selfish aims and begin to work together as only we can work, and achieve as only we can achieve?

That really is the challenge we as a nation face today. We have to see that the spirit of the South Atlantic—the real spirit of Britain—is kindled not only by war but can now be fired by peace.

We have the first prerequisite. We know we can do it—we haven't lost the ability. That is the Falklands Factor. We have proved ourselves to ourselves. It is a lesson we must not now forget. Indeed, it is a lesson which we must apply to peace just as we have learned it in war. The faltering and the self-doubt have given way to achievement and pride. We have the confidence and we must use it.

Just look at the Task Force as an object lesson. Every man had his own task to do and did it superbly. Officers and men, senior NCO and newest recruit—everyone realized that his contribution was essential for the success of the whole. All were equally valuable—each was differently qualified. By working together, each was able to do more than his best. As a team they raised the average to the level of the best and by each doing his utmost, together they achieved the impossible.

That's an accurate picture of Britain at war—not yet of Britain at peace. But the spirit has stirred and the nation has begun to assert itself. Things are not going to be the same again. . . .

PART 3

TRIBUTES

AND

COMMEMORATIONS

Julia Ward Howe
Praises Poet Oliver Wendell Holmes

"O autocratic muse!"

Growing up in New York, Julia Ward Howe (1819–1910)
thrived on literature. She read. She wrote. She wanted to be a
poet.

> Mine eyes have seen the glory of the coming of the Lord;
> He is trampling out the vintage where the grapes of wrath
>   are stored;
> He hath loosed the fateful lightning of His terrible swift
>   sword;
> His truth is marching on.

When Howe published the "Battle Hymn of the Republic"
in 1862, she became more than a poet. She became a literary
sensation—"freedom personified" in the eyes of Lincoln and
others. The Civil War was raging, and Howe's poem, set to the
tune of "John Brown's Body," uplifted the Union cause and
made Howe a national institution.

After the war, she took up the cause of suffrage, establishing
and leading the New England Woman Suffrage Association
with Lucy Stone, and fighting vehemently for marriage rights.
Her own stifling and unhappy marriage came shortly after 1843,

when she married Samuel Gridley Howe—an abolitionist opposed to women leading public lives and less than comfortable with his wife's sudden rise to fame.

Yet the fame endured; in 1908, Howe became the first woman elected to the American Academy of Arts and Letters—an honor her good friend and fellow poet, the renowned Dr. Oliver Wendell Holmes (father of the even more renowned Justice Oliver Wendell Holmes) did not live to see. Holmes died in 1894. In this speech, delivered on December 3, 1879, at a Boston breakfast honoring the poet Holmes on his seventieth birthday, Howe paid tribute to her friend, her mentor—the "man of noble mold."

———•—•———

Ladies and Gentlemen: One word in courtesy I must say in replying to so kind a mention as that which is made, not only of me, but those of my sex who are so happy as to be present here today. I think, in looking on this scene, of a certain congress which took place in Paris more than a year ago. It was called a congress of literary people, *gens de lettres*.

When I heard that this was to take place I immediately bestirred myself to attend its sittings and went at once to the headquarters to find how I might do so. I then learned to my great astonishment that no women were to be included among these *gens de lettres*, that is, literary people. (*Laughter.*)

Now, we have thought it a very modest phrase sometimes to plead that, whatever women may not be, they are people. (*Laughter and applause.*) And it would seem today that they are recognized as literary people, and I am very glad that you gentlemen have found room for the sisterhood today, and have found room to place them so numerously here, and I must say that to my eyes the banquet looks very much more cheerful than it would without them. (*Applause.*) It looks to me as though it had all blossomed out under a new social influence, and beside each dark stem I see a rose. (*Laughter and applause.*)

But I must say at once that I came here entirely unprovided with a speech, and, not dreaming of one, yet I came provided with something. I considered myself invited as a sort of grand-mother—indeed, I am, and I know a grandmother is usually expected to have something in her pocket. And I have a very modest tribute to the illustrious person whom we are met today to honor. With your leave I will read it.

> Thou metamorphic god!
> Who mak'st the straight Olympus thy abode,
> > Hermes to subtle laughter moving,
> > Apollo with serener loving,
> > Thou demi-god also!
> Who dost all the powers of healing know;
> > Thou hero who dost wield
> > The golden sword and shield,—
> > Shield of a comprehensive mind,
> And sword to wound the foes of human kind;
>
> > Thou man of noble mold!
> > Whose metal grows not cold
> Beneath the hammer of the hurrying years;
> > A fiery breath doth blow
> > Across its fervid glow,
> And still its resonance delights our ears;
>
> > Loved of thy brilliant mates,
> > Relinquished to the fates,
> Whose spirit music used to chime with thine,
> > Transfigured in our sight,

Not quenched in death's dark night,
They hold thee in companionship divine.

O autocratic muse!
Soul-rainbow of all hues,
Packed full of service are thy bygone years;
Thy winged steed doth fly
Across the starry sky,
Bearing the lowly burthens of thy tears.

I try this little leap,
Wishing that from the deep,
I might some pearl of song adventurous bring.
Despairing, here I stop,
And my poor offering drop,—
Why stammer I when thou art here to sing?

Mary Lease
Extols the Virtues of Kansas

". . . honest toilers shall constitute a state."

"What you farmers need to do is raise less corn and more hell!" Mary Lease (1850–1933) never said in 1890. She never said it and twice denied it—yet historians have built the reputation of this Populist orator around that simple, single phrase.

Daughter of Irish Catholic immigrants, Lease first used her dramatic, sardonic, and lively oratorical skills on behalf of the Irish National League and later women's rights before becoming a leading voice of the Populist movement in Kansas, and then the nation, in the late nineteenth century. On the hustings for the People's Party, she blasted "tyrannical Eastern money power" and exhorted farmers to vote for Populist candidates. "My God, how any patriotic man today can be a Republican or a Democrat is past my comprehension," she really did say.

This speech, delivered at the 1893 Columbian Exposition in Chicago, is a striking contrast to that tempestuous political style. Lease, representing Kansas's newly elected Populist government, "word paints" an encomium to her state, coupling nineteenth century oratorical pomp with Populist precepts. "Up from her plains, baptized with the blood of martyrs, shall come the prophet of Ezekiel's vision," she says, and ". . . kings shall be no more." It's grandiose—but still a vivid and noble tribute.

He that can paint a picture in marvelous beauty, that can pencil a landscape tinted with the glory of the dawn, that can strike a harp and make its responsive chords burst into a glad melody of song, that can tint a rainbow, give glory to the flowers, sublimity to the sea, majesty to the landscape and with the hand of Liszt bring melody from pattering rain and whispering breeze, evolve the music of the spheres from rustling corn and billowy wheat, may hope to picture Kansas, that old land which men call new.

Before Athens was, or Rome was born, the creeping tides, the rolling breakers, the terror of the tempest, the savagery of the storm, the star-gemmed waves of mighty ocean beat and surged upon her prairie bosom. Speculation as to that time brings us into fellowship with the ages.

What strange sea monsters sported on the wave; what flora; rank, luxuriant, giant palms and somber cypress, nodded on its marshy shore; what white-winged sails or strangely built caravels rocked upon its tide, we may not tell. We question the ages, but few hear the voice which makes reply. We ask the skies and they are dumb. If nature has kept a record of buried continents, dying stars and worlds decayed, of the birth of islands, the emerging of continents from the shoreless sea, her book of lore is closed save to a few.

The past with its atmosphere of floating mist, its clouds of dust, its long dark night, its shoreless expanse of ocean, its convulsions and its cataclysms, has left us dawn and sunset, opened bud, perfected flower, sea and sky, teeming soil, vernal leagues of sun and dew, where the footsteps of angels and the waving of heavenly wings are heard in the rustling corn and the miles and miles of billowy grain. Where night and morning repeat the story of the Resurrection, and spring and autumn write prophecy of immortality on wind-spent plains and sunkissed leagues of rain-thrilled soil.

Strange monsters crawled and swam, jungle serpents and treacherous wild beasts lived and died . . . the tepee of the warrior to the "Pioneer Civilization," the white canvassed schooner of the prairies; the emigrant wagon train plodding toward the setting sun, gave way in turn to the iron horse that with steaming breath and wild halloo awoke the echoes from their slumbers, speeding across the trackless prairies toward farthest limits of the day; and westward, westward evermore God's grand pathfinder plows its way, and Kansas, the geographical center of the Union, the geographical center of the world, with no stain upon her garments, redeemed and consecrated by freedom's baptismal blood, purified and strengthened by chrismal oil of sacrifice, stands preeminent and glorified in the closing hours of the nineteenth century; bearing aloft the torch that already gilds the mountaintops of the Old World; teaching humanity that which makes tyrants tremble and the worn-out monarchies and crumbling crowns of Europe come to marvel and to learn.

Evolution that brought a rich land from the salt marsh of the ocean and transformed slime and mud of the great basin into snowy bloom, golden grain, laid its magic wand upon the people, and Kansans are typical of the growth and improvement and elevation of the world. They are descendants of those

> Who crossed the prairies as of old
> > Our fathers crossed the sea,
> To make the West, as they the East
> > The homeland of the free.

Their ancestors died for freedom, and they themselves are the ambassadors of liberty, the architects and builders of the temple of human rights; the constructors and interpreters of the reverence for God, reverence for man, reverence for women, reverence for law—and upon these four pillars rests the Republic of the United States. They are the most God-fearing, law-abiding, liberty-loving, intelligent people of the earth. A schoolhouse dots every valley, a university of learning crowns every hill. Their school system is based upon the doctrine that each child is entitled to an education, and the state, like a fostering mother, wraps about her children the arms of love, and the wild beast of drunkenness hides from the light of day.

Nature has designed Kansas as debatable ground. The soft south winds, flower-laden, enervating, come stealing from the gulf along our plains and are met by the sturdy western winds that blow straight and strong from the battlements of God, the wondrous Rockies, and ever on our prairies they struggle for supremacy, typical of the warring forces of freedom and slavery, that have made Kansas the amphitheater of human progress and attracted to her the attention of the world.

The immensity of space, the vast illimitable sweep of prairie, the winds that play now high and loud, and now soft and low, across the undulating bosom of the caravanless plains, all, all speak of freedom. Her sacred fires burn in every heart, and, like a furnace blast, sweep through her borders. Let slavery in any form lift its hydra head, and Kansas speaks, and the world listens, for she never speaks in vain.

Should the lion of tyranny invade our soil, we diet him on freedom, give him solid food, labeled "exact justice to all; special privileges to none," and he has no alternative but to digest or die. For us the gates of opportunity are swinging wide, and the eternal sea is scarce wide enough for Kansas sails, and the skies of the land of summer are fluttering with wings of our boundless hope.

Wander we east or west, our thought ever reverts to our well-loved prairie state, and sooner or later our wandering feet return, for we love our land with that constancy of which our loyal sunflower is emblematical.

> For the heart that has truly loved never forgets,
> But as truly loves on to the close
> As the sunflower turns on her god when he sets,
> The same look which she turned when she rose.

Because of the vastness of our inheritance, the boundless scope of our ambitions, we sometimes seem to jostle one another on our onward and upward way, but let outside influence interfere, and we remember at once that we are Kansans, and to be a "Kansan is greater than to be a king."

The freshness of the early dawn is cooling our faces; the rosy clouds and golden light of sunrise just before us. Our sorrows vanish like the Kansas snows and leave no trace. Should enemies assail us, their force is as quickly spent as the Kansas storms. The principles of patriotism and valor and integrity permeates every Kansas heart, and they are as staunch, as tried and true as our Kansas soil that the sunshine and rain have kissed into teaming life and power.

Patrick Henry plead for liberty; Washington fought for it; the philosophy of Jefferson perpetuated it; but Kansans live it.

The grandeur and vastness of our prairies sweeping free has lifted us into broader, grander life, and with Kansas preaching popular government, Kansas in the council halls of the nation, Kansas at the helm of state, the waves of tyranny shall beat and surge in vain, and all the kings of the world and all their blood-fed armies cannot reverse the wheels of human progress.

From Kansas shall come the fulfillment of scripture. Up from her plains, baptized with the blood of martyrs, shall come the prophet Ezekiel's vision, that breathing upon the dry bones of the world's oppressed will clothe them with new life, resur-

recting the wisdom of the seers, the justice of Christ, and all
humanity will enjoy that liberty which the winds of Kansas forever play on aeolian harps, and all the world shall come up the
path which we have blazed and bask in the light which we have
kindled and kings shall be no more, and the world will not tolerate hungry poor or idle rich; neither shall be found tyrants,
small or great, but they who obey the divine injunction to earn
their bread in the sweat of their face; honest toilers shall constitute a state.

Voltairine de Cleyre
Memorializes the Haymarket Martyrs

*"We shall feel their living heartbeats, as we
step upon this swaying bridge. . . ."*

On May 4, 1886, fifteen hundred people gathered in Haymarket
Square in Chicago to denounce police brutality in the wake of
ongoing labor strikes for an eight-hour workday. The impassioned rally, organized by Chicago anarchists, left eleven people
dead and one hundred injured after a bomb exploded and riot-
ing erupted as police tried to disperse the meeting. Eight anarchists were brought to trial, and, though no evidence linked
them to the bomb, the men were convicted of inciting violence. Four were hanged, one committed suicide, and three others, after having served seven years in prison, were pardoned in
1893 by Illinois Governor John P. Altgeld (acting at the urging
of "the common man's attorney," Clarence Darrow).

The trial's "malicious ferocity," in Altgeld's words, and the
fate of the condemned men, haunted a young Voltairine de
Cleyre (1866–1912). Named for Voltaire by her father, the
Michigan-born de Cleyre was schooled in a Catholic convent
before joining the "freethinkers" crusade, flirting briefly with
socialism and finally gravitating to anarchism after the Chicago
riot.

Nearly every year, beginning in 1895, de Cleyre delivered a
memorial oration to the Haymarket martyrs—each one an elo-

quent, upswept eulogy and a pointed defense of her cause. This is the conclusion to her memorial address, presented in Philadelphia on November 17, 1900, de Cleyre's thirty-fourth birthday. The line that borrows from Theodore Roosevelt ("those who live 'the strenuous life' rarely live to be old") is prescient; "the greatest woman anarchist in America," as Emma Goldman called her, suffered a life of unrelieved poverty and chronic illness and died at age forty-five.

. . . These our comrades, who were self-conscious, reasoning, who went with clear eyes to the gallows and died triumphantly as ever any martyr did of old—they of whom even their bitterest enemies had to say "they died like brave me," they will be known and remembered long, even in the Land of Freedom. We shall feel their living heartbeats, as we step upon this swaying bridge; we shall hear their death words crying till the fields of life are won; and up along the banks of the farther shore, there comes a drifting of unborn voices singing, "Blessed are the dead who died for freedom."

Shall I say over again what we have said every year, these thirteen years—that the specific act with which they were charged (conspiracy with the thrower of the Haymarket bomb) was never remotely proven? Shall I repeat that the trial was unfair, the jury prejudiced, the judge committed to conviction, the prosecutor openly bragging they had packed the jury to hang? Governor Altgeld has saved me the trouble of all this. Whoever will dispassionately read his "Reasons for Pardoning Fielden, Neebe, and Schwab," will know it beyond a doubt; they are taken from the court testimony itself—you can ask nothing more.

They were tried and hanged for preaching anarchism; the

bomb-thrower was never known, probably never will be. Whoever it was, he threw it as an act of resistance to the unconstitutional proceeding of the police in breaking up a peaceable meeting. The aggression began with the guardians of law and order, who fired into the crowd, and drew forth a bomb as an answer to their bullets. Right or wrong, it had nothing to do with the right to advocate opinions; but it served as the lever to move the machinery of the law against our comrades.

It is all false that the hanging was done because of their preaching violence; it is not violence the ruling classes object to; for they themselves rule by violence, and take with the strong hand at every door. It is the social change they fear, the equalization of men. Tyranny has often mistaken its means; and the rulers of Illinois repeated history. What they would have destroyed, they multiplied; where they would have cursed, they blessed. And many a one will say with me tonight, in answer to the question, "What made you an anarchist?" "The hanging in Chicago."

Well, they are gone; and we who are here tonight may not have long to stay; for we are moving down past the middle line; and those who live "the strenuous life" rarely live to be old. But few or many our years, we shall spend them working for that which to us is the only thing worth working for—the free life.

To the fervent hopes and efforts of the younger generations, we commit the memories of thirteen years ago, praying them never to forget the price paid by the dead nor the anguish of some yet living; never to forget that the way to honor a sacrifice is to follow up the spirit of it; and that if to you too has come the Vision of Man made one—without countries, nations, divisions, classes, without authorities priestly or civil, with the peace that is real, the equality which means free self-expression—be bold to bear witness to it; picture it; work for it; live for it if you can; die for it if you must. Remember the dungeon and the gallows tonight, and the flesh, warm like yours, that is dust, or corroding in prison cells—and be not silent under pain of condemnation of your own soul, that last judge, to whom all courts are as nothing, to whom you can tell no lies, and who will be with you to the edge of doom. True to your ideal, you may at the end speak to scoffer and persecutor the beautiful lines quoted by our beloved Parsons, near the last:

I am not dead—I am not dead,
I live a life intense, divine!
Yours be the days forever fled,
But all the morrows shall be mine.

Jane Addams
Salutes George Washington

*"What is a great man who has made his mark
upon history?"*

Though the death of her father in 1881 left Jane Addams
(1860–1935) depressed and "without ambition," she found her
calling working for social welfare, woman's suffrage, and peace—
and eventually became known as America's "most useful citizen." Best known for helping to found and run Hull House, a
settlement home established in Chicago in 1889, Addams documented her views on social welfare in voluminous articles,
speeches, and books—including the celebrated *Twenty Years at
Hull House*.

By the early 1900s, polls ranked Addams ahead of Thomas
Edison, Helen Keller, and Theodore Roosevelt in popularity,
but her pacifist views during World War I, appeals for food relief
for German children, and defense of those arrested during the
Red Scare tarnished her image—almost irreparably. Gradually,
her efforts for peace, including the establishment of the
Women's International League for Peace and Freedom, brought
her back into public favor. In 1931, she became the first American woman to win the Nobel Peace prize.

On February 23, 1903, Addams spoke to the Union League
Club in Chicago during a celebration of George Washington's birthday. Much like Frances Wright's patriotic advisement

seventy-five years earlier ("to honor principles rather than men," page 59), Addams distinguishes Washington—the soldier, statesman, citizen—as a man whose principles point to "the life of the larger cause." It is the "wise patriotism" of America's first president, she tells her audience, that should inspire them to seek better conditions and "like opportunity" for all.

—————

We meet together upon these birthdays of our great men, not only to review their lives, but to revive and cherish our own patriotism. This matter is a difficult task. In the first place, we are prone to think that by merely reciting these great deeds we get a reflected glory, and that the future is secure to us because the past has been so fine.

In the second place, we are apt to think that we inherit the fine qualities of those great men, simply because we have had a common descent and are living in the same territory.

As for the latter, we know full well that the patriotism of common descent is the mere patriotism of the clan—the early patriotism of the tribe. We know that the possession of a like territory is merely an advance upon that, and that both of them are unworthy to be the patriotism of a great cosmopolitan nation whose patriotism must be large enough to obliterate racial distinction and to forget that there are such things as surveyor's lines. Then when we come to the study of great men it is easy to think only of their great deeds, and not to think enough of their spirit.

What is a great man who has made his mark upon history? Every time, if we think far enough, he is a man who has looked through the confusion of the moment and has seen the moral issue involved; he is a man who has refused to have his sense of justice distorted; he has listened to his conscience until conscience becomes a trumpet call to like-minded men, so that they gather about him and together, with mutual purpose and mutual aid, they make a new period in history.

Let us assume for a moment that if we are going to make this day of advantage to us, we will have to take this definition of a great man. We will have to appeal to the present as well as to the past. We will have to rouse our national consciences as well as our national pride, and we will have to remember that it lies with the young people of this nation whether or not it is going to go on to a finish in any wise worthy of its beginning.

If we go back to George Washington, and ask what he would be doing were he bearing our burdens now, and facing our problems at this moment, we would, of course, have to study his life bit by bit; his life as a soldier, as a statesman, and as a simple Virginia planter.

First, as a soldier. What is it that we admire about the soldier? It certainly is not that he goes into battle; what we admire about the soldier is that he has the power of losing his own life for the life of a larger cause; that he holds his personal suffering of no account; that he flings down in the gage of battle his all, and says, "I will stand or fall with this cause." That, it seems to me, is the glorious thing we most admire, and if we are going to preserve that same spirit of the soldier, we will have to found a similar spirit in the civil life of the people, the same pride in civil warfare, the spirit of courage, and the spirit of self-surrender which lies back of this.

If we look out upon our national perspective, do we not see certainly one great menace which calls for patriotism? We see all around us a spirit of materialism—an undue emphasis put upon material possessions; an inordinate desire to win wealth; an inordinate desire to please those who are the possessors of wealth. Now, let us say, if we feel that this is a menace, that with all our power, with all the spirit of a soldier, we will arouse high-minded youth of this country against this spirit of materialism. We will say today that we will not count the opening of markets the one great field which our nation is concerned in, but that when our flag flies anywhere it shall fly for righteousness as well as for increased commercial prosperity; that we will see to it that no sin of commercial robbery shall be committed where it floats; that we shall see to it that nothing in our commercial history will not bear the most careful scrutiny and investigation; that we will restore commercial life, however complicated, to such honor and simple honesty as George Washington expressed in his business dealings.

Let us take, for a moment, George Washington as a statesman. What was it he did, during those days when they were framing a constitution, when they were meeting together night after night, and trying to adjust the rights and privileges of every class in the community? What was it that sustained him during all those days, all those weeks, during all those months and years? It was the belief that they were founding a nation on the axiom that all men are created free and equal. What would George Washington say if he found that among us there were causes constantly operating against that equality? If he knew that any child which is thrust prematurely into industry has no chance in life with children who are preserved from that pain and sorrow; if he knew that every insanitary street, and every insanitary house, cripples a man so that he has no health and vigor with which to carry on his life labor; if he knew that all about us are forces making against skill, making against the best manhood and womanhood, what would he say? He would say that if the spirit of equality means anything, it means like opportunity, and if we once lose like opportunity we lose the only chance we have toward equality throughout the nation.

Let us take George Washington as a citizen. What did he do when he retired from office, because he was afraid holding office any longer might bring a wrong to himself and harm to his beloved nation? We say that he went back to his plantation on the Potomac. What were his thoughts during the all too short days that he lived there? He thought of many possibilities, but, looking out over his country, did he fear that there should rise up a crowd of men who held office, not for their country's good, but for their own good? Would he not have foreboded evil if he had known that among us were groups and hordes of professional politicians, who, without any blinking or without any pretense that they did otherwise, apportioned the spoils of office, and considered an independent man as a mere intruder, as a mere outsider; if he had seen that the original meaning of office-holding and the function of government had become indifferent to us, that we were not using our foresight and our conscience in order to find out this great wrong which was sapping the foundations of government? He would tell us that anything which makes for better civic service, which makes for a merit system, which makes for fitness for office, is the only thing which will tell against this wrong, and that this course is the wisest patriotism. What did he write in his last correspondence? He wrote that he felt very unhappy on the subject of slavery, that there was, to his mind, a great menace in the holding of slaves. We know that he neither bought nor sold slaves himself, and that he freed his own slaves in his will. That was a century ago. A man who a century ago could do that, would he, do you think, be indifferent now to the great questions of social maladjustment which we feel all around us? His letters breathe a yearning for a better condition for the slaves as the letters of all great men among us breathe a yearning for the better condition of the unskilled and underpaid. A wise patriotism, which will take hold of these questions by careful legal enactment, by constant and vigorous enforcement, because of the belief that if the meanest man in the Republic is deprived of his rights, then every man in the Republic is deprived of his rights, is the only patriotism by which public-spirited men and women, with a thoroughly aroused conscience, can worthily serve this Republic. Let us say again that the lessons of great men are lost unless they reinforce upon our minds the highest demands which we make upon ourselves; that they are lost unless they drive our sluggish wills forward in the direction of their highest ideals.

Queen Elizabeth II
Remembers the Year that Was

". . . it has turned out to be an annus horribilis."

On November 24, 1992, Queen Elizabeth II delivered this speech at a luncheon at London's Guildhall, honoring the fortieth anniversary of her accession to the throne. Scandals and troubles had beset the monarchy all year—ending in the divorce of the queen's daughter, Anne, from Mark Phillips and the separations of Prince Andrew from Sarah Ferguson and Prince Charles from Diana, Princess of Wales. Add to that a fire, four days before the luncheon, that swept through Windsor Castle, destroying a large section of what had been home to eight generations of British royalty. Though early arrangements for the queen to begin paying income taxes had begun a year earlier, the official announcement, poorly timed, came after the public balked at the news that Windsor's £60 million restoration bill would come from public money.

Looking and sounding sad, her voice hoarse from a heavy cold and the smoke and fumes at Windsor, which she had gone to inspect, the queen made her anniversary remarks to an audience of more than seven hundred well wishers, among them Prime Minister John Major. The criticism of previous months had not escaped her; criticism is good for those in public life, she concedes. But the sovereign with a manifest sense of duty and forty years of service to the realm also appealed for tolerance: criticism mixed with "a touch of gentleness, good humor, and understanding"—a fitting description of her speech.

———— ·•·• ————

Nineteen-ninety-two is not a year I shall look back on with undiluted pleasure. In the words of one of my more sympathetic correspondents*, it has turned out to be an *annus horribilis*. I suspect that I am not alone in thinking it so. Indeed, I suspect that there are very few people or institutions unaffected by these last months of worldwide turmoil and uncertainty. This generosity and whole-hearted kindness of the corporation of the City to Prince Philip and me would be welcome at any time but, at this particular moment, in the aftermath of Friday's tragic fire at Windsor, it is especially so.

And, after this last weekend, we appreciate all the more what has been set before us today. Years of experience, however, have made us a bit more canny than the lady—less well-versed than us in the splendors of City hospitality—who, when she was offered a balloon glass for her brandy, asked for "only half a glass, please."

It is possible to have too much of a good thing. A well-meaning bishop was obviously doing his best when he told Queen Victoria: "Ma'am, we cannot pray too often, nor too fervently, for the royal family." The queen's reply was: "Too fervently, no; too often, yes." I, like Queen Victoria, have always been a believer in that old maxim "moderation in all things."

I sometimes wonder how future generations will judge the events of this tumultuous year. I daresay that history will take a

---

*The Queen's Private Secrretary, classical scholar Sir Edward Ford.

slightly more moderate view than that of some contemporary commentators. Distance is well-known to lend enchantment, even to the less attractive views.

After all, it has the inestimable advantage of hindsight. But it can also lend an extra dimension to judgment, giving it a leavening of moderation and compassion—even of wisdom—that is sometimes lacking in the reactions of those whose task it is in life to offer instant opinions on all things great and small. No section of the community has all the virtues, neither does any have all the vices. I am quite sure that most people try to do their jobs as best they can, even if the result is not always entirely successful. He who has never failed to reach perfection has a right to be the harshest critic.

There can be no doubt, of course, that criticism is good for people and institutions that are part of public life. No institution—city, monarchy, whatever—should expect to be free from the scrutiny of those who give it their loyalty and support, not to mention those who don't.

But we are all part of the same fabric of our national society and that scrutiny, by one part of another, can be just as effective if it is made with a touch of gentleness, good humor, and understanding.

This sort of questioning can also act, and it should do so, as an effective engine for change. The City is a good example of the way the process of change can be incorporated into the stability and continuity of a great institution.

I particularly admire, my Lord Mayor, the way in which the City has adapted so nimbly to what the prayer book calls "the changes and chances of this mortal life." You have set an example of how it is possible to remain effective and dynamic without losing those indefinable qualities, style and character. We only have to look around this great hall to see the truth of that.

Forty years is quite a long time. I am glad to have had the

chance to witness, and to take part in, many dramatic changes in life in this country. But I am glad to say that the magnificent standard of hospitality given on so many occasions to the sovereign by the Lord Mayor of London has not changed at all. It is an outward symbol of one other unchanging factor which I value above all: the loyalty given to me and my family by so many people in this country, and the Commonwealth, throughout my reign.

You, my Lord Mayor, and all those whose prayers—fervent, I hope, but not too frequent—have sustained me through all these years, are friends indeed. Prince Philip and I give you all, wherever you may be, our most humble thanks.

PART 4

SPEECHES
ON
SOCIAL JUSTICE

Maria Stewart
Calls for the Upliftment of Her Race

*"Most of our color have dragged out a
miserable existence of servitude from the cradle
to the grave."*

From the stage of Boston's Franklin Hall, on September 21, 1832, Maria Stewart (1803–1879) became the first American woman to speak publicly before a mixed audience of men and women, blacks and whites—a distinction that preceded the Grimké sisters by five years. The speech was just her second public lecture; her first was to Boston's Afric-American Female Intelligence Society earlier the same year.

Born Maria Miller, a free black from Hartford, Connecticut, Stewart was orphaned at five and "bound out" to a clergyman's family, before marrying James W. Stewart and settling in Boston in 1826. Widowed three years later, she converted to Christianity, which became the catalyst for her public role. "The spirit of God came before me," she said, "and I spake before many."

In this, her historic address, she entreats blacks to rise above "the condition of servants and drudges" and, to the whites in the crowded hall, decries the prejudice that keeps her people from aspiring any higher. Her appeal is impassioned and personal, woven with scriptural references, and draws in her audience with this stunning first question.

W hy ye sit here and die?
If we say we will go to a foreign land, the famine and the pestilence are there, and there we shall die. If we sit here, we shall die. Come let us plead our cause before the whites: if they save us alive, we shall live—and if they kill us, we shall but die.

Methinks I heard a spiritual interrogation—"Who shall go forward, and take off the reproach that is cast upon the people of color? Shall it be a woman?" And my heart made this reply—"If it is thy will, be it even so, Lord Jesus!"

I have heard much respecting the horrors of slavery; but my Heaven forbid that the generality of my color throughout these United States should experience any more of its horrors than to be a servant of servants, or hewers of wood and drawers of water! Tell us no more of southern slavery; for with few exceptions, although I may be very erroneous in my opinion, yet I consider our condition but a little better than that. Yet, after all, methinks there are no chains so galling as those that bind the soul, and exclude it from the vast field of useful and scientific knowledge. Oh, had I received the advantages of an early education, my ideas would, ere now, have expanded far and wide; but, alas! I possess nothing but moral capability—no teachings but the teachings of the Holy Spirit.

I have asked several individuals of my sex, who transact business for themselves, if providing our girls were to give them the most satisfactory references, they would not be willing to grant them an equal opportunity with others? Their reply has been—for their own part, they had no objection; but as it was not the custom, were they to take them into their employ, they would be in danger of losing the public patronage.

And such is the powerful force of prejudice. Let our girls

possess whatever amiable qualities of soul they may; let their characters be fair and spotless as innocence itself; let their natural taste and ingenuity be what they may; it is impossible for scarce an individual of them to rise above the condition of servants. Ah! why is this cruel and unfeeling distinction? Is it merely because God has made our complexion to vary? If it be, oh shame to soft, relenting humanity! "Tell it not in Gath! Publish it not in the streets of Askelon!" Yet, after all, methinks were the American free people of color to turn their attention more assiduously to moral worth and intellectual improvement, this would be the result: prejudice would gradually diminish, and the whites would be compelled to say, unloose those fetters!

> Though black their skins as shades of night
> Their hearts are pure, their souls are white.

Few white persons of either sex, who are calculated for anything else, are willing to spend their lives and bury their talents in performing mean, servile labor. And such is the horrible idea that I entertain respecting a life of servitude, that if I conceived of there being no possibility of my rising above the condition of servant, I would gladly hail death as a welcome messenger. Oh, horrible idea, indeed, to possess noble souls, aspiring after high and honorable acquirements, yet confined by the chains of ignorance and poverty to lives of continual drudgery and toil.

Neither do I know of any who have enriched themselves by spending their lives as house domestics, washing windows, shaking carpets, brushing boots, or tending upon gentlemen's tables. I can but die for expressing my sentiments: and I am willing to die by the sword and pestilence; for I am a true-born American; your blood flows in my veins, and your spirit fires my breast.

I have observed a piece in the *Liberator* a few months since, stating that the colonizationists had published a work respecting us, asserting that we were lazy and idle. I confute them on that point. Take us generally as a people; we are neither lazy nor idle; and considering how little we have to excite or stimulate us, I am almost astonished that there are so many industrious and ambitious ones to be found; although I acknowledge, with extreme sorrow, that there are some who never were and never will be serviceable to society. And have you not a similar class yourselves?

Again, it was asserted that we were "a ragged set, crying for liberty." I reply to it, the whites have so long and so loudly proclaimed the theme of equal rights and privileges, that our souls have caught the flame also, ragged as we are. As far as our merit deserves, we feel a common desire to rise above the condition of servants and drudges. I have learned, by bitter experience, that continual hard labor deadens the energies of the soul, and benumbs the faculties of the mind; the ideas become confined, the mind barren, and, like the scorching sands of Arabia, produces nothing; or like the uncultivated soul, brings forth thorns and thistles.

Again, continual and hard labor irritates our tempers and sours our dispositions; the whole system becomes worn out with toil and fatigue; nature herself becomes almost exhausted, and we care but little whether we live or die. It is true, that the free people of color throughout these United States are neither bought nor sold, nor under the lash of the cruel driver; many obtain a comfortable support; but few, if any, have an opportunity of becoming rich and independent; and the enjoyments we most pursue are unprofitable to us as the spider's web or the floating bubbles that vanish into air. As servants, we are respected; but let us presume to aspire any higher, our employer regards us no longer. And were it not that the King eternal has declared that Ethiopia shall stretch forth her hands unto God, I should indeed despair.

I do not consider it derogatory, my friends, for persons to live out to service. There are many whose inclination leads them to aspire no higher; and I would highly commend the performance of almost anything for an honest livelihood; but where constitutional strength is wanting, labor of this kind, in its mildest form is painful. And, doubtless, many are the prayers that have ascended to heaven from Afric's daughters for strength to perform their work. Oh, many are the tears that have been shed for the want of that strength! Most of our color have dragged out a miserable existence of servitude from the cradle to the grave. And what literary acquirements can be made, or useful knowledge derived, from either maps, books or charts, by those who continually drudge from Monday morning until Sunday noon?

Oh, ye fairer sisters, whose hands are never soiled, whose nerves and muscles are never strained, go learn by experience! Had we had the opportunity that you have had to improve our moral and mental faculties, what would have hindered our intellects from being as bright, and our manners from being as dignified as yours? Had it been our lot to have been nursed in the lap of affluence and ease, and to have basked beneath the smiles and sunshine of fortune, should we not have naturally supposed that we were never made to toil? And why are not our forms as delicate and our constitutions as slender as yours? Is not the workmanship as curious and complete? Have pity upon us, have pity upon us, oh ye who have hearts to feel for others' woes; for the hand of God has touched us. Owing to the disadvantages under which we labor, there are many flowers among us that are

. . . born to bloom unseen
And waste their fragrance on the desert air.

My beloved brethren, as Christ has died in vain for those who will not accept his offered mercy, so will it be vain for the advocates of freedom to spend their breath in our behalf, unless with united hearts and souls you make some mighty efforts to raise your sons and daughters from the horrible state of servitude and degradation in which they be placed. It is upon you that woman depends; she can do but little besides using her influence; and it is for her sake and yours that I have come forward and made myself a hissing and a reproach among the people; for I am also one of the wretched and miserable daughters of the descendants of the fallen Africa.

Do you ask, why are you wretched and miserable? I reply, look at many of the most worthy and most interesting of us doomed to spend our lives in gentlemen's kitchens. Look at our young men—smart, active, and energetic, with souls filled with ambitious fire; if they look forward, alas! What are their prospects? They can be nothing but the humblest laborer, on account of their dark complexion; hence many of them lose their ambition and become worthless.

Look at our middle-aged men, clad in their rusty plaids and coats. In winter, every cent they earn goes to buy wood and pay their rent; their poor wives also toil beyond strength, to help support their families.

Look at our aged sires, whose heads are whitened with the frosts of seventy winters, with their old wood saws on their backs. Alas, what keeps us so? Prejudice, ignorance and poverty.

But ah! methinks our oppression is soon to come to an end; yea, before the majesty of Heaven, our groans and cries have reached the ears of the Lord of Sabbath. And the prayers and tears of Christians will avail the finally impenitent nothing; neither will the prayers and tears of the friends of humanity avail us anything, unless we possess a spirit of virtuous emulation within our breasts.

Did the pilgrims, when they first landed on these shores, quietly compose themselves, and say, "The Britons have all the money and all the power, and we must continue their servants forever?" Did they sluggishly sigh and say, "Our lot is hard; the Indians own the soil, and we cannot cultivate it?" No, they first made powerful efforts to raise themselves, and then God raised up those illustrious patriots, Washington and Lafayette, to assist and defend them. And, my brethren have you made a powerful effort? Have you prayed the legislature for mercy's sake to grant you all the rights and privileges of free citizens, that your daughters may rise to that degree of respectability which true merit deserves, and your sons above the servile situations which most of them fill?

Angelina Grimké
Speaks Above the Shouts of an Angry Mob

"Many times have I wept in the land of my birth over the system of slavery."

Growing up on her father's plantation in South Carolina, Angelina Grimké (1805–1879) became convinced that slavery was evil. Disheartened, she followed her sister Sarah to Philadelphia, where the two women became Quakers and prominent voices for abolition and women's rights. "It is my deep, solemn, deliberate conviction that this is a cause worth dying for," she wrote abolitionist William Lloyd Garrison. Garrison published her letter in his antislavery journal, the *Liberator*, which brought the sisters speaking invitations from abolitionist audiences throughout the North.

Controversy quickly set in, however, when they began to draw mixed audiences. It was audacious enough that the two women spoke publicly, but to speak in the company of men was "beyond impropriety." In 1836, Grimké caused an even greater stir when she wrote, *An Appeal to the Christian Women of the South*, a pamphlet asking women to defy slavery laws. Southern postmasters burned it and warned her never to set foot in the South again.

On May 16, 1838, a few days after marrying abolitionist orator Theodore Weld, Grimké delivered this address at the National Antislavery Convention in Philadelphia. While she spoke, a raging mob howled, stormed, and pelted stones through the windows of the "free expression" building. (They burned the building to the ground the next day.) Grimké, ducking her head, was nonetheless forceful and prophetic and used the moment like background music. Slavery is here, she says. "Hear it! Hear it!" If the mob should attack, "would that be anything compared with what the slaves endure?" She closes, as she often did, by rallying women to the cause.

<hr />

M en, brethren and father—mothers, daughters and sisters, what came ye out for to see? A reed shaken with the wind? Is it curiosity merely, or a deep sympathy with the perishing slave? (*A yell from the mob outside the building.*) Those voices without ought to awaken and call out our warmest sympathies. Deluded beings! "They know not what they do." They know not that they are undermining their own rights and their own happiness, temporal and eternal.

Do you ask, "What has the North to do with slavery?" Hear it! Hear it! Those voices without tell us that the spirit of slavery is *here* and has been roused to wrath by our conventions; for surely liberty would not foam and tear herself with rage, because her friends are multiplied daily, and meetings are held in quick succession to set forth her virtues and extend her peaceful kingdom. This opposition shows that slavery has done its deadliest work in the hearts of our citizens. Do you ask, then, "What has the North to do?" I answer, cast out first the spirit of slavery from your own hearts, and then lend your aid to convert the South. Each one present has a work to do, be his or her situation what it may, however limited their means or insignificant their supposed influence. The great men of this country will not do this work; the church will never do it. A desire to please the world, to keep the favor of all parties and of all conditions, makes them dumb on this and every other unpopular subject.

As a Southerner, I feel that it is my duty to stand up here tonight and bear testimony against slavery. I have seen it! I have seen it! I know it has horrors that can never be described. I was brought up under its wing: I witnessed for many years its demoralizing influences and its destructiveness to human happiness. It is admitted by some that the slave is not happy under the *worst* forms of slavery. But I have *never* seen a happy slave. I have seen him dance in his chains, it is true, but he was not happy. There is a wide difference between happiness and mirth. Man cannot enjoy the former while his manhood is destroyed, and that part of the being which is necessary to the making, and the enjoyment of happiness, is completely blotted out. The slaves, however, may be, and sometimes are mirthful. When hope is extinguished, they say, "Let us eat and drink, for tomorrow we die." (*Just then stones were thrown at the windows—a great noise without and commotion within.*)

What is a mob? What would the breaking of every window be? What would the leveling of this hall be? Any evidence that we are wrong, or that slavery is a good and wholesome institution? What if the mob should now burst in upon us, break up our meeting, and commit violence upon our persons? Would that be anything compared with what the slaves endure? No, no; and we do not remember them "as bound with them," if we shrink in the time of peril, or feel unwilling to sacrifice ourselves, if need be, for their sake. (*Great noise.*) I thank the Lord that there is yet life enough left to feel the truth, even though it rages at it—that conscience is not so completely seared as to be unmoved by the truth of the living God.

Many persons go to the South for a season, and are hospitably entertained in the parlor and at the table of the slaveholder. They never enter the huts of the slaves; they know nothing of the dark side of the picture, and they return home with praises on their lips of the generous character of those with whom they had tarried. Or if they have witnessed the cruelties of slavery, by remaining silent spectator they have naturally become callous—an insensibility has ensued which prepares them to apologize even for barbarity. Nothing but the corrupting influence of slavery on the hearts of the Northern people can induce them to apologize for it; and much will have been done for the destruction of Southern slavery when we have so reformed the North that no one here will be willing to risk his reputation by advocating or even excusing the holding of men as property. The South know it, and acknowledge that as fast as our principles prevail, the hold of the master must be relaxed. (*Another outbreak of mobocratic spirit; and some confusion in the house.*)

How wonderfully constituted is the human mind! How it resists, as long as it can, all efforts to reclaim it from error! I feel that all this disturbance is but an evidence that our efforts are the best that could have been adopted, or else the friends of slavery would not care for what we say and do. The South knows what we do. I am thankful that they are reached by our efforts. Many times have I wept in the land of my birth over the system of slavery. I knew of none who sympathized in my feelings; I was unaware that any efforts were made to deliver the oppressed; no voice in the wilderness was heard calling on the people to repent and do works meet for repentance, and my heart sickened within me. Oh, how should I have rejoiced to know that such efforts as these were being made. I only wonder that I had such feelings. But in the midst of temptation I was preserved, and my sympathy grew warmer, and my hatred of slavery more inveterate, until at last I have exiled myself from my native land, because I could no longer endure to hear the wailing of the slave.

I fled to the land of Penn; for here, thought I, sympathy for the slave will surely be found. But I found it not. The people were kind and hospitable, but the slave had no place in their thoughts. I therefore shut up my grief in my own heart. I remembered that I was a Carolinian, from a state which framed this iniquity by law. Every Southern breeze wafted to me the discordant tones of weeping and wailing, shrieks and groans, mingled with prayers and blasphemous curses. My heart sank within me at the abominations in the midst of which I had been born and educated. What will it avail, cried I, in bitterness of spirit, to expose to the gaze of strangers the horrors and pollutions of slavery, when there is no ear to hear nor heart to feel and pray for the slave? The language of my soul was, "Oh tell it not in Gath, publish it not in the streets of Askelon." But how different do I feel now! Animated with hope, nay, with an assurance of the triumph of liberty and good will to man, I will lift up my voice like a trumpet, and show this people their transgression, their sins of omission towards the slave, and what they can do towards affecting Southern mind, and overthrowing Southern oppression.

We may talk of occupying neutral ground, but on this subject, in its present attitude, there is no such thing as neutral ground. He that is not for us is against us, and he that gathered not with us, scattereth abroad. If you are on what you suppose to be neutral ground, the South looks upon you as on the side of the oppressor. And is there one who loves his country willing to give his influence, even indirectly, in favor of slavery—that curse of nations? God swept Egypt with the besom of destruction, and punished Judea also with a sore punishment, because of slavery. And have we any reason to believe that he is less just now? Or that he will be more favorable to us than to his own "peculiar people"? (*Shouting, stones thrown against the windows.*)

There is nothing to be feared from those who would stop

our mouths, but they themselves should fear and tremble. The current is even now setting fast against them. If the arm of the North had not caused the Bastille of slavery to totter to its foundation, you would not hear those cries. A few years ago, and the South felt secure, and with a contemptuous sneer asked, "Who are the abolitionists? The abolitionists are nothing?" Aye, in one sense they were nothing, and they are nothing still. But in this we rejoice that "God has chosen things that are not to bring to nought things that are." (*Mob again disturbs the meeting.*)

We often hear the question asked: "What shall we do?" Here is an opportunity for doing something now. Every man and every woman present may do something, by showing that we fear not a mob, and in the midst of threatenings and revilings, by opening our mouths for the dumb and pleading the cause of those who are ready to perish.

To work as we should in this cause, we must know what slavery is. Let me urge everyone to buy the books which have been written on this subject and read them, and then lend them to your neighbors. Give your money no longer for things which pander to pride and lust, but aid in scattering "the living coals of truth upon the naked heart of this nation"—in circulating appeals to the sympathies of Christians in behalf of the outraged and suffering slave.

But it is said by some, our "books and papers do not speak the truth." Why, then, do they not contradict what we say? They cannot. Moreover, the South has entreated, nay, commanded us, to be silent; and what greater evidence of the truth of our publications could be desired?

Women of Philadelphia! Allow me as a Southern woman, with much attachment to the land of my birth, to entreat you to come up to this work. Especially let me urge you to petition. *Men* may settle this and other questions at the ballot box, but you have no such right. It is only through petitions that you can reach the legislature. It is, therefore, peculiarly *your* duty to petition. Do you say, "It does no good!" The South already turns pale at the number sent. They have read the reports of the proceedings of Congress and there have seen that among other petitions were very many from the women of the North on the subject of slavery. This fact has called the attention of the South to the subject. How could we expect to have done more yet? Men who hold the rod over slaves rule in the councils of the nation; and they deny our right to petition and remonstrate against abuses of our sex and our kind. We have these rights, however, from our God. Only let us exercise them, and, though often turned away unanswered, let us remember the influence of importunity upon the unjust judge and act accordingly. The fact that the South looks jealously upon our measures shows that they are effectual. There is, therefore, no cause for doubting or despair, but rather for rejoicing.

It was remarked in England that women did much to abolish slavery in her colonies. Nor are they now idle. Numerous petitions from them have recently been presented to the queen to abolish apprenticeship, with its cruelties, nearly equal to those of the system whose place it supplies. One petition, two miles and a quarter long, has been presented. And do you think these labors will be in vain? Let the history of the past answer. When the women of these states send up to Congress such a petition our legislators will arise, as did those of England, and say: "When all the maids and matrons of the land are knocking at our doors we must legislate." Let the zeal and love, the faith and works of our English sisters quicken ours; that while the slaves continue to suffer, and when they shout deliverance, we may feel the satisfaction of *having done what we could.*

Frances Harper
Advocates Liberty for Slaves

---

*"Instead of listening to the cry of agony, they
listen to the ring of dollars and stoop down to
pick up the coin."*

Born a free black in Baltimore, Maryland, poet, writer, and lecturer Frances Harper (1825–1911) was orphaned at three and
widowed after four years of marriage. A teacher, then dressmaker, she eventually took up pen and podium at a time when
America was beginning to self-destruct over the issue of slavery.
Considered a spellbinding orator, Harper spoke out on behalf of
abolition and later black equality—also the causes of women's
rights and temperance—in a lecture career that spanned more
than fifty years.

On May 13, 1857, she delivered this address before the New
York Antislavery Society—one year before Abraham Lincoln
voiced his now-famous phrase: "A house divided against itself
cannot stand." The speech, replete with vivid, expressive language, is a spirited condemnation of the South's materialistic
motivations and the country's constitutional failings. But Harper
will not despair, she tells her audience, because "God is on the
side of freedom."

The themes of this address, also found in other Harper
speeches, later surfaced in one of her best-known works, the
1892 novel *Iola Leroy, or Shadows Uplifted*, a portrait of black life
during the Civil War and Reconstruction.

C ould we trace the record of every human heart, the aspirations of every immortal soul, perhaps we would find no man so imbruted and degraded that we could not trace the word liberty either written in living characters upon the soul or hidden away in some nook or corner of the heart. The law of liberty is the law of God, and is antecedent to all human legislation. It existed in the mind of Deity when He hung the first world upon its orbit and gave it liberty to gather light from the central sun. Some people say, set the slaves free. Did you ever think, if the slaves were free, they would steal everything they could lay their hands on from now till the day of their death— that they would steal more than two thousand millions of dollars? (*Applause.*) Ask Maryland, with her tens of thousands of slaves, if she is not prepared for freedom, and hear her answer: "I help supply the coffee-gangs of the South." Ask Virginia, with her hundreds of thousands of slaves, if she is not weary with her merchandise of blood and anxious to shake the gory traffic from her hands, and hear her reply: "Though fertility has covered my soil, though a genial sky bends over my hills and vales, though I hold in my hand a wealth of water-power enough to turn the spindles to clothe the world, yet, with all these advantages, one of my chief staples has been the sons and daughters I send to the human market and human shambles." (*Applause.*) Ask the farther South, and all the cotton-growing states chime in, "We have need of fresh supplies to fill the ranks of those whose lives have gone out in unrequited toil on our distant plantations."

A hundred thousand new-born babes are annually added to the victims of slavery; twenty thousand lives are annually sacrificed on the plantations of the South. Such a sight should send a thrill of horror through the nerves of civilization and impel the heart of humanity to lofty deeds. So it might, if men had not found out a fearful alchemy by which this blood can be transformed into gold. Instead of listening to the cry of agony, they listen to the ring of dollars and stoop down to pick up the coin. (*Applause.*)

But a few months since a man escaped from bondage and found a temporary shelter almost beneath the shadow of Bunker Hill. Had that man stood upon the deck of an Austrian ship, beneath the shadow of the house of the Hapsburgs, he would have found protection. Had he been wrecked upon an island or colony of Great Britain, the waves of the tempest-lashed ocean would have washed him deliverance. Had he landed upon the territory of vine-encircled France and a Frenchman had reduced him to a thing and brought him here beneath the protection of our institutions and our laws, for such a nefarious deed that Frenchman would have lost his citizenship in France. Beneath the feebler light which glimmers from the Koran, the Bey of Tunis would have granted him freedom in his own dominions. Beside the ancient pyramids of Egypt he would have found liberty, for the soil laved by the glorious Nile is now consecrated to freedom. But from Boston harbour, made memorable by the infusion of three-penny taxed tea, Boston in its proximity to the plains of Lexington and Concord, Boston almost beneath the shadow of Bunker Hill and almost in sight of Plymouth Rock, he is thrust back from liberty and manhood and reconverted into a chattel. You have heard that, down South, they keep bloodhounds to hunt slaves. Ye bloodhounds, go back to your kennels; when you fail to catch the flying fugitive, when his stealthy tread is heard in the place where the bones of the revolutionary sires repose, the ready North is base enough to do your shameful service. (*Applause.*)

Slavery is mean, because it tramples on the feeble and weak. A man comes with his affidavits from the South and hurries me before a commissioner; upon that evidence *ex parte* and alone he hitches me to the car of slavery and trails my womanhood in the dust. I stand at the threshold of the Supreme Court and ask for justice, simple justice. Upon my tortured heart is thrown the mocking words, "You are a Negro; you have no rights which white men are bound to respect"! (*Loud and long-continued applause.*) Had it been my lot to have lived beneath the Crescent instead of the Cross, had injustice and violence been heaped upon my head as a Mohammedan woman, as a member of a common faith, I might have demanded justice and been listened to by the Pasha, the Bey or the Vizier; but when I come here to ask for justice, men tell me, "We have no higher law than the Constitution." (*Applause.*)

But I will not dwell on the dark side of the picture. God is on the side of freedom; and any cause that has God on its side, I care not how much it may be trampled upon, how much it may be trailed in the dust, is sure to triumph. The message of Jesus Christ is on the side of freedom, "I come to preach deliverance to the captives, the opening of the prison doors to them that are bound." The truest and noblest hearts in the land are on the side of freedom. They may be hissed at by slavery's minions, their names cast out as evil, their characters branded with fanaticism, but oh, "To side with truth is noble when we share her humble crust ere the cause bring fame and profit and it's prosperous to be just."

May I not, in conclusion, ask every honest, noble heart, every seeker after truth and justice, if they will not also be on the side of freedom? Will you not resolve that you will abate neither heart nor hope till you hear the death-knell of human bondage sounded, and over the black ocean of slavery shall be heard a song, more exulting than the song of Miriam when it floated o'er Egypt's dark sea, the requiem of Egypt's ruined hosts and the anthem of the deliverance of Israel's captive people? (*Great applause.*)

Zitkala-sä
Speaks to the History of Native Americans

"Look with compassion down, and with thine almighty power move this nation to the rescue of my race."

It was the turn of the century, and young Gertrude Simmons (1876–1938), born a Yankton Sioux in the Dakota Territory, had decided on a penname. Over the remaining thirty-eight years of her life, Zitkala-sä, meaning "red bird," would rise to fame as a writer, lecturer, and advocate of Native American rights.

"Neither a wild Indian nor a tame one," she wrote of herself. Instead, she was a diligent bridge builder between two vast cultures, the "white world" and her own—feeling, at times, estranged from both. The estrangement came early, when, defying her mother's protests, she sought formal education at White's Institute, a Quaker Missionary school, and later Earlham College in Indiana.

After a bitter teaching experience at the Carlisle Indian Institute, where she witnessed "coercion to Christianity" and punishment for speaking in native languages, Zitkala-sä began a lifelong crusade to advance the rights of her people. She established the National Council of American Indians, lobbied for voting rights, and became an earnest campaigner for Franklin Roosevelt.

Of her many speeches, this one—delivered on May 13,

1896—is one of her first and most famous orations. To her sur-
prise, she had won first place in Earlham's oratorical contest and
delivered this address for the state competition in Indianapolis.
With vivid imagery and upswept language, she exhorts her
white audience to understand the history, the motivations, the
plight of her people. "Is patriotism only a virtue in Saxon
hearts?" she asks. To God—"is thy arm so shortened it cannot
save?" Though she peppers the speech with several Christian
references ("His 'Strong Son,' " "thy God my God"), later in
life, she renounced Christianity and returned to spiritual Native
American traditions. Despite racial epithets hurled by the competing schools (a banner mocking the "squaw" from Earlham),
young Gertrude's speech won second place.

T he universe is the product of evolution. An ascending
energy pervades all life. By slow degrees nations have risen
from the mountain foot of their existence to its summit. In the
wild forests of northern Europe two thousand years ago roamed
the blue-eyed Teuton. To the lowlands by the northern sea came
the war-like Saxon, ere long to begin his bloody conquest of
Britain. Yet fierce and barbarous as he was, the irrepressible
germ of progress lay deeply implanted in his nature. His descendants have girdled the globe with their possessions. Today it is
no longer a debatable question whether it shall be Anglo-Saxon
or Cossack, constitutional law or imperial decree, that is des-
tined to mold the character of governments and to determine
the policies of nations.

Out of a people holding tenaciously to the principles of the
Great Charter has arisen in America a nation of free men and
free institutions. On its shores two oceans lavish the products of
the world. Among its rivers, mountains, and lakes, in its stately

forests and on its broad prairies, like rolling seas of green and gold, millions of toiling sovereigns have established gigantic enterprises, great factories, commercial highways, and have developed fruitful farms and productive mines. The ennobling architecture of its churches, schools, and benevolent institutions; its municipal greatness, keeping pace with social progress; its scholars, statesmen, authors, and divines, giving expression and force to the religious and humanitarian zeal of a great people—all these reveal a marvelous progress. Thought is lost in admiration of this matchless scene over which floats in majesty the starry emblem of liberty.

But see! At the bidding of thought the tide of time rolls back four hundred years. The generations of men of all nations, kindred, and tongues, who have developed this civilization in America, return to the bosom of the Old World. Myriad merchantmen, fleets, and armaments shrink and disappear from the ocean. Daring explorers in their frail crafts hie to their havens on the European shore. The fleet of discovery, bearing under the flag of Spain the figure of Columbus, recedes beyond the trackless sea. America is one great wilderness again. Over the trees of the primeval forest curls the smoke of the wigwam. The hills resound with the hunter's shout that dies away with the fleeing deer. On the river glides his light canoe. In the wigwam Laughing Water weaves into moccasins the rainbow-tinted beads. By gleaming council fire brave warriors are stirred by the rude eloquence of their chief. In the evening-glow, the eyes of the children brighten as the aged brave tells his fantastic legends. The reverent and poetic natures of these forest children feel the benign influence of the Great Spirit; they hear his voice in the wind; see his frown in the storm cloud; his smile in the sunbeam. Thus in reverential awe the Red Man lived. His was the life that is the common lot of human kind. Bravely did he struggle with famine and disease. He felt his pulses hasten in the joyous freedom of the hunt. Quick to string his bow for vengeance; ready to bury the hatchet or smoke the pipe of peace; never was he first to break a treaty or known to betray a friend with whom he had eaten salt.

The invasion of his broad dominions by a paler race brought no dismay to the hospitable Indian. Samoset voiced the feeling of his people as he stood among the winter-weary Pilgrims and cried "Welcome, Englishmen." Nor did the Indian cling selfishly to his lands; willingly he divides with Roger Williams and with Penn, who pay him for his own. History bears record to no finer examples of fidelity. To Jesuit, to Quaker, to all who kept their faith with him, his loyalty never failed.

Unfortunately civilization is not an unmixed blessing. Vices begin to creep into his life and deepen the Red Man's degradation. He learns to crave the European liquid fire. Broken treaties shake his faith in the newcomers. Continued aggressions goad him to desperation. The White Man's bullet decimates his tribes and drives him from his home. What if he fought? His forests were felled; his game frightened away; his streams of finny shoals usurped. He loved his family and would defend them. He loved the fair land of which he was rightful owner. He loved the inheritance of his fathers, their traditions, their graves; he held them a priceless legacy to be sacredly kept. He loved his native land. Do you wonder still that in his breast he should brood revenge, when ruthlessly driven from the temples where he worshiped? Do you wonder still that he skulked in forest gloom to avenge the desolation of his home? Is patriotism a virtue only in Saxon hearts? Is there no charity to cover his crouching form as he stealthily opposed his relentless foe?

The charge of cruelty has been brought against the Indian; but the White Man has been the witness and the judge. Anglo-Saxon England, with its progressive blood, its long continued development of freedom and justice, its eight centuries of Christian training, burned the writhing martyr in the fires of

Kenith field from a sense of duty. In the name of religion and liberty, the cultured Frenchman, with his inheritance of Roman justice, ten centuries of Christian ideas, murders his brother on that awful night of St. Bartholomew, and during the Reign of Terror swells the Seine with human blood. Let it be remembered, before condemnation is passed upon the Red Man, that, while he burned and tortured frontiersmen, Puritan Boston burned witches and hanged Quakers, and the Southern aristocrat beat his slaves and set bloodhounds on the tracks of him who dared aspire to freedom. The barbarous Indian, ignorant alike of Roman justice, Saxon law, and the Gospel of Christian brotherhood, in the fury of revenge has brought no greater stain upon his name than these.

But what have two centuries of contact with the foremost wave of Anglo-Saxon civilization wrought for him?

You say they all have passed away,
That noble race—and brave;
That their light canoes have vanished
From off the crested wave:
That mid the forests where they roamed
There rings no hunter's shout;

You say their conelike cabins
That clustered o'er the vale
Have disappeared—as withered leaves
Before the autumn's gale.

If in their stead, we have today a race of blighted promise, will you spurn them? You, whose sires have permitted the most debasing influences to surround these forest children, brutalizing their nobler instincts until sin and corruption have well nigh swept them from the Earth?

Today the Indian is pressed almost to the farther sea. Does

that sea symbolize his death? Does the narrow territory still left to him typify the last brief day before his place on Earth "shall know him no more forever?" Shall might make right and the fittest alone survive? Oh Love of God and of His "Strong Son," thou who liftest up the oppressed and succorest the needy, is thine ear grown heavy that it cannot hear his cry? Is thy arm so shortened, it cannot save? Dost thou not yet enfold him in thy love? Look with compassion down, and with thine almighty power move this nation to the rescue of my race. To take the life of a nation during the slow march of centuries seems not a lighter crime than to crush it instantly with one fatal blow. Our country must not shame her principles by such consummate iniquity. Has the charity which would succor dying Armenia no place for the Indian at home? Has America's firstborn forfeited his birthright to her boundless opportunities? No legacy of barbarism can efface the divine image in man. No tardiness in entering the paths of progress can destroy his divinely given capabilities. No lot or circumstance, except of his own choosing, can invalidate his claim to a place in the brotherhood of man or release more fortunate, more enlightened people from the obligation of a brother's keeper.

Poets sing of a coming federation of the world, and we applaud. Idealists dream that in this commonwealth of all humanity the divine spark in man shall be the only test of citizenship, and we think of their dream and future history. America entered upon her career of freedom and prosperity with the declaration that "all men are born free and equal." Her prosperity has advanced in proportion as she has preserved to her citizens this birthright of freedom and equality. Aside from the claims of a common humanity, can you as consistent Americans deny equal opportunities with yourselves to an American people in their struggle to rise from ignorance and degradation? The claims of brotherhood, of the love that is due a neighbor-race, and of tardy justice have not been wholly lost on your hearts and consciences.

The plaintive melodies, running from his tired but bravely enduring soul, are heard in heaven. The threatening night of oblivion lifts. The great heart of the nation sways us with the olive branch of peace. Some among the noblest of this country have championed our cause. Within the last two decades a great interest in Indian civilization has been awakened; a beneficent government has organized a successful system of Indian educations; training schools and college doors stand open to us. We clasp the warm hand of friendship everywhere. From honest hearts and sincere lips we hear the hearty welcome and God-speed. We come from mountain fastnesses, from cheerless plains, from far-off, low-wooded streams, seeking the "White Man's ways." Seeking your skill in industry and in art, seeking labor and honest independence, seeking the treasures of knowledge and wisdom, seeking to comprehend the spirit of your laws and the genius of your noble institutions, seeking by a new birthright to unite with yours our claim to a common country, seeking the Sovereign's crown that we may stand side by side with you in ascribing royal honor to our nation's flag. America, I love thee. "Thy people shall be my people and thy God my God."

Mother Jones
Exhorts the Miner to His Duty

". . . when we neglect that duty to humanity
we deserve the greatest condemnation."

Labor reformer Mary Harris "Mother" Jones (1830–1930) was swift to correct her admirer: "Get it right. I'm not a humanitarian. I'm a hell raiser." The genteel-faced Jones was "born in revolution," as she put it, to a family deeply entrenched in the quest for Irish independence. After her grandfather was hanged and her father targeted for arrest, young Mary and her family fled Ireland, eventually settling in Toronto. Jones never settled, however, and soon set out on her own as a dressmaker and teacher, traveling from New England to Michigan to Tennessee.

It was in Memphis that she married George Jones, a member of the Iron Molder's Union and organizer for the Knights of Labor. Six years later, her husband and four small children were dead from an outbreak of yellow fever. After staying to nurse remaining victims of the epidemic, Jones moved on to Chicago, setting up a dressmaker's shop—which was later destroyed along with her home in the Great Fire of 1871. Left homeless, she sought refuge in a church basement with other victims, gradually resumed her business, and began attending meetings of the Knights of Labor—never setting down permanent roots again.

Once asked for her address, she said: "I have no abiding place, but wherever a fight is on against wrong, I am always there." "There" would become Virginia, West Virginia, Kansas, Pennsylvania, Colorado, and other states where she crusaded for better labor conditions of behalf of the United Mine Workers of America. A Socialist, Jones made no apologies for her methods of crusade; "the militant, not the meek, shall inherit the earth," she avowed. In 1913, she was accused of inciting violence during a strike in West Virginia and convicted of conspiracy to commit murder, but her sentence was later commuted.

On July 19, 1902, "the miner's angel" had to subdue her penchant for strikes when she spoke at a special UMWA convention in Indianapolis called by union president John Mitchell. Members were gathered to consider a general strike of all coal miners in support of the anthracite coal strikes in Pennsylvania, but Mitchell was against it, declaring that the union should support the strikers but not endanger contracts in other districts—a view that prevailed. In these excerpts from her speech to the convention, Jones invokes the words of Patrick Henry and the intentions of America's founding fathers as she urges members to remain true to the cause of labor.

———————

Mr. Chairman and Fellow Delegates:
I have been wondering whether this great gathering of wealth producers thoroughly comprehended the importance of their mission here today; whether they were really clear as to what their real mission was. I realize, my friends, that the eyes of the people of the Unites States, from one end to the other, are watching you; but you have again given a lesson to the world and a lesson to the statesmen that a general uprising is the last thing you called for; that you will resort to all peaceful, conservative methods before you rise and enter the final protest.

I realize, my friends, what your mission is; but I am one of those who, taking all the conditions into consideration, had I been here would have voted for a gigantic protest. I wanted the powers that be to understand who the miners were; to understand that when they laid down their picks they tied up all other industries, and then the operators would learn what an important factor the miner is toward his support. But, my friends, I believe you have taken the wisest action, that action which the world at large will commend, and which I now commend, believing it is right. . . .

These fights must be won if it costs the whole country to win them. These fights against the oppressor and the capitalists, the ruling classes, must be won if it takes us all to do it. The President said I had made sacrifices. In that I disagree with him, though I do not usually do that, for I hold him very dear. None of us make sacrifices when we do our duty to humanity, and when we neglect that duty to humanity we deserve the greatest condemnation.

There is before you one question, my friends, and you must keep that question before your eyes this fall when you send representatives to the legislative halls. Your instructions to these representatives must be: "Down with government by injunction in the American nation." This generation may sleep its slumber quietly, not feeling its might duty and responsibility . . . but it is the sleep of the slave chained closely to his master. If this generation surrenders its liberties, then the work of our forefathers, which we will lose by doing this, will not be resurrected for two generations to come. . . .

I have wondered many times recently what Patrick Henry would say, Patrick Henry who said, "Give me liberty or give me death," and who also said, "Eternal vigilance is the price of liberty," if he could witness the things that are done in West Virginia in this day and age, in a state that is supposed to be under the Constitution of the United States. I say with him, "Give me liberty or give me death, for for liberty I shall die, even if they riddle my body with bullets after I am dead."

My friends, you must emancipate the miners of West Virginia; they should be the barometer for you in the future. You have a task; go bravely home and take it up like men. Each one of you should constitute himself a missionary, each one should do his duty as a miner and as a member of this organization. Do your duty also as citizens of the United States, do your duty as men who feel a responsibility upon you, and remember, friends, that it is better to die an uncrowned free man than a crowned slave. . . .

Now, my friends, we should all work together in harmony to secure our rights. Don't find fault with each other; rather clasp and fight the battle together. Be true to the teachings of your forefathers who fought and bled and raised the old flag that we might always shout for liberty. Think, my friends! Did the laborers ever take twenty-two capitalists and riddle their bodies with bullets? Did the laborers ever take twenty thousand men, women and children and lock them up in the Bastille and murder them? No, labor has always advanced Christianity. The history of the miner has been bitter and sore; he has traveled the highways and the byways to build up this magnificent organization, and let me beg of you, in God's holy name and in the name of the old flag, let the organization be used for the uplifting of the human race, but do not use it for the uplifting of yourself. Be true to your manhood; be true to your country; be true to the children yet unborn. . . . If you are true to these things, the battle will end in victory for you.

Margaret Chase Smith
Denounces McCarthyism

"I do not want to see the Republican party ride to political victory on the Four Horsemen of Calumny—fear, ignorance, bigotry, and smear."

"Margaret, you look very serious. Are you going to give a speech?" asked Senator Joseph McCarthy. "Yes," she said, "and you will not like it."

Moments later, on June 1, 1950, Senator Margaret Chase Smith (1897–1995) of Maine, the only woman among ninety-five men, set forth a "Declaration of Conscience," denouncing McCarthy's perpetual campaign of anti-Communist witch hunts and "Red" hysteria. "I hold in my hand a list . . ." McCarthy had said three months earlier—a list of "known Communists" he claimed were serving in the highest reaches of the U.S. government. But Smith, along with six other Republican senators was worn thin by "lists with no proof" and were ready to join the Democratic assault against "McCarthyism."

The soft spoken Smith delivered her declaration with ordered arguments. She spoke as a Republican, a woman, a United States Senator, and an American, she told the stilled chamber, and condemned "know nothing, suspect everything" attitudes. Afterward, McCarthy accused his critics of "speaking through a petticoat," and, though Smith's speech won praise from both parties (the "voice of reason," some called her), the reckless war of "Tail Gunner Joe" languished with human consequences until the Senate censured him in 1954.

M r. President, I would like to speak briefly and simply about a serious national condition. It is a national feeling of fear and frustration that could result in national suicide and the end of everything that we Americans hold dear. It is a condition that comes from the lack of effective leadership in the legislative branch or the executive branch of our government. That leadership is so lacking that serious and responsible proposals are being made that national advisory commissions be appointed to provide such critically needed leadership.

I speak as briefly as possible because too much harm has already been done with irresponsible words of bitterness and selfish political opportunism. I speak as simply as possible because the issue is too great to be obscured by eloquence. I speak simply and briefly in the hope that my words will be taken to heart.

Mr. President, I speak as a Republican. I speak as a woman. I speak as a United States senator. I speak as an American.

The United States Senate has long enjoyed worldwide respect as the greatest deliberative body in the world. But recently that deliberative character has too often been debased to the level of a forum of hate and character assassination sheltered by the shield of congressional immunity.

It is ironical that we senators can in debate in the Senate, directly or indirectly, by any form of words, impute to any American who is not a senator any conduct or motive unworthy or unbecoming an American—and without that nonsenator American having any legal redress against us—yet if we say the same thing in the Senate about our colleagues we can be stopped on the grounds of being out of order.

It is strange that we can verbally attack anyone else without restraint and with full protection, and yet we hold ourselves above the same type of criticism here on the Senator floor. Surely the United States Senate is big enough to take self-criticism and self-appraisal. Surely we should be able to take the same kind of character attacks that we "dish out" to outsiders.

I think that it is high time for the United States Senate and its members to do some real soul-searching and to weigh our consciences as to the manner in which we are performing our duty to the people of America and the manner in which we are using or abusing our individual powers and privileges.

I think it is high time that we remembered that we have sworn to uphold and defend the Constitution. I think it is high time that we remembered that the Constitution, as amended, speaks not only of the freedom of speech but also of trial by jury instead of trial by accusation.

Whether it be a criminal prosecution in court or a character prosecution in the Senate, there is little practical distinction when the life of a person has been ruined.

Those of us who shout the loudest about Americanism in making character assassinations are all too frequently those who, by our own words and acts, ignore some of the basic principles of Americanism—the right to criticize; the right to hold unpopular beliefs; the right to protest; the right of independent thought.

The exercise of these rights should not cost one single American citizen his reputation or his right to a livelihood, nor should he be in danger of losing his reputation or livelihood merely because he happens to know someone who holds unpopular beliefs. Who of us does not? Otherwise none of us could call our souls our own. Otherwise thought control would have set in.

The American people are sick and tired of being afraid to speak their minds lest they be politically smeared as Communists or Fascists by their opponents. Freedom of speech is not what it used to be in America. It has been so abused by some that it is not exercised by others.

The American people are sick and tired of seeing innocent people smeared and guilty people whitewashed. But there have been enough proved cases, such as the American case, the Hiss case, the Coplon case, the Gold case, to cause nationwide distrust and strong suspicion that there may be something to the unproved, sensational accusations.

As a Republican, I say to my colleagues on this side of the aisle that the Republican party faces a challenge today that is not unlike the challenge which it faced back in Lincoln's day. The Republican party so successfully met that challenge that it emerged from the Civil War as the champion of a united nation—in addition to being a party which unrelentingly fought loose spending and loose programs.

Today our country is being psychologically divided by the confusion and the suspicions that are bred in the United States Senate to spread like cancerous tentacles of "know nothing, suspect everything" attitudes. Today we have a Democratic administration which has developed a mania for loose spending and loose programs. History is repeating itself—and the Republican party again has the opportunity to emerge as the champion of unity and prudence.

The record of the present Democratic administration has provided us with sufficient campaign issues without the necessity of resorting to political smears. America is rapidly losing its position as leader of the world simply because the Democratic administration has pitifully failed to provide effective leadership.

The Democratic administration has completely confused the American people by its daily contradictory grave warnings and optimistic assurances, which show the people that our Democratic administration has no idea of where it is going.

The Democratic administration has greatly lost the confidence of the American people by its complacency to the threat of communism here at home and the leak of vital secrets to Russia through key officials of the Democratic administration. There are enough proved cases to make this point without diluting our criticism with unproved charges.

Surely these are sufficient reasons to make it clear to the American people that it is time for a change and that a Republican victory is necessary to the security of the country. Surely it is clear that this nation will continue to suffer so long as it is governed by the present ineffective Democratic administration.

Yet to displace it with a Republican regime embracing a philosophy that lacks political integrity or intellectual honesty would prove equally disastrous to the nation. The nation sorely needs a Republican victory. But I do not want to see the Republican party ride to political victory on the Four Horsemen of Calumny—fear, ignorance, bigotry, and smear.

I doubt if the Republican party could do so, simply because I do not believe the American people will uphold any political party that puts political exploitation above national interest. Surely we Republicans are not so desperate for victory.

I do not want to see the Republican party win that way. While it might be a fleeting victory for the Republican party, it would be a more lasting defeat for the American people. Surely it would ultimately be suicide for the Republican party and the two-party system that has protected our American liberties from the dictatorship of a one-party system.

As members of the minority party, we do not have the primary authority to formulate the policy of our government. But we do have the responsibility of rendering constructive criticism, of clarifying issues, of allaying fears by acting as responsible citizens.

As a woman, I wonder how the mothers, wives, sisters, and daughters feel about the way in which members of their families have been politically mangled in Senate debate—and I use the word "debate" advisedly.

As a United States senator, I am not proud of the way in which the Senate has been made a publicity platform for irresponsible sensationalism. I am not proud of the reckless abandon in which unproved charges have been hurled from this side of the aisle. I am not proud of the obviously staged, undignified countercharges which have been attempted in retaliation for the other side of the aisle.

I do not like the way the Senate has been made a rendezvous for vilification, for selfish political gain at the sacrifice of individual reputations and national unity. I am not proud of the way we smear outsiders from the floor of the Senate and hide behind the cloak of congressional immunity and still place ourselves beyond criticism on the floor of the Senate.

As an American, I am shocked at the way Republicans and Democrats alike are playing directly into the Communist design of "confuse, divide, and conquer." As an American, I do not want a Democratic administration whitewash or cover-up any more than I want a Republican smear or witch-hunt.

As an American, I condemn a Republican Fascist just as much as I condemn a Democratic Communist. I condemn a Democratic Fascist just as much as I condemn a Republican Communist. They are equally dangerous to you and me and to our country. As an American, I want to see our nation recapture the strength and unity it once had when we fought the enemy instead of ourselves. . . .

PART 5

SPEECHES

ON

WOMEN'S RIGHTS

Elizabeth Cady Stanton
Keynotes the First Women's Rights Convention

". . . we now demand our right to vote according to the declaration of the government under which we live."

In 1852, Elizabeth Cady Stanton (1815–1902) shocked members of the New York Woman's Temperance Society by demanding a woman's right to divorce drunkard and abusive husbands—a brazen idea whose time had not yet come. Stanton knew she could be controversial. In her diary, reflecting on her friendship with Susan B. Anthony, she wrote: "I tell her that I get more radical as I grow older, while she gets more conservative."

As a girl, Stanton, daughter of a Massachusetts judge, felt the early indignation of being denied admission to the college attended by her brother—though her father provided for a tutor in the classics and allowed her to pluck from the law books in his library. It was Stanton's exposure to the disheartened women who filed into her father's office for help that led her to champion legal rights for women—and become adamant about safeguarding her own. At her 1840 wedding to the prominent abolitionist orator and writer Henry Stanton, she had the word "obey" omitted from the ceremony.

That same year, Stanton, by then active in the abolition movement herself, traveled to London with her husband to the World Anti-Slavery Meeting, which refused to seat women delegates. There she met Quaker minister and social reformer

Lucretia Mott, and together the two women organized America's first women's rights convention, held in Seneca Falls, New York, in 1848. The convention's pinnacle moment came with the presentation of the Declaration of Sentiments, a paraphrased version of the Declaration of Independence. "We hold these truths to be self-evident, that all men *and women* are created equal," it began.

In her keynote address to the convention, given on July 19, 1848, Stanton wields her words like an ax upon the argument that mere biology precludes women from equal rights: "We need not prove ourselves equal . . ." she says. "The right is ours." Sitting in the audience is Anthony, who Stanton would meet two years later.

———

We have met here today to discuss our rights and wrongs, civil and political, and not, as some have supposed, to go into the detail of social life alone. We do not propose to petition the legislature to make our husbands just, generous, and courteous, to seat every man at the head of a cradle, and to clothe every woman in male attire. None of these points, however important they may be considered by leading men, will be touched in this convention. As to their costume, the gentlemen need feel no fear of our imitating that, for we think it in violation of every principle of taste, beauty, and dignity; notwithstanding all the contempt cast upon our loose, flowing garments, we still admire the graceful folds, and consider our costume far more artistic than theirs. Many of the nobler sex seem to agree with us in this opinion, for the bishops, priests, judges, barristers, and lord mayors of the first nation on the globe, and the Pope of Rome, with his cardinals, too, all wear the loose flowing robes, thus tacitly acknowledging that the male attire is neither dignified nor imposing. No, we shall not molest you in your philosophical experiments with stocks, pants, high-heeled boots, and Russian belts. Yours be the glory to discover, by personal experience, how long the kneepan can resist the terrible strapping down which you impose, in how short time the well-developed muscles of the throat can be reduced to mere threads by the constant pressure of the stock, how high the heel of a boot must be to make a short man tall, and how tight the Russian belt may be drawn and yet have wind enough left to sustain life.

But we are assembled to protest against a form of government existing without the consent of the governed—to declare our right to be free as man is free, to be represented in the government which we are taxed to support, to have such disgraceful laws as give man the power to chastise and imprison his wife, to take the wages which she earns, the property which she inherits, and, in case of separation, the children of her love; laws which make her the mere dependent on his bounty. It is to protest against such unjust laws as these that we are assembled today, and to have them, if possible, forever erased from our statute books, deeming them a shame and a disgrace to a Christian republic in the nineteenth century. We have met

> To uplift woman's fallen divinity
> Upon an even pedestal with man's.

And, strange as it may seem to many, we now demand our right to vote according to the declaration of the government under which we live. This right no one pretends to deny. We need not prove ourselves equal to Daniel Webster to enjoy this privilege, for the ignorant Irishman in the ditch has all the civil rights he has. We need not prove our muscular power equal to this same Irishman to enjoy this privilege, for the most tiny, weak, ill-shaped stripling of twenty-one has all the civil rights of the Irishman. We have no objection to discuss the question of equality, for we feel that the weight of argument lies wholly with us, but we wish the question of equality kept distinct from the question of rights, for the proof of the one does not determine the truth of the other. All white men in this country have the same rights, however they may differ in mind, body, or estate.

The right is ours. The question now is: how shall we get possession of what rightfully belongs to us? We should not feel so sorely grieved if no man who had not attained the full stature of a Webster, Clay, Van Buren, or Gerrit Smith could claim the right of the elective franchise. But to have drunkards, idiots, horse-racing, rum-selling rowdies, ignorant foreigners, and silly boys fully recognized, while we ourselves are thrust out from all the rights that belong to citizens, it is too grossly insulting to the dignity of woman to be longer quietly submitted to. The right is ours. Have it, we must. Use it, we will. The pens, the tongues, the fortunes, the indomitable wills of many women are already pledged to secure this right. The great truth that no just government can be formed without the consent of the governed we shall echo and reecho in the ears of the unjust judge, until by continual coming we shall weary him.

There seems now to be a kind of moral stagnation in our midst. Philanthropists have done their utmost to rouse the nation to a sense of its sins. War, slavery, drunkenness, licentiousness, gluttony, have been dragged naked before the people, and all their abominations and deformities fully brought to light, yet with idiotic laugh we hug those monsters to our breasts and rush on to destruction. Our churches are multiplying on all sides, our missionary societies, Sunday schools, and prayer meetings and innumerable charitable and reform organizations are all in operation, but still the tide of vice is swelling, and threatens the destruction of everything, and the battlements of righteousness are weak against the raging elements of sin and death. Verily, the world waits the coming of some new element, some purifying power, some spirit of mercy and love. The voice of woman has been silenced in the state, the church, and the home, but man cannot fulfill his destiny alone, he cannot redeem his race unaided. There are deep and tender chords of sympathy and love in the hearts of the downfallen and oppressed that woman can touch more skillfully than man.

The world has never yet seen a truly great and virtuous nation, because in the degradation of woman the very fountains of life are poisoned at their source. It is vain to look for silver and gold from mines of copper and lead. It is the wise mother that has the wise son. So long as your women are slaves you may throw your colleges and churches to the winds. You can't have scholars and saints so long as your mothers are ground to powder between the upper and nether millstone of tyranny and lust. How seldom, now, is a father's pride gratified, his fond hopes realized, in the budding genius of his son! The wife is degraded, made the mere creature of caprice, and the foolish son is heaviness to his heart. Truly are the sins of the fathers visited upon the children to the third and fourth generation. God, in His wisdom, has so linked the whole human family together that any violence done at one end of the chain is felt throughout its length, and here, too, is the law of restoration, as in woman all have fallen, so in her elevation shall the race be recreated.

"Voices" were the visitors and advisers of Joan of Arc. Do not "voices" come to us daily from the haunts of poverty, sorrow, degradation, and despair, already too long unheeded. Now is the time for the women of this country, if they would save our free institutions, to defend the right, to buckle on the armor that can best resist the keenest weapons of the enemy—contempt and ridicule. The same religious enthusiasm that nerved

Joan of Arc to her work nerves us to ours. In every generation God calls some men and women for the utterance of truth, a heroic action, and our work today is the fulfilling of what has long since been foretold by the Prophet—Joel 2:28: "And it shall come to pass afterward, that I will pour out my spirit upon all flesh; and your sons and your daughters shall prophesy." We do not expect our path will be strewn with the flowers of popular applause, but over the thorns of bigotry and prejudice will be our way, and on our banners will beat the dark storm clouds of opposition from those who have entrenched themselves behind the stormy bulwarks of custom and authority, and who have fortified their position by every means, holy and unholy. But we will steadfastly abide the result. Unmoved we will bear it aloft. Undauntedly we will unfurl it to the gale, for we know that the storm cannot rend from it a shred, that the electric flash will but more clearly show to us the glorious words inscribed upon it, "Equality of Rights."

Sojourner Truth
Asks a Pointed Question

"And ain't I a woman?"

The abolitionist and former slave could handle the heckler who said he didn't mind her talk any more than the bite of a flea. "Perhaps not," she said, "but the Lord willing, I'll keep you scratching." And she could handle the hisses of a white college audience during the Civil War: "Well, children, when you go to heaven and God asks you what made you hate colored people, have you got your answer ready? When I go before the throne of God and God says, 'Sojourner, what made you hate the white people?' I have got my answer ready." Drawing her sleeve to her shoulder, she bared a network of scars from "the master's lash."

Self-assured, with a nearly six-foot frame and low, imposing voice, the powerful, evangelical, insightful Sojourner Truth (c. 1797–1883) feared little—but questioned a great deal, once asking fellow abolitionist Frederick Douglass: "Frederick, is God dead?" Born into slavery as Isabella, she fled her household in upstate New York in 1827 and was later freed under the state's emancipation act. In 1843, "voices" told her to change her name to Sojourner Truth—because she was to "travel up and down the land, showing the people their sins" and declaring the truth because "truth burns up error." The "error" was the denial of natural rights, a philosophical umbrella she used to bridge abolition and women's suffrage. The link surfaces here in this speech to the Ohio Women's Rights Convention in 1851, as she swings from vivid personal experiences of slavery to the forceful and famous repetitive question, "And ain't I a woman?"

———•—•———

Well, children, where there is so much racket there must be something out of kilter, I think that 'twixt the Negroes of the South and the women at the North, all talking about rights, the white men will be in a fix pretty soon. But what's all this here talking about?

That man over there says that women need to be helped into carriages, and lifted over ditches, and to have the best place everywhere. Nobody ever helps me into carriages, or over mud puddles, or gives me any best place! And ain't I a woman? Look at me! Look at my arm. I have plowed and planted, and gathered into barns, and no man could head me! And ain't I a woman? I could work as much and eat as much as a man—when I could get it—and bear the lash as well! And ain't I a woman? I have borne thirteen children, and seen them most all sold off to slavery, and when I cried out with my mother's grief, none but Jesus heard me! And ain't I a woman?

Then they talk about this thing in the head; what's this they call it? (*Intellect, someone whispered.*) That's it, honey. What's that got to do with women's rights or Negro's rights? If my cup won't hold but a pint, and yours holds a quart, wouldn't you be mean not to let me have my little half-measure full?

Then that little man in black there, he says women can't have as much rights as men, 'cause Christ wasn't a woman! Where did your Christ come from? Where did your Christ come from? From God and a woman! Man had nothing to do with him.

If the first woman God ever made was strong enough to turn the world upside down all alone, these women together ought to be able to turn it back, and get it right side up again! And now they is asking to do it, the men better let them.

Obliged to you for hearing me, and now old Sojourner ain't got nothing more to say.

Abby Kelley Foster
Blasts Passivity and Laziness

"Bloody feet, sisters, have worn smooth the path by which you have come up hither."

After hearing Abby Kelley Foster (1810–1887) deliver one of her first public speeches, abolitionist orator Theodore Weld begged her to join his field of lecturers: "Abby, if you don't, God will smite you!" There was little time for discussion. Foster, along with Angelina Grimké, had just spoken before the famous 1838 anti-slavery convention in Philadelphia, where a mob raged and would later torch the building. Fortunately, all escaped, and Foster took up Weld's invitation. Soon, ducking mobs, stones, rotten eggs, and rum bottles were "but a burden of the work."

One of the first women to speak before mixed audiences, the Quaker-raised Foster espoused the causes of abolition and enfranchisement. Along with her husband, abolitionist Stephen S. Foster, she opened the family farm to slaves escaping on the Underground Railroad and, denied the vote, refused to pay taxes to protest taxation without representation.

In 1851, exhausted after a long campaign in New York, the woman with a "felicity of language" and "stentorian lungs" had planned to rest quietly among the audience of the second Woman's Rights Convention, held in Worcester, Massachusetts. But by the third day, October 15, she felt compelled to speak.

She posed her argument: Women are without many rights, she told them, but "I cannot, I will not charge it all upon men." Women must "feel the full stimulus of motive," of her duties, then "she will soon achieve the means." Though Ernestine Rose would respond that rights precede duties "and he who enjoys the most rights, has in return the most duties," the audience loved the speech, and "bloody feet" became the movement's new metaphor for the sacrifices of women in the cause.

M adam President: I rise this evening not to make a speech. I came here without any intention of even opening my mouth in this Convention. But I must utter one word of congratulation, that the cause which we have come here to aid, has given such evidence this evening of its success. When genius, that could find ample field elsewhere, comes forward and lays itself on this altar, we have no reason for discouragement; and I am not without faith that the time is not far distant, when our utmost desires shall be gratified, when our highest hopes shall be realized. I feel that the work is more than half accomplished.

I have an idea, thrown into the form of a short resolution, which I wish to present to this Convention, because no one else has brought it forward. I feel that behind, that underneath, that deeper down than we have yet gone, lies the great cause of the difficulties which we aim to remove. We complain that woman is inadequately rewarded for her labor. It is true. We complain that on the platform, in the forum, in the pulpit, in the office of teacher, and so on to the end of the list, she does not hold that place which she is qualified to fill; and what is the deep difficulty? I cannot, I will not charge it all upon man. I respond to the statement that it is chargeable upon us as well as upon others. It is an old, homely maxim, but yet there is great force in it,

"Where there's a will, there's a way," and the reason why woman is not found in the highest position which she is qualified to fill is because she has not more than half the will. I therefore wish to present the resolution that I hold in my hand:

Resolved, That in regard to most points, woman lacks her rights because she does not feel the full weight of her responsibilities; that when she shall feel her responsibilities sufficiently to induce her to go forward and discharge them, she will inevitably obtain her rights; when she shall feel herself equally bound with her father, husband, brother, and son to provide for the physical necessities and elegances of life, when she shall feel as deep responsibility as they for the intellectual culture and the moral and religious elevation of the race, she will of necessity seek out and enter those paths of physical, intellectual, moral, and religious labor which are necessary to the accomplishment of her object. Let her feel the full stimulus of motive, and she will soon achieve the means.

I believe that the idea embodied in this resolution, though not expressed so clearly as I fain would have had it, points to the great difficulty that lies in our way; and therefore, I feel that it is necessary for us to inculcate, on the rising generation especially (for it is to these that we must chiefly look)—it is necessary for us to inculcate on them particularly this feeling of responsibility. Let mothers take care to impress upon their daughters that they are not to enter upon the marriage relation until they are qualified to provide for the physical necessities of a family. Let our daughters feel that they must never attempt to enter upon the marriage relation until they shall be qualified to provide for the wants of a household, and then we shall see much, if not all, that difficulty which has been complained of here, removed. Women revolt at the idea of marrying for the sake of a home, for the sake of a support—of marrying the purse instead of the man. There is no woman here, who, if the question were put to her,

impossible. "Yes," said my teacher, "you can get that only by
earnest labor, by sacrifice, by weariness." I learned my lesson, I
accomplished my task; and I would to God that every person
had had similar instruction, and learned the necessity of toil—
earnest, self-sacrificing toil. (*Loud cheers.*)

would not say, love is sufficient. She says it is sufficient, and she
believes it; yet behind this lies something else in more than one
case in ten.

Let us therefore inculcate upon our daughters that they
should be able to provide for the wants of a family and that they
are unfit for that relation until they are qualified to do so. If we
teach our daughters that they are as much bound to become
independent as their brothers, and that they should not hang
upon the skirts of a paternal home for support, but secure subsistence for themselves, will they not look out avenues to new
employments? Why, we all feel it, we all know it, if women
could be taught that the responsibilities devolved equally upon
themselves and the other sex, they would seek out the means to
fulfill those responsibilities. That is the duty we owe our daughters today; that is the duty each one owes to herself today, to see
to it that we feel that we must enter into business, such as will
bring in to the support of our families as much as the labor of
our fathers, husbands, and brothers does. Woman's labor is as
intrinsically valuable as any other, and why is it not remunerated
as well? Because, as has been shown here, because there is too
much female labor in the market, compared with the work it is
allowed to undertake. There are other means of support; there
are other modes of acquiring wealth: let woman seek them out
and use them for her own interest, and this evil will in great part
be done away.

Then, again, let every woman feel that she is equally responsible with man for the immorality, for the crime that stalks
abroad in our land, and will she not be up and doing, in order to
put away that vice? Let every woman understand that it is for
her to see that disease be not inflicted on the community, and
will she not seek out means to do it away? If she feels that she is
as competent to banish superstition and prejudice and bigotry
from the world as her brother, will she not be up and doing?

Here is the great barrier to woman's obtaining her rights. Mary Wolstonecraft was the first woman who wrote a book on "Woman's Rights," but a few years later, she wrote another, entitled "Woman's Duty," and when woman shall feel her duty, she will get her rights. We, who are young on this question of Woman's Rights, should entitle our next book "Woman's Duties." Impress on your daughters their duties; impress on your wives, your sisters, on your brothers, on your husbands, on the race, their duties, and we shall all have our rights.

Man is wronged, not in London, New York, or Boston alone. Look around you here in Worcester, and see him sitting amidst the dust of his counting room, or behind the counter, his whole soul engaged in dollars and cents, until the Multiplication Table becomes his creed, his Pater noster, and his Decalogue. Society says, keep your daughters, like dolls, in the parlor; they must not do anything to aid in supporting the family. But a certain appearance in society must be maintained. You must keep up the style of the household. You are in fault if your wife does not uphold the condition to which she was bred in her father's house. I put this before men. If we could look under and within the broadcloth and the velvet, we should find as many breaking hearts, and as many sighs and groans, and as much of mental anguish, as we find in the parlor, as we find in the nursery of any house in Worcester. But woman is vain and frivolous, and man is ignorant; and therefore, he is what he is. Had his daughters, had his wife, been educated to feel their responsibilities, they would have taken their rights, and he would have been a happy and contented man, and would not have been reduced to the mere machine for calculating and getting money that he now is.

My friends, I feel that in throwing out this idea, I have done what was left for me to do. But I did not rise to make a speech—my life has been my speech. For fourteen years I have advocated this cause by my daily life. Bloody feet, sisters, have

worn smooth the path by which you have come (*Great sensation*.) You will not need to speak when y your everyday life. Oh, how truly does Webster action is eloquence! Let us, then, when we go hom complain, but to work. Do not go home to comp men, but go and make greater exertions than ever your everyday duties. Oh! it is easy to be lazy; it is indeed to be indolent; but it is hard, and a martyrd responsibilities. There are thousands of women in th States working for a starving pittance, who know a they are fitted for something better, and who tell talk to them, and urge them to open shops, and do themselves, "I do not want the responsibility of bu too much." Well, then, starve in your laziness!

Oh, Madam President, I feel that we have throw blame on the other side. At any rate, we all deserve have been groping about in the dark. We are trying way, and oh! God give us light! But I am convinced go forward and enter the path, it will grow brighter a unto the perfect day.

I will speak no longer. I speak throughout th those of you who speak but once should take the hope, however, that you do not feel that I speak to yc Oh, no; it is in the hope of inducing you to be willing responsibilities, to be willing to have a sleepless nigh ally, and days of toil and trouble; for he that labors sh reward; he that sows shall reap. My teacher in childh me a lesson, which I hope I never shall forget appointed me a task, and when she asked me if I had I said, "No, it is too hard." "Well," said she, "go into th pick me up an apron full of pebbles." I did it. "It was it," said she. "Oh, yes," I replied. "Go out again," sai pour them down, and bring me in an apron full of g

Lucy Stone
Speaks as a Disappointed Woman

". . . disappointment is the lot of woman."

As a child, Lucy Stone (1818–1893) was suspicious; those passages in the Bible—the ones that proclaim men's dominion over women—had they been properly translated? She resolved to learn Hebrew and Greek just to be sure. A graduate of Oberlin College, Stone drew vast audiences to her lectures on abolition and temperance, but became best known for her advocacy of women's rights.

In 1850, Stone organized the first of many national Woman's Rights Conventions and took a leadership role in the movement alongside Elizabeth Cady Stanton and Susan B. Anthony. A deliberate speaker, skilled at putting illustration to point, she argues here for equality—in a speech delivered at the 1855 convention in Cincinnati, Ohio. It was the same year she married Henry Brown Blackwell and raised eyebrows by keeping her maiden name.

Years later, Stone and other conservative reformers, put out by their colleagues' passive acceptance of the scandalous Victoria Woodhull, split with the movement to form the American Woman Suffrage Association in 1869. Old wounds eventually healed, however, when Alice Blackwell, Stone's daughter, led the formation of a stronger and more united National American

Woman Suffrage Association two decades later; Stone served as chairman of its executive board.

———•◦•———

From the first years to which my memory stretches, I have been a disappointed woman. When, with my brothers, I reached forth after the sources of knowledge, I was reproved with "It isn't fit for you; it doesn't belong to women." Then there was but one college in the world where women were admitted, and that was in Brazil. I would have found my way there, but by the time I was prepared to go, one was opened in the young state of Ohio—the first in the United States where women and Negroes could enjoy opportunities with white men. I was disappointed when I came to seek a profession worthy an immortal being—every employment was closed to me, except those of the teacher, the seamstress, and the housekeeper. In education, in marriage, in religion, in everything, disappointment is the lot of woman. It shall be the business of my life to deepen this disappointment in every woman's heart until she bows down to it no longer. I wish that women, instead of being walking showcases, instead of begging of their fathers and brothers the latest and gayest new bonnet, would ask of them their rights.

The question of woman's rights is a practical one. The notion has prevailed that it was only an ephemeral idea, that it was but women claiming the right to smoke cigars in the streets and to frequent barrooms. Others have supposed it a question of comparative intellect; others still, of sphere. Too much has already been said and written about woman's sphere. Trace all the doctrines to their source and they will be found to have no basis except in the usages and prejudices of the age. This is seen in the fact that what is tolerated in woman in one country is not tolerated in another. In this country women may hold prayer meetings, et cetera, but in Mohammedan countries it is written upon their mosques, "Women and dogs, and other impure animals, are not permitted to enter." Wendell Phillips says, "The best and greatest thing one is capable of doing, that is his sphere."

I have confidence in the Father to believe that when He gives us the capacity to do anything He does not make a blunder. Leave women, then, to find their sphere. And do not tell us before we are born even, that our province is to cook dinners, darn stockings, and sew on buttons. We are told woman has all the rights she wants; and even women, I am ashamed to say, tell us so. They mistake the politeness of men for rights—seats while men stand in this hall tonight, and their adulations; but these are mere courtesies.

We want rights. The flour merchant, the house builder, and the postman charge us no less on account of our sex; but when we endeavor to earn money to pay all these, then, indeed, we find the difference. Man, if he have energy, may hew out for himself a path where no mortal has ever trod, held back by nothing but what is in himself; the world is all before him, where to choose; and we are glad for you, brothers, men, that it is so. But the same society that drives forth the young man, keeps woman at home—a dependent—working little cats on worsted, and little dogs on punctured papers; but if she goes heartily and bravely to give herself to some worthy purpose, she is out of her sphere and she loses caste. Women working in tailor shops are paid one-third as much as men. Someone in Philadelphia has stated that women make fine shirts for twelve and a half cents apiece; that no woman can make more than nine a week, and the sum thus earned, after deducting rent, fuel, et cetera, leaves her just three and a half cents a day for bread. Is it a wonder that women are driven to prostitution? Female teachers in New York are paid fifty dollars a year, and for every such situation there are five hundred applicants. I know not what you believe of God, but I believe He gave yearnings and longings to be filled, and that He did not mean all our time should be devoted to feeding and clothing the body.

The present condition of woman causes a horrible perversion of the marriage relation. It is asked of a lady, "Has she married well?" "Oh, yes, her husband is rich." Woman must marry for a home, and you men are the sufferers by this; for a woman who loathes you may marry you because you have the means to get money which she cannot have. But when woman can enter the lists with you and make money for herself, she will marry you only for deep and earnest affection. . . .

The widening of woman's sphere is to improve her lot. Let us do it, and if the world scoff, let it scoff—if it sneer, let it sneer. . . .

Sojourner Truth
Keeps Things Stirring

". . . I have a right to have just as much as a man."

American abolitionist Sojourner Truth never learned to read or write. "I don't read such small stuff as letters," she said. "I read men and nations." In 1867, her nation was just two years away from ratifying the Fifteenth Amendment, which would forbid denial of the vote "on account of race, color, or previous condition of servitude."

Though the former slave eventually decided not to begrudge suffrage for black men, on May 9, 1867, in this speech to the American Equal Rights Association in New York, she laments the "great stir about colored men getting their rights, but not a word about the colored women." Truth marshalls arguments against this disparity—and after "forty years a slave and forty years free," will stay in the battle for equal rights for women.

Sixteen years later, the woman in the Quaker dress and white bonnet, the woman who spoke with uplifted hands and homespun phrases, the freed woman praised by Lincoln, died at her home in Battle Creek, Michigan.

My friends, I am rejoiced that you are glad, but I don't know how you will feel when I get through. I come from another field—the country of the slave. They have got their liberty—so much good luck to have slavery partly destroyed; not entirely. I want it root and branch destroyed. Then we will all be free indeed. I feel that if I have to answer for the deeds done in my body just as much as a man, I have a right to have just as much as a man. There is a great stir about colored men getting their rights, but not a word about the colored women; and if colored men get their rights, and not colored women theirs, you see the colored men will be masters over the women, and it will be just as bad as it was before. So I am for keeping the thing going while things are stirring; because if we wait till it is still, it will take a great while to get it going again. White women are a great deal smarter, and know more than colored women, while colored women do not know scarcely anything. They go out washing, which is about as high as a colored woman gets, and their men go about idle, strutting up and down; and when the women come home, they ask for their money and take it all, and then scold because there is no food. I want you to consider on that, chil'n. I call you chil'n; you are somebody's chil'n, and I am old enough to be mother of all that is here. I want women to have their rights. In the courts women have no right, no voice; nobody speaks for them. I wish woman to have her voice there among the pettifoggers. If it is not a fit place for women, it is unfit for men to be there.

I am above eighty years old; it is about time for me to be going. I have been forty years a slave and forty years free, and would be here forty years more to have equal rights for all. I suppose I am kept here because something remains for me to do; I suppose I am yet to help to break the chain. I have done a great deal of work; as much as a man, but did not get so much pay. I used to work in the field and bind grain, keeping up with would not say, love is sufficient. She says it is sufficient, and she believes it; yet behind this lies something else in more than one case in ten.

Let us therefore inculcate upon our daughters that they should be able to provide for the wants of a family and that they are unfit for that relation until they are qualified to do so. If we teach our daughters that they are as much bound to become independent as their brothers, and that they should not hang upon the skirts of a paternal home for support, but secure subsistence for themselves, will they not look out avenues to new employments? Why, we all feel it, we all know it, if women could be taught that the responsibilities devolved equally upon themselves and the other sex, they would seek out the means to fulfill those responsibilities. That is the duty we owe our daughters today; that is the duty each one owes to herself today, to see to it that we feel that we must enter into business, such as will bring in to the support of our families as much as the labor of our fathers, husbands, and brothers does. Woman's labor is as intrinsically valuable as any other, and why is it not remunerated as well? Because, as has been shown here, because there is too much female labor in the market, compared with the work it is allowed to undertake. There are other means of support; there are other modes of acquiring wealth: let woman seek them out and use them for her own interest, and this evil will in great part be done away.

Then, again, let every woman feel that she is equally responsible with man for the immorality, for the crime that stalks abroad in our land, and will she not be up and doing, in order to put away that vice? Let every woman understand that it is for her to see that disease be not inflicted on the community, and will she not seek out means to do it away? If she feels that she is as competent to banish superstition and prejudice and bigotry from the world as her brother, will she not be up and doing?

Here is the great barrier to woman's obtaining her rights. Mary Wolstonecraft was the first woman who wrote a book on "Woman's Rights," but a few years later, she wrote another, entitled "Woman's Duty," and when woman shall feel her duty, she will get her rights. We, who are young on this question of Woman's Rights, should entitle our next book "Woman's Duties." Impress on your daughters their duties; impress on your wives, your sisters, on your brothers, on your husbands, on the race, their duties, and we shall all have our rights.

Man is wronged, not in London, New York, or Boston alone. Look around you here in Worcester, and see him sitting amidst the dust of his counting room, or behind the counter, his whole soul engaged in dollars and cents, until the Multiplication Table becomes his creed, his Pater noster, and his Decalogue. Society says, keep your daughters, like dolls, in the parlor; they must not do anything to aid in supporting the family. But a certain appearance in society must be maintained. You must keep up the style of the household. You are in fault if your wife does not uphold the condition to which she was bred in her father's house. I put this before men. If we could look under and within the broadcloth and the velvet, we should find as many breaking hearts, and as many sighs and groans, and as much of mental anguish, as we find in the parlor, as we find in the nursery of any house in Worcester. But woman is vain and frivolous, and man is ignorant; and therefore, he is what he is. Had his daughters, had his wife, been educated to feel their responsibilities, they would have taken their rights, and he would have been a happy and contented man, and would not have been reduced to the mere machine for calculating and getting money that he now is.

My friends, I feel that in throwing out this idea, I have done what was left for me to do. But I did not rise to make a speech—my life has been my speech. For fourteen years I have advocated this cause by my daily life. Bloody feet, sisters, have worn smooth the path by which you have come up hither. (*Great sensation.*) You will not need to speak when you speak by your everyday life. Oh, how truly does Webster say, action, action is eloquence! Let us, then, when we go home, go not to complain, but to work. Do not go home to complain of the men, but go and make greater exertions than ever to discharge your everyday duties. Oh! it is easy to be lazy; it is comfortable indeed to be indolent; but it is hard, and a martyrdom, to take responsibilities. There are thousands of women in these United States working for a starving pittance, who know and feel that they are fitted for something better, and who tell me, when I talk to them, and urge them to open shops, and do business for themselves, "I do not want the responsibility of business—it is too much." Well, then, starve in your laziness!

Oh, Madam President, I feel that we have thrown too much blame on the other side. At any rate, we all deserve enough. We have been groping about in the dark. We are trying to feel our way, and oh! God give us light! But I am convinced that as we go forward and enter the path, it will grow brighter and brighter unto the perfect day.

I will speak no longer. I speak throughout the year, and those of you who speak but once should take the platform. I hope, however, that you do not feel that I speak to you in anger. Oh, no; it is in the hope of inducing you to be willing to assume responsibilities, to be willing to have a sleepless night occasionally, and days of toil and trouble; for he that labors shall have his reward; he that sows shall reap. My teacher in childhood taught me a lesson, which I hope I never shall forget. She had appointed me a task, and when she asked me if I had learned it, I said, "No, it is too hard." "Well," said she, "go into the road and pick me up an apron full of pebbles." I did it. "It was easy to do it," said she. "Oh, yes," I replied. "Go out again," said she, "and pour them down, and bring me in an apron full of gold." It was impossible. "Yes," said my teacher, "you can get that only by earnest labor, by sacrifice, by weariness." I learned my lesson, I accomplished my task; and I would to God that every person had had similar instruction, and learned the necessity of toil—earnest, self-sacrificing toil. (*Loud cheers.*)

Lucy Stone
Speaks as a Disappointed Woman

". . . disappointment is the lot of woman."

As a child, Lucy Stone (1818–1893) was suspicious; those passages in the Bible—the ones that proclaim men's dominion over women—had they been properly translated? She resolved to learn Hebrew and Greek just to be sure. A graduate of Oberlin College, Stone drew vast audiences to her lectures on abolition and temperance, but became best known for her advocacy of women's rights.

In 1850, Stone organized the first of many national Woman's Rights Conventions and took a leadership role in the movement alongside Elizabeth Cady Stanton and Susan B. Anthony. A deliberate speaker, skilled at putting illustration to point, she argues here for equality—in a speech delivered at the 1855 convention in Cincinnati, Ohio. It was the same year she married Henry Brown Blackwell and raised eyebrows by keeping her maiden name.

Years later, Stone and other conservative reformers, put out by their colleagues' passive acceptance of the scandalous Victoria Woodhull, split with the movement to form the American Woman Suffrage Association in 1869. Old wounds eventually healed, however, when Alice Blackwell, Stone's daughter, led the formation of a stronger and more united National American

Woman Suffrage Association two decades later; Stone served as chairman of its executive board.

———·•·———

From the first years to which my memory stretches, I have been a disappointed woman. When, with my brothers, I reached forth after the sources of knowledge, I was reproved with "It isn't fit for you; it doesn't belong to women." Then there was but one college in the world where women were admitted, and that was in Brazil. I would have found my way there, but by the time I was prepared to go, one was opened in the young state of Ohio—the first in the United States where women and Negroes could enjoy opportunities with white men. I was disappointed when I came to seek a profession worthy an immortal being—every employment was closed to me, except those of the teacher, the seamstress, and the housekeeper. In education, in marriage, in religion, in everything, disappointment is the lot of woman. It shall be the business of my life to deepen this disappointment in every woman's heart until she bows down to it no longer. I wish that women, instead of being walking showcases, instead of begging of their fathers and brothers the latest and gayest new bonnet, would ask of them their rights.

The question of woman's rights is a practical one. The notion has prevailed that it was only an ephemeral idea, that it was but women claiming the right to smoke cigars in the streets and to frequent barrooms. Others have supposed it a question of comparative intellect; others still, of sphere. Too much has already been said and written about woman's sphere. Trace all the doctrines to their source and they will be found to have no basis except in the usages and prejudices of the age. This is seen in the fact that what is tolerated in woman in one country is not tolerated in another. In this country women may hold prayer meetings, et cetera, but in Mohammedan countries it is written upon their mosques, "Women and dogs, and other impure animals, are not permitted to enter." Wendell Phillips says, "The best and greatest thing one is capable of doing, that is his sphere."

I have confidence in the Father to believe that when He gives us the capacity to do anything He does not make a blunder. Leave women, then, to find their sphere. And do not tell us before we are born even, that our province is to cook dinners, darn stockings, and sew on buttons. We are told woman has all the rights she wants; and even women, I am ashamed to say, tell us so. They mistake the politeness of men for rights—seats while men stand in this hall tonight, and their adulations; but these are mere courtesies.

We want rights. The flour merchant, the house builder, and the postman charge us no less on account of our sex; but when we endeavor to earn money to pay all these, then, indeed, we find the difference. Man, if he have energy, may hew out for himself a path where no mortal has ever trod, held back by nothing but what is in himself; the world is all before him, where to choose; and we are glad for you, brothers, men, that it is so. But the same society that drives forth the young man, keeps woman at home—a dependent—working little cats on worsted, and little dogs on punctured papers; but if she goes heartily and bravely to give herself to some worthy purpose, she is out of her sphere and she loses caste. Women working in tailor shops are paid one-third as much as men. Someone in Philadelphia has stated that women make fine shirts for twelve and a half cents apiece; that no woman can make more than nine a week, and the sum thus earned, after deducting rent, fuel, et cetera, leaves her just three and a half cents a day for bread. Is it a wonder that women are driven to prostitution? Female teachers in New York are paid fifty dollars a year, and for every such situation there are five hundred applicants. I know not what you believe of God, but I believe He gave yearnings and longings to be filled, and that He did not mean all our time should be devoted to feeding and clothing the body.

The present condition of woman causes a horrible perversion of the marriage relation. It is asked of a lady, "Has she married well?" "Oh, yes, her husband is rich." Woman must marry for a home, and you men are the sufferers by this; for a woman who loathes you may marry you because you have the means to get money which she cannot have. But when woman can enter the lists with you and make money for herself, she will marry you only for deep and earnest affection. . . .

The widening of woman's sphere is to improve her lot. Let us do it, and if the world scoff, let it scoff—if it sneer, let it sneer. . . .

Sojourner Truth
Keeps Things Stirring

". . . I have a right to have just as much as a man."

American abolitionist Sojourner Truth never learned to read or write. "I don't read such small stuff as letters," she said. "I read men and nations." In 1867, her nation was just two years away from ratifying the Fifteenth Amendment, which would forbid denial of the vote "on account of race, color, or previous condition of servitude."

Though the former slave eventually decided not to begrudge suffrage for black men, on May 9, 1867, in this speech to the American Equal Rights Association in New York, she laments the "great stir about colored men getting their rights, but not a word about the colored women." Truth marshalls arguments against this disparity—and after "forty years a slave and forty years free," will stay in the battle for equal rights for women.

Sixteen years later, the woman in the Quaker dress and white bonnet, the woman who spoke with uplifted hands and homespun phrases, the freed woman praised by Lincoln, died at her home in Battle Creek, Michigan.

My friends, I am rejoiced that you are glad, but I don't know how you will feel when I get through. I come from another field—the country of the slave. They have got their liberty—so much good luck to have slavery partly destroyed; not entirely. I want it root and branch destroyed. Then we will all be free indeed. I feel that if I have to answer for the deeds done in my body just as much as a man, I have a right to have just as much as a man. There is a great stir about colored men getting their rights, but not a word about the colored women; and if colored men get their rights, and not colored women theirs, you see the colored men will be masters over the women, and it will be just as bad as it was before. So I am for keeping the thing going while things are stirring; because if we wait till it is still, it will take a great while to get it going again. White women are a great deal smarter, and know more than colored women, while colored women do not know scarcely anything. They go out washing, which is about as high as a colored woman gets, and their men go about idle, strutting up and down; and when the women come home, they ask for their money and take it all, and then scold because there is no food. I want you to consider on that, chil'n. I call you chil'n; you are somebody's chil'n, and I am old enough to be mother of all that is here. I want women to have their rights. In the courts women have no right, no voice; nobody speaks for them. I wish woman to have her voice there among the pettifoggers. If it is not a fit place for women, it is unfit for men to be there.

I am above eighty years old; it is about time for me to be going. I have been forty years a slave and forty years free, and would be here forty years more to have equal rights for all. I suppose I am kept here because something remains for me to do; I suppose I am yet to help to break the chain. I have done a great deal of work; as much as a man, but did not get so much pay. I used to work in the field and bind grain, keeping up with the cradler; but men doing no more, got twice as much pay; so with the German women. They work in the field and do as much work, but do not get the pay. We do as much, we eat as much, we want as much. I suppose I am about the only colored woman that goes about to speak for the rights of the colored women. I want to keep the thing stirring, now that the ice is cracked. What we want is a little money. You men know that you get as much again as women when you write, or for what you do. When we get our rights we shall not have to come to you for money, for then we shall have money enough in our own pockets; and may be you will ask us for money. But help us now until we get it. It is a good consolation to know that when we have got this battle fought we shall not be coming to you any more. You have been having our rights so long, that you think, like a slaveholder, that you own us. I know that it is hard for one who has held the reins for so long to give up; it cuts like a knife. It will feel all the better when it closes up again. I have been in Washington about three years, seeing about these colored people. Now colored men have the right to vote. There ought to be equal rights now more than ever, since colored people have got their freedom. I am going to talk several times while I am here; so now I will do a little singing. I have not heard any singing since I came here.

(*Accordingly, suiting the action to the word, Sojourner sang, "We are going home."*)

There, children, in heaven we shall rest from all our labors; first do all we have to do here. There I am determined to go, not to stop short of that beautiful place, and I do not mean to stop till I get there, and meet you there, too.

Elizabeth Cady Stanton
Sees the Male Element as a Destructive Force

*"Society is but the reflection of man himself,
untempered by woman's thought."*

Elizabeth Cady Stanton and her lifelong friend, Susan B. Anthony, together compiled and edited the first three volumes of the *History of Woman Suffrage*, a sweeping record of the women's movement in the nineteenth century. In the first volume, Stanton writes: "I am the better writer, she the better critic. She supplied the facts and statistics, I the philosophy and the rhetoric, and together we made arguments which have stood unshaken by the storms of thirty long years; arguments that no man has answered."

One of those arguments Stanton set forth in her speech to the Woman Suffrage Convention in Washington, D.C., in 1868: "The male element is a destructive force." It had been twenty years since the gathering at Seneca Falls, and Stanton still fired for the vote, contending in this address that enfranchisement would allow women to better the socially poor conditions wrought by "what is called the stronger sex." Two years before this speech, Stanton became the first woman to run for Congress. Like Anthony's subsequent symbolic and illegal vote in the 1872 general election, Stanton ran as a way to mock a legal system that allowed a woman to run for office but not vote for anyone holding one.

Stanton's speaking style, typical of—but less encumbered by—the grandiose language of her day, conveys the punch of deft wording ("black codes and gloomy creeds"), metaphor ("written by the finger of God on her soul"), and sheer tenor to make this an effective speech.

I urge a sixteenth amendment, because "manhood suffrage," or a man's government, is civil, religious, and social disorganization. The male element is a destructive force, stern, selfish, aggrandizing, loving war, violence, conquest, acquisition, breeding in the material and moral world alike discord, disorder, disease, and death. See what a record of blood and cruelty the pages of history reveal! Through what slavery, slaughter, and sacrifice, through what inquisitions and imprisonments, pains and persecutions, black codes and gloomy creeds, the soul of humanity has struggled for the centuries, while mercy has veiled her face and all hearts have been dead alike to love and hope!

The male element has held high carnival thus far; it has fairly run riot from the beginning, overpowering the feminine element everywhere, crushing out all the diviner qualities in human nature, until we know but little of true manhood and womanhood, of the latter comparatively nothing, for it has scarce been recognized as a power until within the last century. Society is but the reflection of man himself, untempered by woman's thought; the hard iron rule we feel alike in the church, the state, and the home. No one need wonder at the disorganization, at the fragmentary condition of everything, when we remember that man, who represents but half a complete being, with but half an idea on every subject, has undertaken the absolute control of all sublimary matters.

People object to the demands of those whom they choose to call the strong-minded, because they say "the right of suffrage will make the women masculine." That is just the difficulty in which we are involved today. Though disfranchised, we have few women in the best sense; we have simply so many reflections, varieties, and dilutions of the masculine gender. The strong, natural characteristics of womanhood are repressed and ignored in dependence, for so long as man feeds woman she will try to please the giver and adapt herself to his condition. To keep a foothold in society, woman must be as near like man as possible, reflect his ideas, opinions, virtues, motives, prejudices, and vices. She must respect his statutes, though they strip her of every inalienable right, and conflict with that higher law written by the finger of God on her own soul.

She must look at everything from its dollar-and-cent point of view, or she is a mere romancer. She must accept things as they are and make the best of them. To mourn over the miseries of others, the poverty of the poor, their hardships in jails, prisons, asylums, the horrors of war, cruelty, and brutality in every form, all this would be mere sentimentalizing. To protest against the intrigue, bribery, and corruption of public life, to desire that her sons might follow some business that did not involve lying, cheating, and a hard, grinding selfishness, would be arrant nonsense.

In this way man has been molding woman to his ideas by direct and positive influences, while she, if not a negation, has used indirect means to control him, and in most cases developed the very characteristics both in him and herself that needed repression. And now man himself stands appalled at the results of his own excesses, and mourns in bitterness that falsehood, selfishness, and violence are the law of life. The need of this hour is not territory, gold mines, railroads, or specie payments but a new evangel of womanhood, to exalt purity, virtue, morality, true religion, to lift man up into the higher realms of thought and action.

We ask woman's enfranchisement, as the first step toward the recognition of that essential element in government that can only secure the health, strength, and prosperity of the nation. Whatever is done to lift woman to her true position will help to usher in a new day of peace and perfection for the race.

In speaking of the masculine element, I do not wish to be understood to say that all men are hard, selfish, and brutal, for many of the most beautiful spirits the world has known have been clothed with manhood; but I refer to those characteristics, though often marked in woman, that distinguish what is called the stronger sex. For example, the love of acquisition and conquest, the very pioneers of civilization, when expended on the earth, the sea, the elements, the riches and forces of nature, are powers of destruction when used to subjugate one man to another or to sacrifice nations to ambition.

Here that great conservator of woman's love, if permitted to assert itself, as it naturally would in freedom against oppression, violence, and war, would hold all these destructive forces in check, for woman knows the cost of life better than man does, and not with her consent would one drop of blood ever be shed, one life sacrificed in vain.

With violence and disturbance in the natural world, we see a constant effort to maintain an equilibrium of forces. Nature, like a loving mother, is ever trying to keep land and sea, mountain and valley, each in its place, to hush the angry winds and waves, balance the extremes of heat and cold, of rain and drought, that peace, harmony, and beauty may reign supreme. There is a striking analogy between matter and mind, and the present disorganization of society warns us that in the dethronement of woman we have let loose the elements of violence and ruin that she only has the power to curb. If the civilization of the age calls for an extension of the suffrage, surely a government of the most virtuous educated men and women would better represent the whole and protect the interests of all than could the representation of either sex alone.

Susan B. Anthony
Defines "Citizenship" Under the Constitution

"Are women persons?"

Sixteen years before her death, Susan Brownell Anthony (1820–1906) tried to revive the deflated spirit of her fellow suffragists: "Cheer up, the world will not always view our question as it does now! By and by there will be victory." At eighty-six and still without voting rights, Anthony's tenacity shone in her last public words: "Failure is impossible." It was "that hope which hoped on when others saw nothing to hope for; that splendid optimism which never knew despair," Carrie Chapman Catt said at Anthony's funeral, that made "her greater than others."

Born into a Massachusetts's Quaker family, the third of six children, Anthony became a teacher as a way of easing financial burdens at home. In 1849, bored and dismayed by her lack of opportunities in the classroom, she set out on a career as a crusader for social reforms—a path that led to Elizabeth Cady Stanton, who would become a lifelong friend. Joining forces, they helped pass legislation in New York that gave women the power to control their own earnings and property and, in 1869, formed the National Woman Suffrage Association.

Three years later, Susan B. Anthony registered to vote and led fifteen women to the polls on election day; she was, she argued when arrested, simply taking the Fourteenth Amendment "at its word"—that all people born in the United States were citizens. Her subsequent trial, her conviction, her fine of $100 (which she refused to pay), and her cause swelled the columns of the country's newspapers.

As a speaker, Anthony saw herself as "neither an orator nor a philosopher," but in this speech, delivered in 1873 after her conviction, she shows a forthright style that excels over flourish. Her gift was that she could be blunt; she could mock the logical: "Are women persons?" She advances that, unquestionably, they are and thus are entitled to every respect under the law.

———•———

F riends and fellow citizens: I stand before you tonight under indictment for the alleged crime of having voted at the last presidential election, without having a lawful right to vote. It shall be my work this evening to prove to you that in thus voting, I not only committed no crime, but, instead, simply exercised my citizen's rights, guaranteed to me and all United States citizens by the National Constitution, beyond the power of any state to deny.

The preamble of the Federal Constitution says:

"We, the people of the United States, in order to form a more perfect union, establish justice, insure domestic tranquility, provide for the common defense, promote the general welfare, and secure the blessings of liberty to ourselves and our posterity, do ordain and establish this Constitution for the United States of America."

It was we, the people; not we, the white male citizens; nor yet we, the male citizens; but we, the whole people, who formed the Union. And we formed it, not to give the blessings of liberty, but to secure them; not to the half of ourselves and the half of our posterity, but to the whole people—women as well as men. And it is a downright mockery to talk to women of their enjoyment of the blessings of liberty while they are denied the use of the only means of securing them provided by this democratic-republican government—the ballot.

For any state to make sex a qualification that must ever result in the disfranchisement of one entire half of the people is to pass a bill of attainder, or an *ex post facto* law, and is therefore a violation of the supreme law of the land. By it the blessings of liberty are forever withheld from women and their female posterity. To them this government has no just powers derived from the consent of the governed. To them this government is not a democracy. It is not a republic. It is an odious aristocracy; a hateful oligarchy of sex; the most hateful aristocracy ever established on the face of the globe; an oligarchy of wealth, where the right govern the poor. An oligarchy of learning, where the educated govern the ignorant, or even an oligarchy of race, where the Saxon rules the African, might be endured; but this oligarchy of sex, which makes father, brothers, husband, sons, the oligarchs over the mother and sisters, the wife and daughters of every household—which ordains all men sovereigns, all women subjects—carries dissension, discord, and rebellion into every home of the nation.

Webster, Worcester, and Bouvier all define a citizen to be a person in the United States, entitled to vote and hold office.

The only question left to be settled now is: Are women persons? And I hardly believe any of our opponents will have the hardihood to say they are not. Being persons, then, women are citizens; and no state has a right to make any law, or to enforce any old law, that shall abridge their privileges or immunities. Hence, every discrimination against women in the constitutions and laws of the several states is today null and void, precisely as is every one against Negroes.

Frances Willard
Makes a Plea for "Home Protection"

"I have passed the Rubicon of Silence . . ."

More than twenty thousand people filed past the casket of Frances Willard (1839–1898) as her body lay in state at the Women's Temple in Chicago in 1898. "No woman in America was better known, none was more universally loved" than Frances Willard, read her obituary.

Her cause was temperance—a fight against "the nemesis of home's arch enemy, King Alcohol," the "demon rum" that left men abusive and idle and women and children cowering at home in poverty. President of Evanston College in 1871, Willard came to the movement in small steps, first joining crusaders as they knelt in prayer upon sawdust-covered saloon floors, singing "Rock of Ages"—even convincing some barkeepers to give up their "morally destructive" businesses. Then, in 1874, she helped form the Woman's Christian Temperance Union and became its president five years later. Her "white ribbon army" grew to nearly two million members.

Willard also advocated women's suffrage and worked for many years to link the goals of both her causes as a way of ensuring "home protection." In this speech, delivered at the Woman's Congress in Philadelphia in 1876, she argues that the ballot could give women the "power to protect, along life's

treacherous highways, those whom they have so long loved."
The peroration is quintessential Willard—an appeal to emotion
("heartbroken wives," "sorrowful little children") in high style. It
was not unusual for Willard to speak before crowds of four to
five thousand people and, as she did in this address, leave them
spellbound.

L onger ago than I shall tell, my father returned one night to
the far-off Wisconsin home where I was reared, and, sitting
by my mother's chair, with a child's attentive ear I listened to
their words. He told us of the news that day that had brought
about Neal Dow, and the great fight for prohibition down in
Maine, and then he said: "I wonder if poor, rum-cursed Wisconsin will ever get a law like that!" And mother rocked awhile
in silence, in the dear old chair I love, and then she gently said:
"Yes, Josiah, there'll be such a law all over the land some day,
when women vote."

My father had never heard her say as much before. He was a
great conservative; so he looked tremendously astonished, and
replied in his keen, sarcastic voice: "And pray, how will you
arrange it so that women shall vote?" Mother's chair went to
and fro a little faster for a minute, and then, looking not into his
face, but into the flickering flame of the grate, she slowly
answered: "Well, I say to you, as the Apostle Paul said to his
jailor: 'You have put us into prison, we being Romans, and you
must come and take us out.' "

That was a seed-thought in a girl's brain and heart. Years
passed on, in which nothing more was said upon the dangerous
theme. My brother grew to manhood, and soon after he was
twenty-one years old he went with Father to vote. Standing by
the window, a girl of sixteen years, a girl of simple, homely fan-

cies, not at all strong-minded, and altogether ignorant of the world, I looked out as they drove away, my father and brother, and as I looked I felt a strange ache in my heart, and tears sprang to my eyes. Turning to my sister Mary, who stood beside me, I saw that the dear little innocent seemed wonderfully sober, too. I said, "Don't you wish that we could go with them when we are old enough? Don't we love our country just as well as they do?" and her little frightened voice piped out: "Yes, of course we ought. Don't I know that; but you mustn't tell a soul—not mother, even; we should be called strong-minded."

In all the years since then, I have kept those things, and many others like them, and pondered them in my heart; but two years of struggle in this temperance reform have shown me, as they have ten thousand other women, so clearly and so impressively my duty, that I have passed the Rubicon of Silence, and am ready for any battle that shall be involved in this honest declaration of the faith that is within me. "Fight behind masked batteries a little longer," whisper good friends and true. So I have been fighting hitherto; but it is a style of warfare altogether foreign to my temperament and mode of life. Reared on the prairies, I seemed pre-determined to join the cavalry force in this great spiritual war, and I must tilt a free lance henceforth on the splendid battlefield of this reform; where the earth shall soon be shaken by the onset of contending hosts; where legions of valiant soldiers are deploying; where to the grand encounter marches today a great army, gentle of men and mild of utterance, but with hearts for any fate; where there are trumpets and bugles calling strong souls onward to a victory which Heaven might envy, and

Where, behind the dim Unknown,
Standeth God within the shadow,
Keeping watch above His own.

I thought that women ought to have the ballot as I paid the hard-earned taxes upon my mother's cottage house—but I never said as much—somehow the motive did not command my heart. For my own sake, I had not courage; but I have for thy sake, dear native land, for thy necessity is as much greater than mine as thy transcendent hope is greater than the personal interest of thy humble child. For love of you, heart-broken wives, whose tremulous lips have blessed me; for love of you, sweet mother, who in the cradle's shadow kneel this night, beside your infant sons; and you, sorrowful little children, who listen at this hour, with faces strangely old, for him whose footsteps frighten you; for love of you have I thus spoken.

All, it is women who have given the costliest hostages to fortune. Out into the battle of life they have sent their best beloved, with fearful odds against them, with snares that men have legalized and set for them on every hand. Beyond the arms that held them long, their boys have gone forever. Oh! by the danger they have dared; by the hours of patient watching over beds where helpless children lay; by the incense of ten thousand prayers wafted from their gentle lips to Heaven, I charge you give them power to protect, along life's treacherous highway, those whom they have so long loved. Let it no longer be that they must sit back among the shadows, hopelessly mourning over their strong staff broken, and their beautiful rod; but when the sons they love shall go forth to life's battle, still let their mothers walk beside them, sweet and serious, and clad in the garments of power.

Belva Lockwood
Calls Forth History

"Gentlemen, the flood tide is with you!"

Belva Ann Lockwood (1830–1917) fought her first battle for equal opportunity with her father, who believed too much education turned girls into "old maids"; it was the first of many obstacles this later twice-married, twice-widowed lawyer would overcome.

In 1879, Lockwood became the first woman admitted to the bar of the U.S. Supreme Court and, in 1906, won a five-million-dollar settlement against the United States on behalf of the Eastern and Emigrant Cherokee Indians—at the time, the largest settlement ever granted. She was also the first woman to appear on a national ballot for president of the United States—running as a candidate in 1884 and 1888, as a member of the Equal Rights Party. A little ditty from the *Lockport Union* pledged support:

> My soul is tired of politics;
> Its vicious ways, its knavish tricks;
> I will not vote for any man
> But whoop it up for Belva Ann!

An eloquent advocate on behalf of labor, temperance, the peace movement, and women's rights, this "Portia of the

Republic," as some called her, became a fixture in the halls of Congress, lobbying members to her assorted causes. In this undated speech, an excerpt of remarks delivered before a congressional committee, Lockwood is expressive and, ever the lawyer, citing historical precedent, she makes the case for equal rights for women.

———•———

Gentlemen of the Committee: We come before you today, not with any studied eloquence, far-fetched erudition, or new theories for the metamorphosis of our government, or the overthrow of our social economy and relations, but we come, asking for our whole commonwealth, for the fathers who begat us, and the brothers at our side; for the mothers who bore us, and the sisters who go hand in hand with us; for the orphan and the widow unprotected; for the wretched inebriate and the outcast Magdalene; for the beggars who throng our streets, and the inmates of our jails and asylums: for these we ask you that we too may have a hand and a voice, a share in this matter which so nearly concerns not only our temporal but even our eternal salvation. We ask you that we may have an interest that shall awaken from its apathy fully one-half of the moral and intellectual resources of the country, fully one-half of its productive interest—an interest which contains in the germ the physical power and vital force of the whole nation. Weakness cannot beget power, ignorance cannot beget wisdom, disease cannot produce health. Look at our women of today, with their enfeebled bodies, dwarfed intellects, laxness of moral force; without enough of healthy stimulus to incite them to action; and compare them with our grandmothers of the Revolution and the Martha Washington school. Here you find a woman who dared to control her own affairs; who superintended a farm of six hundred acres; giving personal instructions to the workmen, writing her own bills and receipts, and setting an example of industry and frugality to the neighboring women who called to see her.

I need not, gentlemen, enumerate to you to prove what I wish to prove today, the countless numbers of women who have participated creditably in government from the days of our Savior until the present time. You know that Victoria rules in England; and the adoration of the English heart today for its queen found expression but a few weeks since in one of our popular lecture halls, when the audience, composed partly of Englishmen, were asked to sing "God Save the Queen." The wisdom of the reign of Elizabeth, "good Queen Bess," as she has been called, gave to England her prestige—the proud preeminence which she holds today among the nations of the earth. Isabella I of Spain, the patron saint of America, without whose generosity our country today might have been a wilderness, was never nobler than when, after Ferdinand's refusal, after the refusal of the crowned authority of England, the disapproval of the wise men of her own kingdom, she rose in her queenly majesty, and said, "I undertake it for my own crown of Castile, and will pledge my jewels to raise the necessary funds." Maria Theresa, of Austria, who assumed the reins of government with her kingdom divided and disturbed, found herself equal to the emergency, brought order out of chaos, and prosperity to her kingdom. Christine, of Sweden, brought that kingdom to the zenith of its power. Eugenie, Empress of the French, in the late disastrous revolution, assumed the regency of the Empire in defiance of her ministry, and when forced to flee, covered her flight with a shrewdness that would have done credit to Napoleon himself. Florence Nightingale brought order and efficiency into the hospitals of the Crimea; and Clara Barton, with her clear head and generous heart, has lifted up the starving women of Strasburg, and made it possible for them to be self-sustaining. I need not cite to you Catharine of Russia, Cleopatra, or the Queen of Sheba, who came to admire the wisdom of Solomon; or the Roman matrons, Zenobia, Lucretia, Tullia; or revert to the earliest forms of government when the family and the church were lawgivers; remind you of Lydia, the seller of purple and fine linen, who ruled her own household, called to the church; of Aquilla and Priscilla, whom Paul took with him and left to control the church at Ephesus, after they had been banished from Rome by the decree of Claudius; or of Phoebe, the deaconess. It is a well-known fact that women have been sent as ministers and ambassadors, the latter a power fuller than our country grants, to treat on important State matters between the crowned heads of Europe. In many cases they have represented the person of the monarch or emperor himself. France, since the beginning of the reign of Louis XIV, through the period of the ascendancy of Napoleon I down to the reign of Napoleon III, has employed women in diplomacy. Instances may be recorded in a work entitled "Napoleon and His Court," by Madame Junot, and also in our own consular works. The late Empress of France has been said to be especially gifted in this respect. It has been the custom of Russia for the past century, and still continues to be, to send women on diplomatic errands. In this empire, also, where the voting is done by households, a woman is often sent to represent the family.

Women are now writing a large proportion of the books and newspapers of the country, are editing newspapers and commanding ships. They are admitted to law schools, medical schools, and the higher order of colleges, and are knocking at Amherst and Yale. Yea, more, they are admitted to the practice of law, as in Iowa, Missouri, Kansas, Wyoming and Utah; admitted to the practice of medicine everywhere, and more recently to consultation. One hundred women preachers are already ordained and are preaching throughout the land. Women are elected as engrossing and enrolling clerks in legislatures, as in Wisconsin, Missouri and Indiana; appointed as justices of the peace, as in Maine, Wyoming and Connecticut: as bankers and brokers, as in New York and St. Louis. They are filling as school-teachers three-fourths of the schools of the land.

This is more than true of our own city. Shall we not then have women school trustees and superintendents? Already they are appointed in the East and in the West, and women are permitted to vote at the school elections. Who has a deeper interest in the schools than the mothers?

Look at the hundreds of women clerks in the government departments. They are all eligible, since the passage of the Arnell bill, to the highest clerkships. Look at the postmistresses throughout the land. Each one a bonded officer of the government, appointed by the president and confirmed by the Senate, the highest executive power in the land. "The power of the president to appoint, and of the Senate to confirm, has never been questioned by our highest Courts. Being bonded officers, they must necessarily qualify before a judicial officer."

And now, gentlemen of the Committee on Laws and Judiciary, whatever may be your report on these bills for justice and equality to women, committed to your trust, I hope you will bear in mind that you have mothers, wives, sisters, daughters, who will be affected by your decision. They may be amply provided for today, and be beggared tomorrow. Remember that "life is short and time is fleeting," but principles never die. You hold in your hands a power and an opportunity today to render yourselves immortal—an opportunity that comes but once in a lifetime. Shakespeare says: "There is a tide in the affairs of men which, taken at the flood, leads on to fortune." Gentlemen, the flood tide is with you! Shall this appeal be in vain? I hold in my hands the names of hundreds of men and women of our city

pledged to this work, and they will not relax their efforts until it
is accomplished.

> Truth crushed to earth will rise again;
>> The eternal years of God are hers;
> But Error, wounded, writhes in pain
>> And dies, amid her worshipers.

Emmeline Pankhurst
Exhorts British Women to Be Militant

"I incite this meeting to rebellion."

"Those of you who can break windows—break them," urges British suffragist Emmeline Pankhurst in this speech. It was a bold thing to say after just getting out of prison for "window smashing." Six months earlier, Pankhurst, leader of the Women's Social and Political Union, had led several hundred hammer-wielding women down the elegant streets of Bond and Regent—with a special stop at No. 10 Downing. "I hope our demonstration will be enough," she said. "If not, I will go further."

For more than a decade, beginning in 1903, Pankhurst, along with her daughters Christabel and Sylvia, advocated destruction of property as a way of securing suffrage—"militancy or the vote," she had told England's Lord Asquith. Her first of many arrests came in 1908, when members of the Union tried to rush the House of Commons. Her second followed a year later—at the same time prisons introduced force-feeding to confront rampant hunger strikes.

On October 12, 1912, at London's Royal Albert Hall, in her first public address after leaving prison for the "smashing" incident, Pankhurst delivered a triumphant but rather extended address laying blame for militancy at the hands of an unresponsive government. We join her in this extract as she forcefully signals a newer and stronger policy of aggression—a promise that she will "go further."

There is a great deal of criticism, ladies and gentlemen, of this movement. It always seems to me when the antisuffrage members of the government criticize militancy in women that it is very like beasts of prey reproaching the gentler animals who turn in desperate resistance when at the point of death. Criticism from gentlemen who do not hesitate to order out armies to kill and slay their opponents, who do not hesitate to encourage party mobs to attack defenseless women in public meetings—criticism from them hardly rings true.

Then I get letters from people who tell me that they are ardent suffragists but who say that they do not like the recent developments in the militant movement and implore me to urge the members not to be reckless with human life. Ladies and gentlemen, the only recklessness the militant suffragists have shown about human life has been about their own lives and not about the lives of others, and I say here and now that it has never been and never will be the policy of the Women's Social and Political Union recklessly to endanger human life. We leave that to the enemy. We leave that to the men in their warfare. It is not the method of women. No, even from the point of view of public policy, militancy affecting the security of human life would be out of place.

There is something that governments care far more for than human life, and that is the security of property, and so it is through property that we shall strike the enemy. From henceforward the women who agree with me will say, "We disregard your laws, gentlemen, we set the liberty and the dignity and the welfare of women above all such considerations, and we shall continue this war, as we have done in the past; and what sacrifice of property, or what injury to property accrues will not be our fault. It will be the fault of that government who admits the justice of our demands but refuses to concede them without evidence, so they have told us, afforded to governments of the past, that those who asked for liberty were in earnest in their demands! . . .

Be militant each in your own way. Those of you who can express your militancy by going to the House of Commons and refusing to leave without satisfaction, as we did in the early days—do so. Those of you who can express militancy by facing party mobs at Cabinet Ministers' meetings, when you remind them of their falseness to principle—do so. Those of you who can express your militancy by joining us in our antigovernment by-election policy—do so. Those of you who can break windows—break them. Those of you who can still further attack the secret idol of property, so as to make the government realize that property is as greatly endangered by women's suffrage as it was by the Chartists of old—do so. And my last word is to the government: I incite this meeting to rebellion.

Jeannette Rankin
Urges a "Small Measure of Democracy" for Women

"How shall we answer their challenge, gentlemen?"

"As a woman, I can't go to war and I refuse to send anyone else," said this lifelong pacifist. A Republican from Montana, Jeannette Rankin (1880–1973) was the first woman elected to the United States Congress and one of fifty-six members who voted in 1917 against "Mr. Wilson's War" on Germany. Though the vote cost her reelection, she returned to Congress in 1940, but was forced to retire a year later after casting the only vote against war following the Japanese attack on Pearl Harbor. Her final antiwar gesture came in Washington, D.C., in 1968, when she led 5,000 women—the "Jeannette Rankin Brigade"—in a protest march against American involvement in Vietnam.

Less than a year into Rankin's first congressional term, Wilson endorsed women's suffrage and the House again took up the issue of a U.S. Woman Suffrage amendment. Members invited the "lady from Montana" to open the debate, which she did with this speech, delivered on January 10, 1918. Rankin used little range of motion while she spoke; she remembered being told that, while men should use the whole arm when making a point, women should "just use the forearm." So, reservedly but forcefully, she argues here for "votes for women," couching her words within the dramatic context of the First World War.

The amendment passed the House, but the Senate rejected the resolution for a third time.

———•—•———

M r. Speaker, we are facing today a question of political evolution. International circumstances have forced this question to an issue. Our country is in a state of war; the nation has had a terrible shock. The result has been a sudden change in our national consciousness. The things we have been taking for granted for years are suddenly assuming a new significance for us. . . .

We have men—men for the army, for the navy, for the air; men for the industries, the mines, the fields; men for the government. And the national leaders are now reaching out and drawing men of talent, picking those with the best minds, with expert knowledge, and with broad perspective to aid in war work.

But something is still lacking in the completeness of our national effort. With all our abundance of coal, with our great stretches of idle, fertile land, babies are dying from cold and hunger; soldiers have died for lack of a woolen shirt.

Might it not be that men who have spent their lives thinking in terms of commercial profit find it hard to adjust themselves to thinking in terms of human needs?

Might it not be that a great force which has always been thinking in terms of human needs, and that always will think in terms of human needs, has not been mobilized?

Is it not possible that the women of the country have something of value to give the country at this time?

It would be strange indeed if the women of this country, through all these years, had not developed an intelligence, a feeling, a spiritual force to themselves which they hold in readiness to give the world. It would be strange indeed if the influence of women through direct participation in the political struggles, through which all social and industrial development proceeds, would not lend a certain virility, a certain influx of new strength and understanding and sympathy and ability to the exhausting effort we are now making to meet the problem before us.

For seventy years, the women leaders of this country have been asking the government to recognize this possibility. Every great woman who stands out in our history—Susan B. Anthony, Elizabeth Cady Stanton, Clara Barton, Mary Livermore, Harriet Beecher Stowe, Frances Willard, Lucy Stone, Jane Addams, Ella Flagg Young, Alice Stone Blackwell, Anna Howard Shaw, Mrs. Catt—all have asked the government to permit women to serve more effectively the national welfare.

All have felt that the energy, the thought, and the suffering that was spent in trying to obtain permission to serve directly should as quickly as possible be turned to the actual service. And in the meantime they did all they could indirectly. They learned to read and to know each other. They became interested in each other's problems, for they found them to be their own problems. As they were the stabilizing influence in the home and kept the family unity, so they have become a great possible stabilizing influence in society, asking now to help keep the unity of the nation to its highest standard of service.

They have stood back of the men. They have pioneered with them, rejoiced with them over their successes, and, when they failed, encouraged them and helped them to begin again. The women have done all that they were allowed to do, all that the men planned for them to do. But through all their work they have pleaded for the political machinery which would enable them to do more

Today as never before, the nation needs its women—needs the work of their hands and their hearts and their minds. Their energy must be utilized in the most effective service they can

give. Are we now going to refuse these women the opportunity
to serve, in the face of their plea—in the face of the nation's
great need? Are you, gentlemen, representing the South, you
who have struggled with your Negro problem for half a century, going to retaliate after fifty years for the injustice you
believe that was done you so long ago? Have you not learned, in
your struggle for adjustment in the South, to be broad and fair
and open-minded in dealing with another franchise problem
that concerns the whole nation? . . .

We declared war, not state by state, but by federal action. We
mobilized and equipped our army, not state by state, but through
Congress. Shall our women, our home defense, be our only
fighters in the struggle for democracy who shall be denied federal action?

It is time for our old political doctrines to give way to the
new visions, the new aspects of national and international relations which have come to us already since the war began. For
we have had new visions; we have been aroused to a new way of
looking at things. Our president, with his wisdom and astute-
ness, has helped us to penetrate new problems, to analyze situations, to make fine distinctions. He startled us by urging us to
distinguish between the German government and the German
people. We who have been steeped in democratic ideals since
the days when our forefathers signed the Declaration of Independence find it difficult to think of government as something
separate from the people.

Yet as we learn to make this distinction for Germany, will
not our minds revert to our own situation and be puzzled? How
can people in other countries who are trying to grasp our plan
of democracy avoid stumbling over our logic when we deny the
first steps in democracy to our women? May they not see a distinction between the government of the United States and the
women of the United States?

Deep down in the hearts of the American people is a living faith in democracy. Sometimes it is not expressed in the most effective way. Sometimes it seems almost forgotten. But when the test comes, we find it still there, groping and aspiring and helping men and women to understand each other and their common need. It is our national religion and it prompts in us the desire for that measure of justice which is based on equal opportunity, equal protection, equal freedom for all. In our hearts we know that desire can be realized only when "those who submit to authority have a voice in their own government"—whether that government be political, industrial or social.

Today there are men and women in every field of endeavor who are bending all their energies toward a realization of this dream of universal justice. They believe that we are waging a war for democracy. The farmer who knows the elements of democracy becomes an idealist when he contemplates the possibility of feeding the world during this crisis. The woman who knits all day to keep from thinking of the sacrifice she is making wonders what this democracy is which she is denied and for which she is asked to give. The miner is dreaming his dreams of industrial democracy as he goes about 2,000 feet underground, bringing forth from the rock precious metals to help in the prosecution of the war.

The girl who works in the Treasury no long works until she is married. She knows not that she will work on and on and on. The war has taken from her opportunities for the joys that young girls look forward to. Cheerfully and willingly, she makes her sacrifice. And she will pay to the very end in order that the future need not find women paying again for the same cause.

The boys at the front know something of the democracy for which they are fighting. These courageous lads who are paying with their lives testified to the sincerity of their fight when they sent home their ballots in the New York election, and voted two to one in favor of woman suffrage and democracy at home. (*Applause.*)

These are the people of the nation. These are the fiber and sinew of war—the mother, the farmer, the miner, the industrial worker, the soldier. These are the people who are giving their all for the cause of democracy. These are the people who are resting their faith in the Congress of the United States because they believe that Congress knows what democracy means. These people will not fight in vain.

Can we afford to allow these men and women to doubt for a single instant the sincerity of our protestations of democracy? How shall we answer their challenge, gentlemen? How shall we explain to them the meaning of democracy if the same Congress that voted for war to make the world safe for democracy refuses to give this small measure of democracy to the women of our country?

Hillary Rodham Clinton
Honors the First Women's Rights Convention

"What matters is whether sentiment and resolutions, once made, are fulfilled or forgotten."

Asked in 1992 who would be his "Robert F. Kennedy," his most trusted political adviser and confidant, president-elect Bill Clinton pointed, rhetorically, to his wife. Theirs would be "an unprecedented partnership," he said. Lawyer, social activist, author, and first lady of the United States, Hillary Rodham Clinton (b.1947), as a child, wanted to be an astronaut; no girls allowed, she was told by the space program. Instead, the graduate of Wellesley College and Yale Law School became an attorney, working for children's rights, and later devising impeachment strategies against Richard Nixon, as a staff member of the House Judiciary Committee.

After serving twelve years as first lady of Arkansas, the self-assured, socially conscious, politically outspoken Mrs. Clinton was both excoriated and extolled when she assumed her White House role in 1993. She was the woman vying for co-president, said opponents; she was the woman who could bring social change, said admirers.

Early White House scandals wrought during her husband's presidential tenure—and questions concerning her own participation—did not help her image. Yet, in the closing years of her husband's troubled administration, his legacy marred by impeachment, Hillary Clinton emerged as her supporters wanted her to—as her own woman: a passionate "policywonk" and goodwill ambassador, giving voice to the causes of human rights, child welfare, and the economic empowerment of women. She also became the first American first lady to seek political office—running for the U.S. Senate from New York in 2000.

On July 16, 1998, at the 150th anniversary of the first women's rights convention in Seneca Falls, New York, the first lady spoke to a convocation of thousands, honoring Elizabeth Cady Stanton, Susan B. Anthony, and other early pioneers of the cause. Her oratorical style here is straightforward; her speech, laudatory but admonishing. Women are not exercising their right to vote, she tells her audience. While the women of the first convention "were silenced by someone else," she says. "Today, women, we silence ourselves." But first, she sets the scene.

———————

F or a moment, I would like you to take your minds back 150 years. Imagine if you will that you are Charlotte Wood-ward, a nineteen-year-old glove maker working and living in Waterloo. Every day you sit for hours sewing gloves together, working for small wages you cannot even keep, with no hope of going on in school or owning property, knowing that if you marry, your children and even the clothes on your body will belong to your husband.

But then one day in July 1848, you hear about a women's rights convention to be held in nearby Seneca Falls. It's a convention to discuss the "social, civil, and religious conditions and rights of women." You run from house to house and you find other women who have heard the same news. Some are excited, others are amused or even shocked, and a few agree to come with you, for at least the first day.

When that day comes—July 19, 1848—you leave early in the morning in your horse-drawn wagon. You fear that no one else will come, and at first, the road is empty, except for you and your neighbors. But suddenly, as you reach a crossroads, you see a few more wagons and carriages, then more and more, all going towards Wesleyan Chapel. Eventually you join the others to form one long procession on the road to equality.

Who were the others traveling that road to equality, traveling to that convention? Frederick Douglass, the former slave and great abolitionist, was on his way there and he described the participants as "few in numbers, moderate in resources, and very little-known in the world. The most we had to connect us was a firm commitment that we were in the right and a firm faith that the right must ultimately prevail." In the wagons and carriages, on foot or horseback, were women like Rhoda Palmer. Seventy years later in 1918, at the age of 102, she would cast her first ballot in a New York state election.

Also traveling down that road to equality was Susan Quinn, who at fifteen will become the youngest signer of the Declaration of Sentiments. Catherine Fish-Steben, a veteran of activism starting when she was only twelve going door to door collecting anti-slavery petitions. She also, by the way, kept an antitobacco pledge on the parlor table and asked all her young male friends to sign up. She was a woman truly ahead of her time, as all the participants were.

I often wonder, when reflecting back on the Seneca Falls Convention, who of us—men and women—would have left our homes, our families, our work, to make that journey 150 years ago. Think about the incredible courage it must have taken to join that procession. Ordinary men and women, mothers and fathers, sisters and brothers, husbands and wives, friends and neighbors. And just like those who have embarked on other journeys throughout American history, seeking freedom or escaping religious or political persecution, speaking out against slavery, working for labor rights, these men and women were motivated by dreams of better lives and more just societies.

At the end of the two-day convention, one hundred people—sixty-eight women and thirty-two men—signed the Declaration of Sentiments that you can now read on the wall at Wesleyan Chapel. Among the signers were some of the names we remember today: Elizabeth Cady Stanton and Lucretia Mott, Martha Wright and Frederick Douglass and young Charlotte Woodward. The "Seneca Falls One Hundred," as I like to call them, shared the radical idea that America fell far short of her ideals stated in our founding documents, denying citizenship to women and slaves.

Elizabeth Cady Stanton, who is frequently credited with originating the idea for the convention, knew that women were not only denied legal citizenship, but that society's cultural values and social structures conspired to assign women only one occupation and role, that of wife and mother. Of course, the reality was always far different. Women have always worked, and worked both in the home and outside the home for as long as history can record. And even though Stanton herself had a comfortable life and valued deeply her husband and seven children, she knew that she and all other women were not truly free if they could not keep wages they earned, divorce an abusive husband, own property, or vote for the political leaders who governed them. Stanton was inspired along with the others who met to rewrite our Declaration of Independence, and they boldly asserted, "We hold these truths to be self-evident that all men and women are created equal."

"All men and all women." It was the shout heard around the world, and if we listen, we can still hear its echoes today. We can hear it in the voices of women demanding their full civil and political rights anywhere in the world. I've heard such voices and their echoes from women around the world, from Belfast to Bosnia to Beijing, as they work to change the conditions for women and girls and improve their lives and the lives of their families. We can even hear those echoes today in Seneca Falls. We come together this time not by carriage, but by car or plane, by train or foot, and yes, in my case, by bus. We come together not to hold a convention, but to celebrate those who met here 150 years ago, to commemorate how far we have traveled since then, and to challenge ourselves to persevere on the journey that was begun all those many years ago.

We are, as one can see looking around this great crowd, men and women, old and young, different races, different backgrounds. We come to honor the past and imagine the future. That is the theme the president and I have chosen for the White House Millennium Council's efforts to remind and inspire Americans as we approach the year 2000. This is my last stop on the Millennium Council's tour to "Save America's Treasures"— those buildings, monuments, papers, and sites—that define who we are as a nation. They include not only famous symbols like the Star-Spangled Banner, and not only great political leaders like George Washington's revolutionary headquarters, or creative inventors like Thomas Edison's invention factory, but they include also, the women of America who wrote our nation's past and must write its future.

Women like the ones we honor here, and in fact, at the end of my tour yesterday, I learned that I was following literally in the footsteps of one of them, Lucretia Mott, who, on her way to Seneca Falls, stopped in Auburn to visit former slaves and went on to the Seneca Indian Nations to meet with clan mothers, as I did.

Last evening, I visited the home of Marianne and Thomas

M'Clintock in Waterloo, where the Declaration of Sentiments was drafted, and which the Park Service is planning to restore for visitors if the money needed can be raised. I certainly hope I can return here sometime in the next few years to visit that restoration.

Because we must tell and retell, learn and relearn these women's stories, and we must make it our personal mission, in our everyday lives, to pass these stories on to our daughters and sons. Because we cannot—we must not—ever forget that the rights and opportunities that we enjoy as women today were not just bestowed upon us by some benevolent ruler. They were fought for, agonized over, marched for, jailed for and even died for by brave and persistent women and men who came before us.

Every time we buy or sell or inherit property in our own name—let us thank the pioneers who agitated to change the laws that made that possible.

Every time we vote, let us thank the women and men of Seneca Falls, Susan B. Anthony and all the others, who tirelessly crossed our nation and withstood ridicule and the rest to bring about the Nineteenth Amendment to the Constitution.

Every time we enter an occupation—a profession of our own choosing and receive a paycheck that reflects earnings equal to a male colleague, let us thank the signers and women like Kate Mullaney, whose house I visited yesterday, in Troy, New York.

Every time we elect a woman to office—let us thank groundbreaking leaders like Jeannette Rankin and Margaret Chase Smith, Patti Caraway, Louise Slaughter, Bella Abzug, Shirley Chisholm—all of whom proved that a woman's place is truly in the House, and in the Senate, and one day, in the White House, as well.

And every time we take another step forward for justice in

this nation—let us thank extraordinary women like Harriet Tubman, whose home in Auburn I visited yesterday, and who herself escaped from slavery, and then risked her life, time and again, to bring at least two hundred other slaves to freedom as well.

Harriet Tubman's rule for all of her underground railroad missions was to keep going. Once you started—no matter how scared you got, how dangerous it became—you were not allowed to turn back. That's a pretty good rule for life. It not only describes the women who gathered in Wesleyan Chapel in 1848, but it could serve as our own motto for today. We, too, cannot turn back. We, too, must keep going in our commitment to the dignity of every individual—to women's rights as human rights. We are on that road of the pioneers to Seneca Falls: they started down it 150 years ago. But now, we too, must keep going.

We may not face the criticism and derision they did. They understood that the Declaration of Sentiments would create no small amount of misconception, or misrepresentation and ridicule; they were called mannish women, old maids, fanatics, attacked personally by those who disagreed with them. One paper said, "These rights for women would bring a monstrous injury to all mankind." If it sounds familiar, it's the same thing that's always said when women keep going for true equality and justice.

Those who came here also understood that the convention and the Declaration were only first steps down that road. What matters most is what happens when everyone packs up and goes back to their families and communities. What matters is whether sentiment and resolutions, once made, are fulfilled or forgotten. The Seneca Falls One Hundred pledged themselves to petition, and lit the pulpit and used every instrumentality within their power to affect their subjects. And they did. But they also knew they were not acting primarily for themselves. They knew they probably would not even see the changes they advocated in their own lifetime. In fact, only Charlotte Woodward lived long enough to see American women finally win the right to vote.*

Those who signed that Declaration were doing it for the girls and women—for us—those of us in the twentieth century.

Elizabeth Cady Stanton wrote a letter to her daughters later in life enclosing a special gift and explaining why. "Dear Maggie and Patti, this is my first speech," she wrote. "It contains all I knew at that time; I give this manuscript to my precious daughters in the hopes that they will finish the work that I have begun." And they have. Her daughter, Harriet Blatch, was the chief strategist of the suffrage movement in New York. Harriet's daughter, Nora Barney, was one of the first women to be a civil engineer. Nora's daughter, Rhoda Jenkins, became an architect. Rhoda's daughter, Coline Jenkins-Sahlin is an elected official in Greenwich, Connecticut. And her daughter, Elizabeth is a thirteen-year-old, who wrote about the six generations of Stantons in a book called, *33 Things Every Girl Should Know.*

So, far into the twentieth century, the work is still being done; the journey goes on. Now, some might say that the only purpose of this celebration is to honor the past, that the work begun here is finished in America, that young women no longer face legal obstacles to whatever education or employment choices they choose to pursue. And I certainly believe and hope all of you agree that we should, every day, count our blessings as American women.

I know how much change I have seen in my own life. When I was growing up back in the fifties and sixties, there were still barriers that Mrs. Stanton would have recognized—

---

*National woman suffrage was proclaimed in 1920.

scholarships I couldn't apply for, schools I couldn't go to, jobs I couldn't have—just because of my sex. Thanks to federal laws like the Civil Rights Act of 1964 and Title IX, and the Equal Pay Act, legal barriers to equality have fallen.

But if all we do is honor the past, then I believe we will miss the central point of the Declaration of Sentiments, which was, above all, a document about the future. The drafters of the Declaration imagined a different future for women and men, in a society based on equality and mutual respect. It falls to every generation to imagine the future, and it our task to do so now.

We know, just as the women 150 years ago knew, that what we imagine will be principally for our daughters and sons in the twenty-first century. Because the work of the Seneca Falls Convention is, just like the work of the nation itself, never finished, so long as there remain gaps between our ideals and reality. That is one of the great joys and beauties of the American experiment. We are always striving to build and move toward a more perfect union, that we on every occasion keep faith with our founding ideals, and translate them into reality. So what kind of future can we imagine together?

If we are to finish the work begun here—then no American should ever again face discrimination on the basis of gender, race, or sexual orientation anywhere in our country.

If we are to finish the work begun here—then seventy-six cents in a woman's paycheck for every dollar in a man's is still not enough. Equal pay for equal work can once and for all be achieved.

If we are to finish the work begun here—then families need more help to balance their responsibilities at work and at home. In a letter to Susan B. Anthony, Elizabeth Cady Stanton writes, "Come here and I will do what I can to help you with your address, if you will hold the baby and make the pudding." Even then, women knew we had to have help with child care. All families should have access to safe, affordable, quality child care.

If we are to finish the work begun here—then women and children must be protected against what the Declaration called the "chastisement of women," namely domestic abuse and violence. We must take all steps necessary to end the scourge of violence against women and punish the perpetrators. And our country must join the rest of the world, as so eloquently Secretary Albright called for on Saturday night here in Seneca Falls, "Join the rest of the world and ratify the convention on the elimination of discrimination against women."

If we are to finish the work begun here—we must do more than talk about family values, we must adopt policies that truly value families—policies like a universal system of health care insurance that guarantees every American's access to affordable, quality health care. Policies like taking all steps necessary to keep guns out of the hands of children and criminals. Policies like doing all that is necessary at all levels of our society to ensure high-quality public education for every boy or girl, no matter where that child lives.

If we are to finish the work begun here—we must ensure that women and men who work full-time earn a wage that lifts them out of poverty and all workers who retire have financial security in their later years through guaranteed Social Security and pensions.

If we are to finish the work begun here—we must be vigilant against the messages of a media-driven consumer culture that convinces our sons and daughters that what brand of sneakers they wear or cosmetics they use is more important than what they think, feel, know, or do.

And if we are to finish the work begun here—we must, above all else, take seriously the power of the vote and use it to make our voices heard. What the champions of suffrage understood was that the vote is not just a symbol of our equality, but that it can be, if used, a guarantee of results. It is the way we express our political views. It is the way we hold our leaders and governments accountable. It is the way we bridge the gap between what we want our nation to be and what it is.

But when will the majority of women voters of our country exercise their most fundamental political right? Can you imagine what any of the Declaration signers would say if they learned how many women fail to vote in elections? They would be amazed and outraged. They would agree with a poster I saw in 1996. On it, there is a picture of a woman with a piece of tape covering her mouth and under it, it says, "Most politicians think women should be seen and not heard. In the last election, fifty-four million women agreed with them."

One hundred fifty years ago, the women at Seneca Falls were silenced by someone else. Today, women, we silence ourselves. We have a choice. We have a voice. And if we are going to finish the work begun here we must exercise our right to vote in every election we are eligible to vote in.

Much of who women are and what women do today can be traced to the courage, vision, and dedication of the pioneers who came together at Seneca Falls. Now it is our responsibility to finish the work they began. Let's ask ourselves, at the 200th anniversary of Seneca Falls, will they say that today's gathering also was a catalyst for action? Will they say that businesses, labor, religious organizations, the media, foundations, educators, every citizen in our society came to see the unfinished struggle of today as their struggle?

Will they say that we joined across lines of race and class, that we raised up those too often pushed down, and ultimately found strength in each other's differences and resolved in our common cause? Will we, like the champions at Seneca Falls, recognize that men must play a central role in this fight? How can we ever forget the impassioned plea of Frederick Douglass, issued in our defense of the right to vote?

How can we ever forget that young legislator from Tennessee by the name of Harry Burns, who was the deciding vote in ratifying the Nineteenth Amendment. He was planning on voting no, but then he got a letter from his mother with a simple message. The letter said, "Be a good boy, Harry, and do the right thing." And he did! Tennessee became the last state to ratify, proving that you can never, ever overestimate the power of one person to alter the course of history, or the power of a little motherly advice.

Will we look back and see that we have finally joined the rest of the advanced economies by creating systems of education, employment, child care, and health care that support and strengthen families and give all women real choices in their lives?

At the 200th anniversary celebration, will they say that women today supported each other in the choices we make? Will we admit once and for all there is no single cookie-cutter model for being a successful and fulfilled woman today, that we have so many choices? We can choose full-time motherhood or no family at all, or like most of us, seek to strike a balance between our family and our work, always trying to do what is right in our lives. Will we leave our children a world where it is self-evident that all men and women, boys and girls are created equal? These are some of the questions we can ask ourselves.

Help us imagine a future that keeps faith with the sentiments expressed here in 1848. The future, like the past and the present, will not and cannot be perfect. Our daughters and granddaughters will face new challenges which we today cannot even imagine. But each of us can help prepare for that future by doing what we can to speak out for justice and equality for women's rights and human rights, to be on the right side of history, no matter the risk or cost, knowing that eventually the sentiments we express and the causes we advocate will succeed because they are rooted in the conviction that all people are entitled by their creator and by the promise of America to the freedom, rights, responsibilities, and opportunity of full citizenship. That is what I imagine for the future. I invite you to imagine with me and then to work together to make that future a reality.

PART 6

SPEECHES
TO THE
COURT

Hortensia
Speaks Before the Roman Tribunal

". . . we will not be in any way concerned in a civil war."

When the triumvirs of Rome failed to raise "needed" funds from the men they had proscribed, they decided to tax the property of the 1,400 wealthiest women—among them, Hortensia (b. 85 B.C.), daughter of the renowned orator, Quintus Hortensius.

The women appealed for help—unfortunately, to a rude and dismissive Fulvia, Marc Antony's wife, who turned them out of her house. Desperate, they stormed their way before a public tribunal and persuaded Hortensia to speak on their behalf, which she did—defiantly but quickly. The triumvirs were furious and had the women driven away, but, fearing insurrection from a sympathetic and vocal crowd, they reduced the number of women subject to tax to four hundred.

Hortensia's speech, delivered in 42 B.C., earned the esteemed praise of Quintillian, a first-century literary critic, and is preserved (and likely embellished) by the second-century Greek historian, Appian.

———•◦•———

T he unhappy women you see here, imploring your justice and bounty, would never have presumed to appear in this place, had they not first made use of all other means their natural modesty could suggest. Though our appearing here may seem contrary to the rules proscribed to our sex, which we have hitherto strictly observed, the loss of our fathers, children, brothers, and husbands may sufficiently excuse us, especially when their unhappy deaths are made a pretense for our further misfortunes.

You plead that they had offended and provoked you; but what injury have we women done, that we must be impoverished? If we are blameable as the men, why not proscribe us also? Have we declared you enemies to your country? Have we suborned your soldiers, raised troops against you, or oppressed you in pursuit of those honors and offices which you claim?

We pretend not to govern the republic, nor is it our ambition which has drawn our present misfortune on our heads; empires, dignities and honors, are not for us. Why should we then contribute to a war in which we have no interest?

It is true, indeed, that in the Carthaginian war our mothers assisted the republic, which was at the time reduced to the utmost distress; but neither their houses, their lands, nor their moveables were sold for this service; some rings, and a few jewels, furnished the supply. Nor was it constraint or violence that forced from them what they contributed, rather theirs was the voluntary offering of generosity.

What danger at present threatens Rome? If the Gauls or Parthians were encamped on the banks of the Tiber or the Arno, you should find us not less zealous in the defense of our country than our mothers were before us; but it becomes not us, and we are resolved that we will not be in any way concerned in a civil war.

Neither Marius, nor Caesar, nor Pompey, ever thought of obliging us to take part in the domestic troubles which their ambition had raised; nay, nor did ever Sylla himself, who first set up tyranny in Rome. And yet you assume the glorious title of reformers of the state, a title which will turn to your eternal infamy, if, without the least regard to the laws of equity, you persist in your wicked resolution of plundering those of their lives and fortunes, who have given you no just cause of offense.

Emma Goldman
Addresses Her Jury

"We say that if America has entered the war to make the world safe for democracy, she must first make democracy safe in America."

In 1885, sixteen-year-old Russian factory worker Emma Goldman (1869–1940) emigrated to the United States, where the trial and execution of the Haymarket anarchists in Chicago the following year would heighten her already radical views. She became an anarchist and agitated for social change, which earned her the sobriquet "Red Emma," and, with Alexander Berkman in 1906, founded *Mother Earth,* an anarchist monthly.

Goldman and Berkman opposed America's entry into World War I. As Uncle Sam screamed "I Want You!" from recruitment posters, in support of Woodrow Wilson's call for conscription, the two radicals founded a No-Conscription League and distributed more than 100,000 copies of a "No-Conscription" manifesto at antiwar meetings. They were arrested within weeks and charged with conspiracy to obstruct the draft. At their trial in June 1917, they conducted their own defense, which included this speech by Goldman to the jury.

Throughout the address, Goldman is forceful and formal in her repeated use of the phrase "gentlemen of the jury" and, to good effect, holds her audience with a series of rhetorical questions. Yet the woman, who as a young speaker had "wept with joy" because, as she said, "I could sway people with words," found none of that here. Goldman and Berkman were convicted, fined $10,000, and deported after serving two years in prison. After her death, Goldman was buried at Waldheim Cemetery in Chicago, near the graves of the Haymarket martyrs.

———— ·•· ————

G entlemen, when we asked whether you would be prejudiced against us if it were proven that we propagated ideas and opinions contrary to those held by the majority, you were instructed by the Court to say, "If they are within the law." But what the Court did not tell you is, that no new faith—not even the most humane and peaceable—has ever been considered "within the law" by those who were within power. The history of human growth is at the same time the history of every new idea heralding the approach of a brighter dawn, and the brighter dawn has always been considered illegal, outside of the law.

Gentlemen of the jury, most of you, I take it, are believers in the teachings of Jesus. Bear in mind that he was put to death by those who considered his views as being against the law. I also take it that you are proud of your Americanism. Remember that those who fought and bled for your liberties were in their time considered as being against the law, as dangerous disturbers and troublemakers. They not only preached violence, but they carried out their ideas by throwing tea into the Boston harbor. They said that "Resistance to tyranny is obedience to God." They wrote a dangerous document which continues to be dangerous to this day, and for the circulation of which a young man was sentenced to ninety days prison in a New York Court, only the other day. They were the Anarchists of *their* time—they were never within the law.

Your government is allied with the French Republic. Need

I call your attention to the historic fact that the great upheaval in France was brought about by extra-legal means? The Dantes, the Robespierres, the Marats, the Herberts, aye even the man who is responsible for the most stirring revolutionary music, the Marseillaise (which fortunately has deteriorated into a war tune), even Camille Desmoulines, were never within the law. But for those great pioneers and rebels, France would have continued under the yoke of the idle Louis XVI, to whom the sport of shooting jack rabbits was more important than the destiny of the people of France. . . .

Never can a new idea move within the law. It matters not whether that idea pertains to political and social changes or to any other domain of human thought and expression—to science, literature, music; in fact, everything that makes for freedom and joy and beauty must refuse to move within the law. How can it be otherwise? The law is stationary, fixed, mechanical, "a chariot wheel" which grinds all alike without regard to time, place and condition, without ever taking into account cause and effect, without ever going into the complexity of the human soul.

Progress knows nothing of fixity. It cannot be pressed into a definite mold. It cannot bow to the dictum, "I have rule," "I am the regulating finger of God." Progress is ever renewing, ever becoming, ever changing—*never is it within the law.*"

If that be crime, we are criminals even like Jesus, Socrates, Galileo, Bruno, John Brown and scores of others. We are in good company, among those whom Havelock Ellis, the greatest living psychologist, describes as the political criminals recognized by the whole civilized world, except America, as men and women who out of deep love for humanity, out of a passionate reverence for liberty and an all-absorbing devotion to an ideal are ready to pay for their faith even with their blood. We cannot do otherwise if we are to be true to ourselves—we know that the political criminal is the precursor of human progress—the political criminal of today must needs be the hero, the martyr and the saint of the new age.

But, says the prosecuting attorney, the press and the unthinkable rabble, in high and low station, "that is a dangerous doctrine and unpatriotic at this time." No doubt it is. But are we to be held responsible for something which is as unchangeable and unalienable as the very stars hanging in the heavens unto time and all eternity?

Gentlemen of the jury, we respect your patriotism. We would not, if we could, have you change its meaning for yourself. But may there not be different kinds of patriotism as there are different kinds of liberty? I for one cannot believe that love of one's country must needs consist in blindness to its social faults, in deafness to its social discords, in articulation of its social wrongs. Neither can I believe that the mere accident of birth in a certain country or the mere scrap of a citizen's paper constitutes the love of country.

I know many people—I am one of the them—who were not born here, nor have they applied for citizenship, and who yet love America with deeper passion and greater intensity than many natives whose patriotism manifests itself by pulling, kicking, and insulting those who do not rise when the national anthem is played. Our patriotism is that of the man who loves a woman with open eyes. He is enchanted by her beauty, yet he sees her faults. So we, too, who know America, love her beauty, her richness, her great possibilities; we love her mountains, her canyons, her forests, her Niagara, and her deserts—above all do we love the people that have produced her wealth, her artists who have created beauty, her great apostles who dream and work for liberty—but with the same passionate emotion we hate her superficiality, her cant, her corruption, her mad, unscrupulous worship at the altar of the Golden Calf.

We say that if America has entered the war to make the

world safe for democracy, she must first make democracy safe in America. How else is the world to take America seriously, when democracy at home is daily being outraged, free speech suppressed, peaceable assemblies broken up by overbearing and brutal gangsters in uniform; when free press is curtailed and every independent opinion gagged. Verily, poor as we are in democracy, how can we give of it to the world? We further say that a democracy conceived in the military servitude of the masses, in their economic enslavement, and nurtured in their tears and blood, is not democracy at all. It is despotism—the cumulative result of a chain of abuses which, according to that dangerous document, the Declaration of Independence, the people have the right to overthrow.

The District Attorney has dragged in our Manifesto, and he has emphasized the passage, "Resist conscription." Gentlemen of the jury, please remember that that is not the charge against us. But admitting that the Manifesto contains the expression, "Resist conscription," may I ask you, is there only one kind of resistance? Is there only the resistance which means the gun, the bayonet, the bomb or flying machine? Is there not another kind of resistance? May not the people simply fold their hands and declare, "We will not fight when we do not believe in the necessity of war"? May not the people who believe in the repeal of the Conscription Law, because it is unconstitutional, express their opposition in word and by pen, in meetings and in other ways? What right has the District Attorney to interpret that particular passage to suit himself? Moreover, gentlemen of the jury, I insist that the indictment against us does not refer to conscription. We are charged with a conspiracy against registration. And in no way or manner has the prosecution proven that we are guilty of conspiracy or that we have committed an overt act.

Gentlemen of the jury, you are not called upon to accept our views, to approve of them or to justify them. You are not even called upon to decide whether our views are within or against the law. You are called upon to decide whether the prosecution has proven that the defendants Emma Goldman and Alexander Berkman have conspired to urge people not to register. And whether their speeches and writings represent overt acts.

Whatever your verdict, gentlemen, it cannot possibly affect the rising tide of discontent in this country against the war which, despite all boasts, is a war for conquest and military power. Neither can it affect the ever increasing opposition to conscription which is a military and industrial yoke placed upon the necks of the American people. Least of all will your verdict affect those to whom human life is sacred, and who will not become a party to the world slaughter. Your verdict can only add to the opinion of the world as to whether or not justice and liberty are a living force in this country or a mere shadow of the past.

Your verdict may, of course, affect us temporarily, in a physical sense—it can have no effect whatever upon our spirit. For even if we were convicted and found guilty and the penalty were that we be placed against a wall and shot dead, I should nevertheless cry out with the great Luther: "Here I am and here I stand and I cannot do otherwise."

And gentlemen, in conclusion let me tell you that my co-defendant, Mr. Berkman, was right when he said the eyes of America are upon you. They are upon you not because of sympathy for us or agreement with Anarchism. They are upon you because it must be decided sooner or later whether we are justified in telling people that we will give them democracy in Europe, when we have no democracy here? Shall free speech and free assemblage, shall criticism and opinion—which even the espionage bill did not include—be destroyed? Shall it be a shadow of the past, the great historic American past? Shall it be trampled underfoot by any detective, or a policeman, anyone who decides upon it? Or shall free speech and free press and free assemblage continue to be the heritage of the American people?

Gentlemen of the jury, whatever your verdict will be, as far as we are concerned, nothing will be changed. I have held ideas all my life. I have publicly held my ideas for twenty-seven years. Nothing on earth would ever make me change my ideas except one thing; and that is, if you will prove to me that our position is wrong, untenable, or lacking in historic fact. But never would I change my ideas because I am found guilty. I may remind you of two great Americans, undoubtedly not unknown to you, gentlemen of the jury; Ralph Waldo Emerson and Henry David Thoreau. When Thoreau was placed in prison for refusing to pay taxes, he was visited by Ralph Waldo Emerson and Emerson said: "David, what are you doing in jail?" and Thoreau replied: Ralph, what are you doing outside, when honest people are in jail for their ideals?" Gentlemen of the jury, I do not wish to influence you. I do not wish to appeal to your passions. I do not wish to influence you by the fact that I am a woman. I have no such desires and no such designs. I take it that you are sincere enough and honest enough and brave enough to render a verdict according to your convictions, beyond the shadow of a reasonable doubt.

Please forget that we are Anarchists. Forget that it is claimed that we propagated violence. Forget that something appeared in *Mother Earth* when I was thousands of miles away, three years ago. Forget all that, and merely consider the evidence. Have we been engaged in a conspiracy? Has that conspiracy been proven? Have we committed overt acts? Have those overt acts been proven? We for the defense say they have not been proven. And therefore your verdict must be not guilty.

But whatever your decision, the struggle must go on. We are but the atoms in the incessant human struggle towards the light that shines in the darkness—the ideal of economic, political and spiritual liberation of mankind!

Elizabeth Gurley Flynn
Disputes the Smith Act

*"It is a terrible thing to see one's country in
the grip of fear . . ."*

Beginning with her first public speech at age sixteen, American
agitator and labor organizer Elizabeth Gurley Flynn (1890–1964)
waxed militant through a life that spanned the labor struggles of
the turn of the century to the activism of the early 1960s.
Daughter of Irish revolutionaries, Flynn joined the Socialist
Party while a teenager growing up in Bronx, New York, and
quickly gained fame for her impassioned speeches on behalf of
the International Workers of the World. "I agitate a listener," she
said. "I know how to get the power out of my diaphragm
instead of my vocal cords, and I'm happy to be free to give capitalism hell."

"The Rebel Girl" spent the next few decades mobilizing
strikes, fighting for free speech, and for seven years, helping to
defend the ultimately doomed Italian anarchists Nicola Sacco
and Bartolomeo Vanzetti. She joined the Communist Party in
1936, prompting her ouster four years later from the American
Civil Liberties Union, an organization she helped found.

In the 1950s, as McCarthyism flourished, Flynn was one of
several Communist leaders brought to trial and convicted on
charges of violating the Smith Act, legislation that made it
unlawful to advocate the violent overthrow of the government—and often widely interpreted during the rampant years

of "red" hysteria. Before receiving her sentence, Flynn made this speech to the court on February 2, 1953, in Foley Square, New York. She was less fiery than usual, but still articulate as she mocked the "frightened rich" and the government's "hollow and costly Pyrrhic, victory" over "a few individuals." She was sentenced to three years in prison.

Your Honor, my first impulse was to remain silent during this last act of our trial which I feel could have been foretold in April 1952. I had had many opportunities as a *pro se* counsel to speak and to testify at length. The time available here today really belongs to my comrades, who thus far have not been heard. Your Honor undoubtedly has the list of our names and sentences already in mind, and this procedure will probably cause no change.

In spite of a sense of futility which grew with every passing day of this frustrating trial, I must speak out, however. Silence might be construed as acceptance of a verdict which is justified neither by the so-called evidence of a motley array of bought and paid-for informers, stool pigeons and renegades, as unworthy of belief as a Judas Iscariot or a Benedict Arnold, nor by the law as expounded in your charge to the jury. Therefore I say again, Your Honor, that I and none of my comrades are guilty of any conspiracy to advocate overthrow of the United States government by force and violence. Silence might be construed as defeatism when the truth is that I am so serene in our consciousness of innocence of any crimes, that I can be imprisoned but I cannot be corrected, reformed or changed. My body can be incarcerated but my thoughts will remain free and unaffected.

All human history has demonstrated that ideas, thoughts, cannot be put in prison. They can only be met in the forum of public discussion.

Someone sent me a picture of Thomas Jefferson which now adorns my cell in the House of Detention. It says: "Difference of opinion leads to enquiry of truth. We value too much freedom of opinion not to cherish its exercise."

The political, industrial and social conditions under capitalism which created our ideas remain. They will produce similar ideas in the minds of countless others and further strengthen them in ours. Never did prison affect resolute people who live and work and die if necessary by their ideas. We Communists are such people. I have faith in the ultimate justice of the American people once the fog of lies, hysteria, prejudice and, worst of all, *fear* is swept away. It is a terrible thing to see one's country in the grip of fear—needless, stupid, foolish fear; fear of imaginary enemies, fear of our allies and friends; fear of the accusing fingers of stool pigeons, fear of losing one's job or one's citizenship or one's place in a community. The whole governmental bureaucracy, wasting billions of dollars, boasting, bragging, bullying, is whistling in the dark of fear, trying to make the whole world afraid of us. But some bright morning the American people, Your Honor, will come out of this fog and remember the wise words of Franklin Delano Roosevelt, "We have nothing to fear but fear itself." It has happened before. They will ask themselves, "Who is afraid?"

It is from a small handful of frightened rich that this contagion has spread—the men of the trusts, who never loved their country more than their stocks and bonds, whose patriotism is always on a percentage basis, who would rule and exploit and use violence against not only their fellow countrymen but the human race. They would plunge the world into a sea of blood by atomic warfare in order to maintain their own mean and mercenary rule, their way of life, and foist it upon other people who want none of it. Great as the danger looms, I have faith that fascism will never come to pass in our country. I am proud of the role that our Party has played in signalizing that danger since 1935. American Communists shed their blood in Spain and in every theater of action during World War II against fascism. Great as the threat of war looms, I am confident it is not inevitable and I am proud of the role of the Communists who are foremost here and throughout the world in the struggle for peace.

We defendants tried for many months to present what we really stand for and do—our intent. The scales were weighted against us. The government seeks to convict, and thwarts all efforts to present the facts. The voice of truth is stifled here by precedents, procedures, laws of evidence. Sometimes, for a few moments, it breaks through like the synthetic sunlight that occasionally is reflected here from the upper-story window. But life and progress move on outside, Your Honor.

You know our analysis of the jury system. I will not attempt to repeat it. How impossible it was for a single juror to enter that box with an open mind or a courageous spirit! Poisoned with prejudice, fearful of their futures, incapable of assimilating scientific concepts, hypnotized by legalistic language, smothered in data they could neither remember nor comprehend, they grasped the straw man of the government's case to their bosoms as set forth in its closing summation. It was all they cared to remember. It is no illusion, however, for us to say confidently, Your Honor, we are on the winning side. We have the welfare of our country and its people at heart. We know that millions of Americans hate fascism and want peace, that the working class of our country moves forward, that the Negro people are on the march for their full democratic rights and will not turn back.

Time was when the Communists alone raised slogans for peace, for security, for jobs, for democracy, for unionism, which are on the minds and lips of millions of Americans today. Our lives, our work, our aspirations are part of the American scene for the past half century. Our predecessors go back a century and more. Somewhere and soon the Smith Act will go into the discard as did the Alien and Sedition Laws of 1800, the Fugitive Slave Laws of the sixties, the Criminal Syndicalist Laws of the 1920s.

The fog engulfing courtrooms, middle class juries and the press will lift among the masses of plain people, the ones who never get on federal juries because their appearance and manner doesn't satisfy a hard-boiled political appointee who splits his infinitives, doubles his negatives and toadies to the prosperous.

A people's movement is arising in our country like a strong, fresh prairie wind against repressive legislation, loyalty oaths, congressional investigations, witch-hunts, political trials and the like. The people will repeal the Smith Act and see that its victims are released, and that will be long before a transition to socialism, Your Honor.

It is a hard and bitter path that American reaction is plotting out for the American people, but they will not go far along the path. Our voices have been and will be raised in protest at every step of the way. If our individual voices are silenced, others will be raised.

I asked you a question on Friday, Your Honor, which I now repeat: If the Communist Party is not illegal, its membership and officership is not illegal, if advocating socialism is not illegal, if advocating a day-to-day program of "good deeds," as the government cynically calls it, is not illegal, what in all conscience is illegal here? Of what are we guilty?

In all my long life . . . I never expected that I would go to jail for books, and not even whole books but scraps and pieces, and if I return to my normal life of the last forty-seven years, of working and speaking on unionism, democratic rights, the rights of the Negro people and of women, on peace and against fascism and war, and on socialism, what happens then, Your Honor? Does the government tote out all the by-then tattered and torn books, the trained marionettes of aging stool pigeons, and does the whole thing start over again?

Does this question not demonstrate that constitutional rights are tied up in the Smith Act, not only for Communists but for any who speak out on these matters?

Your Honor, all the material property I possess, as far as a fine is concerned, are books accumulated since I first bought a paper-covered copy of Tom Paine's *Common Sense* at the age of sixteen. They are good books—poetry, drama, history, political economy, fiction, philosophy, art, music, travel, literature. Marx and Engels are there beside Shakespeare, Shaw, Emerson, Hegel, Mark Twain; Lenin and Stalin are there beside Thoreau, Jefferson, the Beards, the Webbs, Hugo, Hardy and many others. What happens to them, Your Honor? They are my "guilt by association" partners that I use for my speeches and my articles.

There is force and violence on those shelves but not where the government looked for it. It is in Irish history—Connelly, O'Casey and others telling of the long and bloody struggle against British rule. It is in American labor history, in Colorado, West Virginia, Homestead, South Chicago and on the Embarcadero of San Francisco. It is in American history—the Revolution, the wars against the American Indians, the Civil War, the Spanish-American War. It is in the struggles of the Negro people. It is in the Bible, too—which is on my shelf, Your Honor—violence against the Jewish Tribes, and the old prophets, against Jesus and his Disciples, and the early Christian martyrs.

And it all proves our thesis, that force and violence come from the ruling class and not from the people.

There is a Homeric irony, Your Honor, in the ending of this hollow and costly Pyrrhic victory for the government, that the books, the ideas, the thoughts remain outside, spreading on the wings of the morning, while only we, a few individuals, go to prison, and that history will write a different verdict and will agree that "we are many and they are few."

PART 7

DECLARATIONS
OF THE
FOURTH ESTATE

Dorothy Thompson
Chides Hitler's Definition of a Free Press

"Had the predecessors of Mr. Hitler held Mr. Hitler's view of the press, never, never, never would he have come to power!"

American journalist Dorothy Thompson (1893–1961) campaigned for women's suffrage, wrote "phony blurbs for soap and mouthwash," and married celebrated writer Sinclair Lewis before becoming "the woman Adolf Hitler expelled from Germany."

Thompson, who interviewed the dictator in 1931, had written a barrage of stories condemning his violent anti-Semitism and forewarning the rise of the Third Reich. "My offense was to think that Hitler was just an ordinary man," she wrote later. "That is a crime against the reigning cult in Germany, which says that Mr. Hitler is a Messiah sent of God to save the German people—an old Jewish idea. To question this mystic mission is so heinous that if you are German you can be sent to jail. I, fortunately, am an American, so I merely was sent to Paris. Worse things can happen to one."

Her dramatic expulsion sparked instant international fame, her own column ("On the Record," which she wrote for nearly two decades), and thousands of requests to speak—opportunities she used to continue her attacks against "tyrants of free expression." Witness this speech to the New York Herald Tribune Forum on October 4, 1937, in which she finds irony in her expeller—a man whose very power, she argues, advanced on the freedoms he took away from others.

———•+•———

There was a time, not long ago, when all men who pretended to call themselves civilized agreed that the search for truth was one of the noblest human activities. . . . They by no means agreed on what the truth was. A great many of them doubted whether anything remotely resembling final truth about anything could ever be found. They thought of truth, as George Eliot thought of justice when she said, "Justice, like the Kingdom of God, is not without us as a fact, but within us, as a deep yearning."

But they all agreed that to love truth and pursue it was an intellectual and spiritual exercise without which men sank beneath the level of human dignity. Certainly, the great Hebrew prophets believed this. So did the Greeks of the high period of Athens. So did the men of the Renaissance; and so did the great spirits of the eighteenth and nineteenth centuries. . . .

The passion of Western man has been the love of truth and freedom. "Look round on all the glorious face of nature. On freedom it is founded. See how rich through freedom it has grown!" Those are not the words of an Anglo-Saxon liberal. They are the words of . . . Friedrich Schiller.

"Freedom is so beautiful a word, that even if it did not exist, one would have to believe in it." Those words are not the words of an Anglo-Saxon or an American. They are the words of Goethe.

And the man who for all of us is the very incorporation of the concept of freedom of conscience, freedom of conscience for every individual human soul, is the man who said, "Here I stand. I cannot do otherwise." He didn't say, "Here I stand as a loyal German." He didn't say, "Here I stand firm in the faith of Adolph Hitler." He said, "Here I stand, I, alone, a human soul, clothed in the dignity of the right to own that soul, and the responsibility for what I do with that soul." His name was Martin Luther.

And if it be overoptimistic to believe that the spirit of Schiller and Goethe and Luther—and of Herder and Hoelderlin—and of Shakespeare and Byron and Shelley and Jefferson and Voltaire and Montesquieu and Socrates and Aeschylus and Washington and John Stuart Mill—if it be overoptimistic to believe that this spirit will survive the spirit of every dictatorship in the world today—then I am overoptimistic. All of these people were one kind of man. They were German and French and English and American. You can find their lesser or greater prototypes in every nation and in every culture. All of them believed that man must be free. He mustn't be free in order to make a more prosperous country, or contribute to greater national glory, or make a more stabilized social order. He must be free in order to be a man at all!

It is extremely important for us constantly to remind ourselves that liberal democracy is based upon a philosophical conception of the nature of man. We have a free press for the same reason that we have the right of habeas corpus, trial by jury, the independent university, and the constitutional right of freedom of worship.

Liberal democracy, of which all these things are only logical results, is based upon an extremely lofty idea of man and his mission on this planet. It presumes that man is a creature of reason, endowed with mental and spiritual faculties, as well as with a stomach, an urge to reproduce himself and a herd instinct. It believes that he has the power to exercise choice, to take responsibility for his own actions, and the social results of those actions. It assumes that out of many minds, working in conjunction, it is possible to get a basis for the ordering of human affairs which, although it will not be perfect, will nevertheless approximate justice.

And the chief instrument for achieving that approximation of justice is not the vote, nor even representative government, and certainly not, necessarily, the parliamentary system. The chief instrument is free expression of the opinions, desires, complaints, approvals, dreams, ideas and hopes of the individuals and groups who constitute the governed. . . .

Let me give you a simple illustration of what I mean. Our German speaker today . . . believes that Mr. Hitler's rule is wholly beneficient for Germany. He believes that Mr. Hitler has regenerated a people gone soft and discouraged. But is it not clear that Mr. Hitler himself, his whole position and power, for better or for worse, is the creation of free speech, a free press, and the right of free assemblage that existed under the German republic? Had the predecessors of Mr. Hitler held Mr. Hitler's view of the press, never, never, never would he have come to power! For fifteen years, Mr. Hitler used the instruments of a free press, and the right of free speech (and so did Mussolini) to air the shortcomings, and what he considered the sins, of the German republic.

In 1923 Mr. Hitler attempted a coup d'état, which amounted to treason. He was imprisoned, but within a year his sentence was commuted. Many people in Germany wished to give him his physical liberty, on condition that he never again speak, write, or conduct a campaign or agitation. The man who protested against this, and demanded the right of free expression for Adolf Hitler was Paul Loebe, the social-democratic president of the German Reichstag, who insisted that the principle of free expression was an integral part of German republicanism. Had the German Republic not been so quixotically, some say so suicidally, generous, there would be no Third Reich.

But now, what this regime is doing, and what the Russian and Italian regimes are doing, is to take away the possibility of there being any future Lenins, or Hitlers, or Mussolinis. Themselves born of rebellion, they are mortgaging the possibility of this generation or any future generation to rebel. They ask us to assume that never again will there be such evils in society, such maladjustments of the governmental system, as to demand a radical change—the kind of change that can only be brought about in one of two ways: by free expression and an evolving public opinion, or by dark, underground, secret conspiracy, and the overthrow of the government by violence. In our modern tyrannies, only the last way—the way of revolution by violence—is left to future Lenins, Mussolinis, or Hitlers.

I have said that freedom of the press cannot be divorced from other civil liberties. That, too, is obvious. No matter how much freedom I am theoretically given in Russia, I am not a free journalist if tomorrow the authorities of the state can arrest me without a warrant, imprison me without an indictment, and try me without a hearing before a jury. I am not free for the simple reason that I am scared. I may be theoretically given the right to criticize the government, but unfortunately I do not know at what moment, and by what edict I may become guilty, not of criticism, but of high treason and lose certainly my job, and possibly my life. I therefore take no chances in any fundamental kind of criticism. . . .

I cannot leave unchallenged certain things that have been said today . . . that the vital functions of the press are to gather all important news; to create an intelligent attitude toward important national issues, and to supply readers with the entertainment they like.

I would first of all challenge that the German press—or the Italian press or the Russian—do any of these things. They may gather all important news, but they certainly don't publish it. I should think, for instance, that it is important news how many people, at any given moment, are in prison or concentration camps for political reasons. But those facts are not published.

I should think that it would interest the German people to know how much of their money is being spent—but the German budget has not been published anywhere in over three years.

Whether the German press gives the people the entertainment they like, I doubt, from the simple fact that the circulation of the German press has gone down by hundreds of thousands since Hitler came into power. . . .

But I would challenge, even more importantly, whether these are the only vital functions of the press! The most vital function of the press is to provide a means of expression for public opinion. A means by which any individual citizen—like the hundreds who write letters to the papers—or any group of citizens, whether they represent a political party, a dissident group, or a group collaborating with the government, may express their opinions and criticisms, approvals, new ideas and reactions, to the many-faceted society in which they live. The free press is a continual forum for public debate.

That is its essential function in a democracy. That is why it gathers news. . . .

We are told that the controlled press is more tactful toward other countries and other peoples, and that it does not publish sordid and spicy details of other peoples' lives. I am not, from this platform, going to defend many of what I consider to be the abuses of the free press. But, good gracious, is the German press tactful about Russia? Was it tactful during the Dollfuss regime, about Austria? Is it tactful about Czechoslovakia? Has it recently been tactful about Poland?

As for sordid and spicy detail . . . The German papers, in order to prove the degeneracy of democracies, constantly play up sexual scandals in Hollywood and lynchings in the South. How about the trials of the priests, with all the details of degeneration in monasteries, when the German government was at war with the Vatican? If, now, the Nazi government makes peace with the Vatican, in order to straighten out its relations with Mussolini and Franco, these scandals about priests will suddenly disappear because the policy has changed. Not because of tactfulness.

As for us, who still have some freedom of expression, it is our duty to guard it, and to work to remedy the abuses of it, in the realization that the concomitant of freedom is responsibility.

Freedom of conscience implies that man has a conscience. The justification of freedom is belief in human reason, love of truth, and passion for justice. If these things die out in a people, then they will lose their freedom, and it will take new heroes to restore it.

Clare Boothe Luce
Takes the American Press to Task

---

*"What is wrong with .the American press is
what is in part wrong with American society."*

Playwright, journalist, politican, diplomat Clare Boothe Luce
(1903–1987) takes on the American press in this speech—given
April 21, 1960, before the Women's National Press Club in
Washington, D.C. "I stand here at this rostrum invited to throw
rocks at you," she says tentatively. Well, not tentatively; Clare
Boothe Luce rarely said anything tentatively. She spoke with a
wit and willfulness that stooped to conquer—and many times
did—which was okay with this audience of journalists because
Clare was one of them, and, after all, they were the ones who
posed the question: "What's Wrong with the American Press?"

Clare Boothe Luce began her career as an editor at *Vogue*
and *Vanity Fair* in the early thirties, and after one failed trip to
the altar, married Henry Luce, the influential publisher of *Time,
Life,* and *Fortune* magazines. She won fame in 1936 for her satir-
ical play, *The Women,* and later won headlines, and bylines, as a
war correspondent in Indochina. A conservative Republican,
she became "Congresswoman to the Nation" in the early forties
(technically just Connecticut, but by then she had attracted a
formidable national constituency). And a decade later, Eisenhower appointed her U.S. ambassador to Italy, the first woman
to hold an ambassadorship to a major European power.

The woman of many hats (both figurative and literal) knew how to deliver a speech—and proved it by graciously, wisely beginning this asked-for condemnation with laudatory praise. The "best press in the world," she assures them—and more important, a free press, "an unguided press" (as her public rival Dorothy Thompson speaks to on pages 219–25). What is wrong with the American press, she argues, is its willingness to follow the "debasement of popular taste"—to "soak the common-denominator reader-sponge with what it wants." Her advisement for "a new, vigorous, masculine leadership" might make some flinch, but the louder clarion call—for a press that will enlighten rather than follow public taste—is one that still holds force.

———•••———

I am happy and flattered to be a guest of honor on this always exciting and challenging occasion. But looking over this audience tonight, I am less happy than you might think and more challenged than you could know. I stand here at this rostrum invited to throw rocks at you. You have asked *me* to tell *you* what's wrong with *you*—the American press. The subject not only is of great national significance but also has, one should say, infinite possibilities—and infinite perils to the rock thrower.

For the banquet speaker who criticizes the weaknesses and pretensions, or exposes the follies and sins, of his listeners—even at their invitation—does not generally evoke an enthusiastic— no less a friendly—response. The delicate art of giving an audience hell is always one best left to the Billy Grahams and the Bishop Sheens.

But you are an audience of journalists. There is no audience anywhere who should be more bored—indeed, more revolted—

by a speaker who tried to fawn on it, butter it up, exaggerate its virtues, play down its faults, and who would more quickly see through any attempt to do so. I ask you only to remember that I am not a volunteer for this subject tonight. You asked for it!

For what is good journalism all about? On a working, finite level it is the effort to achieve illuminating candor in print and to strip away cant. It is the effort to do this not only in matters of state, diplomacy, and politics but also in every smaller aspect of life that touches the public interest or engages proper public curiosity. It is the effort to explain everything from a summit conference to why the moon looks larger coming over the horizon than it does when it has fully risen in the heavens. It is the effort, too, to describe the lives of men—and women— big and small, close at hand or thousands of miles away, familiar in their behavior or unfamiliar in their idiosyncrasies. It is—to use the big word—the pursuit of and the effort to state the truth.

No audience knows better than an audience of journalists that the pursuit of the truth, and the articulation of it, is the most delicate, hazardous, exacting, and *inexact* of tasks. Consequently, no audience is more forgiving (I hope) to the speaker who fails or stumbles in his own pursuit of it. The only failure this audience could never excuse in any speaker would be the failure to try to tell the truth, as he sees it, about his subject.

In my perilous but earnest effort to do so here tonight, I must begin by saying that if there is much that is wrong with the American press, there is also much that is right with it.

I know, then, that you will bear with me, much as it may go against your professional grain, if I ask you to accept some of the *good* with the bad—even though it may not make such good copy for your newspapers.

For the plain fact is that the U.S. daily press today is not inspiringly good; it is just far and away the best press in the world.

To begin with, its news-gathering, news-printing, news-dissemination techniques and capacities are without rivals on the globe.

The deserving American journalist himself enjoys a far more elevated status than his foreign counterpart anywhere. And this, not only because Americans passionately believe that a free press is vital to the preservation of our form of democracy, but because the average American journalist has, on the record, shown himself to be less venal, less corrupt, and more responsible than the average journalist of many foreign lands.

No capital under the sun has a press corps that is better equipped, and more eager to get the news, the news behind the news, and the news ahead of the news, the inside-outside-topside-bottomside news, than the Washington press corps.

I must add only half-jokingly that if the nation's dailies are overwhelmingly pro-Republican in their editorial policy, then the Washington press corps is a large corrective for this political imbalance. Not because Washington reporters are *all* Democrats. Rather because they place on the administration in power their white-hot spotlight of curiosity and exposure. So that no one—Republican or Democrat—can sit complacently in office in this capital unobserved by the men and women of the press who provide the news and information that can make or break an elected or appointed officeholder.

Certainly no press corps contains more journalists of competence and distinction, zeal and dedication. What minds regularly tap more "reliable sources" in government, politics, diplomacy? What breasts guard and unguard more "high level" confidences more jealously? What hearts struggle more conscientiously and painfully to determine to what extent truth telling, or shall we say "leaking," will serve or unserve the public interest? What typewriters send out more facts, figures, statistics, views, and opinions about great public questions and great public figures?

And in what other country of the world are there so many great newspapers? Who could seriously challenge the preeminence among the big-city quality press of the *New York Times*? Where in the world is there a "provincial" newspaper (I use the term only in its technical sense) greater than, to take only one outstanding example, the *Milwaukee Journal*? Even the biggest and splashiest of the foreign English-language press, the *London Daily Mirror*, cannot touch in popular journalism the *New York Daily News*. (And since we are talking in superlatives—good and bad—is there a worse paper in England, Japan, France, or India than the *New York Sunday Enquirer*?)

While the range between the best and the worst is very wide, America's some eighteen hundred newspapers nevertheless average out a higher quality, variety, and volume of information than any other press in the world.

Certainly no other press has greater freedom, more freely granted by the people, to find the news and to print it as it finds it. The American press need not be caught in the subtle toils of subsidies by groups or interests. It does not have to fight government newsprint allocations—that overt or covert censorship exercised in many so-called free countries. Except as the American press is guided by the profit motive, which is in turn guided by the public demand for its papers, it is an unguided press.

All this is what is right with the American press. And the result of this situation is that our people have more ways to be well informed about issues and events near and far than any people in the world. And they are, by and large, better informed.

But now let us come to the question of the evening: "What is wrong with the American press?" We cannot answer this question unless we will voluntarily abandon our relative measurement of it against the press of *other* countries. We must measure it, in absolute terms, against its own highest ideal of freedom, responsibility, and—let us not forget—success.

It is easy to point to many instances in which the American

press—especially its individual members—tend to abuse their freedom and shirk their responsibility.

For example, one could note that nowadays the banner of press freedom is more often raised in matters of printing crime, sex, and scandal stories than it is in matters of printing the truth about great national figures, policies, and issues. Or that too many members of the working press uncritically pass on—even if they do not personally swallow—too much high-level government and political cant, tripe, and public relations; or that there are too many journalists who seem willing to sell their birthright of candor and truth in order to become White House pets, party pets, corporation pets, Pentagon or State Department or trade union or governor's mansion pets; who wistfully yearn after gray eminency, or blatantly strive for publicity for themselves, on lecture platforms or political rostrums.

While agreeing with most journalists that people are not as much interested in the issues as they should be, one could at the same time note that neither are many journalists. One could mention that such journalists seem to have forgotten that *men, not names* alone, make news, and that men are made by the clarity with which they state issues, and the resolution with which they face them. One could express the hope that more journalists would encourage rather than avoid controversy and argument, remembering that controversy and argument are not the enemies of democracy but its friends. One could wish for fewer journalist prodigies of the well-written factual story, and more gifted talents for drawing explanations from the facts, or that working pressmen would be more creative in reporting the news, or that they would reflect less in themselves of what in this decade they have so roundly condemned in American leadership: apathy, cynicism, lukewarmness, and acceptance of the status quo about everything, from juvenile delinquency to nuclear destruction. One could pray, above all, for journalists who cared less about ideologies and more about ideas.

But such criticisms and complaints—important as they may be—cover only one area of the American press. It is, alas, a relatively small area. A large, unmeasurable percentage of the total editorial space in American newspapers is concerned not with public affairs or matters of stately importance. It is devoted instead to entertainment, titillation, amusement, voyeurism, and tripe.

The average American newspaper reader wants news, but he wants lots of things from his newspaper besides news: he wants the sports page, the comics, fashion, homemaking, advice-to-the-lovelorn, do-it-yourself psychiatry, gossip columns, medical, cooking, and decorating features, TV, movie, and theater coverage, Hollywood personality stories, Broadway and society prattle, church columns, comics, bridge columns, crossword puzzles, big-money contests. Above all, he wants news that concerns not a bit the public weal but that people just find "interesting" reading.

I confess to enjoying much of this myself. And I do not mean to suggest that every newspaper must read like the London *Times*. But the plain fact is that we are witnessing in America what Professor William Ernest Hocking and others have called the debasement of popular taste.

Is it necessary? An editor of my acquaintance was asked recently whether the new circulation rise of his increasingly wild-eyed newspaper was being achieved at the expense of good journalism. He replied, "But you don't understand; our first journalistic need is to survive." I submit that a survival achieved by horribly debasing the journalistic coin is short-lived. The newspaper that engages in mindless, untalented sensationalism gets caught up in the headlong momentum it creates in its readers' appetites. It cannot continue satisfying the voracious appetites it is building. Such journalism may suddenly burn brightly with success; but it will surely burn briefly.

We have the familiar example of television closely at hand.

The American press has rightly deplored the drivel, duplicity, and demeaning programming that has marked much of television's commercial trust. A critic, of course, need not necessarily always have clean hands. The press is right to flail what is wrong in television, just as it is obliged to recognize the great service television has provided in areas where its public affairs, news, and good programs have succeeded in adding something new and enriching to American life.

But if the press criticizes what is wrong in television without recognizing the moral for itself, it will have missed a valuable and highly visible opportunity for self-improvement.

The double charge against the American press may thus be stated: its failure to inform the public better than it does is the evasion of its responsibility; its failure to educate and elevate the public taste rather than following that taste like a blind, wallowing dinosaur is an abuse of its freedom.

In view of the river of information which flows daily from the typewriters of American correspondents at home and abroad, why are the American people not better informed? Whose fault is it? At first glance it would seem to be the fault of the publishers, and especially editors. But the publisher or editor who does not give his readers plenty of what they want is going to lose circulation to a competitor who does. Or if he has a news monopoly in his city, and feels too free to shortchange them on these things, he is going to lose circulation as his reader-slack is taken up by the radio, the TV, and the magazines.

Add that even the news the reader wants in most cities, especially the smaller cities throughout the United States, is primarily local news. He remains, even as you and I, more interested in the news of his neighbors, his community, and his city than he is in the news out of Washington, Paris, or Rome.

Can we quarrel with this? We cannot. The Declaration of Independence itself set the pattern of the American way, and with it American reading habits. Life, liberty, and the pursuit of *happiness* were to be man's prime and legitimate goals. Perhaps the history of our country would have been better—and happier—if "the pursuit of truth, information, and enlightenment" had been his third great goal. But that was not the way our founding fathers saw things. And that is not the way the American public sees them now.

The fact is that while "man" is a rational animal, *all* men and *all* women are not preeminently rational, logical, and thoughtful in their approach to life. They do not thirst, above all, for knowledge and information about the great domestic and international issues, even though these issues may profoundly affect not only their pocketbooks but their very lives.

Today, as yesterday, people are primarily moved in their choice of reading by their daily emotions, their personal, immediate, existential prejudices, biases, ambitions, desires, and—as we know too well in the Freudian age—by many subconscious yearnings and desires, and irrational hates and fears.

Very well then: let us accept the fact.

Should the American press bow to it? Accept it? Cater to it? Foster it?

What else (the cynical and sophisticated will ask) is there to do?

The American press, no less than the TV and radio, is big business. It is now, as never before, a mass medium. As big business, it faces daily vast problems of costliness and competition. As a mass medium, it cannot handle these problems without seeking to satisfy the public's feelings, desires, and wants. It publishes in the noisiest and most distracted age in our history. It seems doomed to satisfy endlessly the tastes of the nation—pluralistic, pragmatic, emotional, sensuous, and predominantly irrational. By its big-business mass media nature it seems compelled to seek ever more and more to saturate the mass markets, to soak the common-denominator reader-sponge with what it wants.

Certainly we must face this fact: if the American press, as a mass medium, has formed the minds of America, the mass has also formed the medium. There is action, reaction, and interaction going on ceaselessly between the newspaper-buying public and the editors. What is wrong with the American press is what is in part wrong with American society.

Is this, then, to exonerate the American press for its failures to give the American people more tasteful and more illuminating reading matter? Can the American press seek to be excused from responsibility for public lack of information as TV and radio often do, on the grounds that, after all, "we have to give the people what they want or we will go out of business"?

No. Not without abdicating its own American birthright, it cannot. The responsibility *is* fixed on the American press. Falling directly and clearly on publisher and editor, this responsibility is inbuilt into the freedom of the press itself. The freedom guaranteed by the Constitution under the First Amendment carries this responsibility with it.

"Freedom," as Clemenceau said, "is nothing in the world but the opportunity for self-discipline"—that is to say, voluntarily to assume responsibility.

There are many valiant publishers, editors, and journalists in America who have made and are making courageous attempts to give readers a little more of what they *should* have, and a little less of what they want—or, as is more often true, what they only *think* they want, because they have no real knowledge of what is available to them. America owes these publishers and editors and journalists an incomparable debt of gratitude.

What is really wrong with the American press is that there are not enough such publishers and editors. There is hardly an editor in this room who could not—if he passionately would— give every day, every year, a little more honest, creative effort to his readers on the great issues which face us—the issues which, in the years to come, must spell peace or disaster for our democracy. A beginning would be to try courageously, which is to say *consistently,* to keep such news (however brief) on the front page, playing it in some proportion to its real importance. For a newspaper which relegates to the back pages news which is vital to the citizenry as a whole, in favor of sensational "circulation building" headlines about ephemeral stories of crime, lust, sex, and scandal, is *actively* participating in the debasement of public taste and intelligence. Such a newspaper, more especially its editor, is not only breaking faith with the highest of democratic journalism, he is betraying his nation. And, you may be surprised to hear me say, he may even be courting commercial failure.

For there is enough in American life in these exciting sixties to keep interested and absorbed many of the readers who have been written off as impossible to reach except through cheap sensationalism. The commercial challenge is not to achieve success by reaching backward into cliché-ridden ideas, stories, and situations. It is rather to recognize that uniquely now in this country there is natural and self-propelled drive toward a better life, more sustaining and relevant interests. There is, in sum, an infinity of new subjects that make exciting, inviting, and important exploration for the American press.

There can be no doubt that honorable and patriotic publishers and devoted and dedicated editors can increase little by little, in season and out, the public's appetite for better information. There can also be no doubt that they can also decrease, little by little, in the rest of their papers the type of stories which appeals to the worst in human nature by catering to the lowest-common-denominator taste in morals and ethics.

Teddy Roosevelt once said that a good journalist should be part Saint Paul and part Saint Vitus.

A good editor today must be part Santa Claus, part Saint Valentine, part Saint Thomas (the doubter), part Saint Paul, and certainly he must be part Saint Jude. Saint Jude, as you know, is the patron saint of those who ask for the impossible.

It is not impossible to ask that the American press begin to reverse its present trend, which Dean Ed Barrett of the Columbia School of Journalism calls "giving the public too much froth because too few want substance." If this trend is not reversed (which it can be only by your determined effort), the American press will increasingly become the creature, rather than the creator, of man's tastes. It will become a passive, yielding, and, curiously, an effeminate press. And twixt the ads for the newest gas range, and the firmest girdle, the cheapest vacuum cleaner, and the best buy in Easter bonnets; twixt the sports page, the fashion page, the teenage columns, the children's comics; twixt the goo, glop, and glamour handouts on Elvis Presley and Elizabeth Taylor, and above all twixt the headlines on the sexiest murders, and the type of political editorializing which sees the great presidential issues of the day as being between the case of the "boyish forelock" versus the "tricky ski-jump nose," the press will lose its masculine prerogative, which is to educate, inform, engage the interest of, and guide the minds of free men and women in a great democracy.

As I know that the American Society of Newspaper Editors holds hard to the belief in masculine superiority in the realm of the intellect, and could only view with horror the picture of the fourth estate as the "kept man" of the emotional masses, I—for one—am certain this will not happen.

Let us watch then, with hope, for the signs of a new, vigorous, masculine leadership in the American press. For if you fail, must not America also fail in its great and unique mission, which is also yours: to lead the world towards life, liberty, and the pursuit of enlightenment—so that it may achieve happiness? It is that goal which the American press must seize afresh— creatively, purposefully, energetically, and with a zeal that holds a double promise: the promise of success and the promise of enlightenment.

Katharine Graham
Gives a Vigilant Press Its Due During Watergate

"What has sustained and enlarged the scandal has not been the press, but the facts which emerged and the way those involved have reacted to each new disclosure."

"We are not here to be popular," wrote Katharine Graham (b. 1917) of the press. "We are here to be respected and above all, to be believed." One of the most influential figures in American journalism, Graham, whose father bought the *Washington Post* in 1933, became publisher of the paper after her husband's suicide in 1963, and chairman of The Washington Post Company ten years later.

Graham's decision to publish the Pentagon Papers in 1971, following on the heels of the *New York Times,* sent the *Post* into a court fight with the Nixon administration—and Graham into the public eye. But it was her support of the *Post*'s now historic investigation into Watergate that made her famous—at times, uncomfortably so. "I have often been credited with courage for backing our editors in Watergate," she said. "The truth is that I never felt there was much choice."

On March 20, 1974, Graham spoke at Colby College in Waterville, Maine, to accept journalism's Elijah Parish Lovejoy award. Lovejoy, a 1826 Colby graduate, publisher, and abolitionist—considered America's first martyr to journalistic freedom—was mortally wounded while defending his printing press against a proslavery mob.

In her speech, delivered with the drama of Watergate still unfolding, Graham makes the case—both constitutional and public—for a vigilant press. She begins by discounting the press as "a fourth branch of government," then leads into a review of Watergate events (juxtaposing "what was being said" with "what was being done"). The final point to ponder, she tells her audience, is "whether by reporting events, the press has somehow exceeded its charter or abused its liberty, and, by so doing, damaged the nation." To accept that it has, she argues in a forceful peroration, "is to concede too much about the strength and resiliency of this country." Five months after Graham's speech, Richard Nixon resigned; Gerald Ford became president; and the great republic moved on.

———

Though Waterville and Washington may seem to be worlds apart, I really think that you and I are in the same business: the business of education. The Lovejoy Award, for instance, encourages qualities which are as vital to your academic inquiries as to the efforts of the press—the qualities of integrity, craftsmanship, character, intelligence and courage. Those are demanding goals, which we may seldom reach but which we must never stop reaching for.

The challenges facing the press today are great. It is true that presses are not sacked and burned, or thrown in rivers, as they were in Elijah Lovejoy's day. And nowadays reporters, editors and publishers are rarely forced to defend their First Amendment freedoms with their lives.

But while modern-day assaults may be less physical, they are no less real. To an extent, that is a consequence of the kind of work in which we are engaged. For any news organization which really does its job is bound to be a target of complaint from people in the news, people with an obvious interest in the way their words and deeds are transmitted to the public.

There is, however, one category of complaint which is especially troubling to me. That is the criticism which comes from individuals who are disinterested, whose achievements we respect and whose comments therefore carry special weight.

One in this category is the former special prosecutor, Archibald Cox. In a recent speech, according to a wire service report, Mr. Cox said that "the media certainly is turning gradually to a more active role in shaping the course of events . . . the selection of the news items emphasized often reflects the sort of notion that the press is the fourth branch of government, and it should play a major role in government."

Such complaints are as old as the republic, but have acquired a new currency because of Watergate. So I would like to address myself to them this evening.

Consider first the charge that the press has become a "fourth branch of government." As far as being a fourth branch of government is concerned, I'm sure the other three wouldn't have us—nor would we want to be counted among them. The label, "The Fourth Estate," which was first used by Edmund Burke, is much more accurate, for it reflects the true role of the press as a vital institution of democracy—but an institution kept apart from government, endowed with a singular status and entrusted with a singular role.

The Constitution makes the difference plain. The powers of each of the three branches of government are generally, and in some cases quite specifically, defined. Their limits and relationships are carefully arranged. Qualifications for holding office are prescribed. The basic source of all authority—the people and their representatives—is emphasized throughout. All this was done to avoid the accumulation and abuse of power.

The press, in contrast, is mentioned in the Constitution only once—and then as an institution whose freedom may not be abridged. The term, "the press," is not defined. No limits are placed on its membership, its methods or its reach. Nothing illustrates better that the founding fathers sought to keep the forces of inquiry, the transmitters of information, the instruments of free debate as varied, numerous and independent as possible. Freedom of speech and of the press was the essential counterweight to government, the basic check against abuses of official power. And what the founders feared—and so sought to prevent—was not that government might be inconvenienced by the press, but that the press might be harassed and regulated by the government.

So in a very real sense, it is a gross inversion of the constitutional scheme to complain that the press is too probing or too independent now. Yet there are many who make that argument, with the best of intentions; many who make the ritual bow in the direction of the Bill of Rights, and then go on to say, "Yes, but the press is overdoing it." We should be more respectful, they assert. We ought to be questioning. We ought to serve more as bulletin boards for those in power, and be content simply to pass along the news which officials and agencies volunteer.

This notion of a passive, cooperative press reminds me somewhat of the notion of two-party government which was once propounded by a great legislator from Maine, Thomas Reed, Speaker of the House of Representatives in the late nineteenth century. The proper scheme of things, Speaker Reed once said, was for one party to govern and the other one to watch.

The press, however, is not supposed to watch in any docile or passive sense. It is meant to be a watchdog, informing the public of what is really going on and thus keeping those who govern perhaps more honest, certainly more accountable—and thus dishonest only at some peril to their tenure and their power.

This is hardly an easy task. For one thing, the sheer bulk and complexity of modern government make it hard: more of what is really important is obscured in the great streams of chaff blown out each day by agencies, departments, offices and bureaus. One fiercely independent journalist, I. F. Stone, made much of his reputation by digging up and putting together facts which had been buried—in the public records of the government.

For another thing, the government—and especially the president—has come to enjoy awesome powers of communication which can be employed at will. As we have seen recently, a president can command live coverage on all television and radio networks, on virtually any subject, at short notice. He can choose his forum and select the live audience to applaud or ask him questions. His remarks will not only be carried across the airwaves; they will also be reprinted, at least in large part, in the daily newspapers of the land. Presidential pronouncements thus enjoy a weight and circulation which no other view or version of the facts is likely to attain.

This gives the government enormous power to reveal what it wants when it wants, to give the people only the authorized version of events—and, equally important, to conceal that which is unfavorable, untimely or embarrassing. And that power to conceal, to keep information bottled up, is a kind of license to abuse the public trust.

Nothing illustrates this better than Watergate. Toward the beginning of the first Nixon administration, John Mitchell once warned the press that we would be better advised to watch what the administration did rather than what it said.

So, with the hindsight we have now gained so painfully, let's look back at what was being said—and what we now know was being done—on a few specific days.

Let's take, for instance, June 25, 1970. What was being said? President Nixon addressed the Jaycees in St. Louis, and he said,

"Some believe the nation is coming apart at the seams; that we are gripped with fear and repression and even panic . . . it is time to stand up and speak about what is right in America." And he said: "If we ask people to respect the laws, we must have laws and those who enforce the laws who deserve respect."

What was being done on that same day? Tom Charles Huston, a White House aide, was giving Mr. Nixon a top-secret domestic security plan which authorized illegal breaking and entering, mail covers, wiretapping and other covert operations. That plan, as we now know, was approved by the president and was in effect for five days.

Or take another day, March 22, 1971. What was being said? In a live television interview with Howard K. Smith, Mr. Nixon expressed great concern about the cost of political campaigns. The problem, he said, was how to devise curbs on campaign spending "which will . . . be comprehensive and . . . not give an advantage to incumbents over challengers."

What was being done? On that same day the milk producers delivered one of their large gifts to the Republican campaign chests. The next day, Mr. Nixon met with them, and then decided to raise milk price supports—a decision which only an incumbent could make.

Or consider a third day, September 3, 1971. What was being said? Mr. Nixon spoke to the nation's dairy farmers and praised them because, as he put it, "You haven't whimpered helplessly about uncontrollable economic forces, nor waited passively for government to bail you out."

What was being done? Shortly thereafter, on September 11, White House aide Gordon Strachan, in a memo to H. R. Haldeman, noted that the dairy industry had promised campaign contributions of $90,000 a month but had only paid about half that amount.

Of course, after the Watergate break-in, when the cover-up

was under way, the contrast between words and deeds became even sharper. Take for instance, September 19, 1972—four days after the seven original Watergate conspirators had been indicted. What was being said? Vice President Agnew was letting it be known that he suspected—and I quote—"Someone set up these people and encouraged them to undertake this caper to embarrass them and to embarrass the Republican party."

What was being done? According to the recent indictment, on that same day Anthony Ulasewicz delivered $53,000 to Dorothy Hunt, while Fred LaRue arranged a payment of about $20,000 to William Bittman.

Take another day, November 13, 1972. What was being said? Charles Colson was attacking the *Washington Post*. "The charge of subverting a whole political process," he declared, "that is a fantasy, a work of fiction rivaling only *Gone with the Wind* in circulation and *Portnoy's Complaint* for indecency." Mr. Colson went on to upbraid the *Post*'s executive editor, saying that "Mr. Bradlee now sees himself as the self-appointed leader of . . . the tiny fringe of arrogant elitists who infect the healthy mainstream of American journalism with their own peculiar view of the world."

And what was being done? Two days later, according to the more recent Watergate indictment, Mr. Colson had a telephone conversation with Howard Hunt about the need for more payments to the defendants.

Take one more day, January 14, 1973. What was being said then? John Mitchell, through his attorney, was reacting to reports that the seven original Watergate defendants were being paid. That, he said, and I quote, was "outrageously false and preposterous."

And what was being done? Fred LaRue was arranging another payment, this time to Gordon Liddy's representative.

What do all these discrepancies show? In some cases, the contrast between words and deeds may have been a matter of expediency; in other cases, part of the cover-up; in others, the product of ignorance about what one's colleagues were up to; in some, part of an effort to shift attention from the news to the media.

But they all point to one conclusion: the inadequacy, and indeed the danger, of relying only or even principally on what those in government say as a measure of what those in government do.

By now, of course, the nation has found out about the Huston Plan, the milk money, the payments, the cover-up, and the other illegal and improper acts which go under the heading of "Watergate." The people know in large part because they have found out through the medium of the press and/or because the press generated other forms of inquiry.

Does this make the press "activist"? In a way, it does, but I would argue that it is the proper way. And, to go back to where I began, this whole painful experience points up the flaw in Mr. Cox's argument against so-called press activism.

On this matter of activism, I would note two things. First, if the media have been paramount in uncovering pieces of the scandal, it is because at the beginning the other agencies of inquiry were not doing their jobs. The Congress, the Justice Department and the courts were all thwarted or blocked or delayed, especially at the time when an airing of events might have had the most impact—before the election in November 1972.

House hearings were delayed after the Justice Department turned on the pressure and argued that public probes might prejudice the pending criminal case. A federal judge ruled, for the same reason, that the civil suit brought by the Democratic National Committee had to be delayed. And the criminal case, in turn, was limited and delayed, in part because some officials were playing games with the evidence and trying hard to frustrate the official investigation.

So that left the press. But if Watergate shows how essential it is for the press to be vigorous, persistent and free, the experience also points up the limits of what we can do.

In saying this, I don't mean to take away anything from the superb performance of Bob Woodward and Carl Bernstein, and the team of experienced editors who guided and checked their work during those months of hard, lonely digging. But the fact is that their work was productive only because a number of people, many inside government and mostly Republicans, were willing to talk with them—to tell them pieces of the truth, often at great peril to their jobs.

And it's also worth reflecting on that, even after their stories about secret funds and political sabotage had appeared, a great deal remained hidden. Many of the key revelations came from elsewhere—from James McCord, as a result of Judge Sirica's pressure, from John Dean, from the hearings on L. Patrick Gray's nomination to be head of the FBI, from the work of the Senate committee, from the lawsuits of the Democrats, Common Cause and Ralph Nader, from the work of the special prosecution team and the grand juries. And what may have been *the* crucial event—the discovery that a voice-activated tape system had been installed in the White House—came not from the work of the press, but from a Senate staff question put to a man, Alexander Butterfield, who had been thought of as a peripheral figure.

When you consider everything that has flowed from that one interview—the court suits over executive privilege, the "Saturday Night Massacre," the missing tapes and the 18½-minute gap, the arguments about what Mr. Nixon said on March 21, the impeachment investigation—one thing becomes evident. It is that what has finally given Watergate such scope and momentum has not been the press but the force of events and the ultimate determination of responsible people to make our system of justice work. What has sustained and enlarged the scandal has not been the press, but the facts which emerged and the way those involved have reacted to each new disclosure.

To paraphrase Mr. Cox, *events* have shaped events. There would, after all, have been no stories if there had been nothing to report.

This leaves the final point: whether by reporting events, the press has somehow exceeded its charter or abused its liberty, and, by so doing, has damaged the nation.

The question is whether the country would be better off if the Watergate story had stayed in the *Post's* local section, where it spent its early days; if Woodward and Bernstein had gone back to other stories after the White House called the matter an isolated, third-rate burglary; if the press had given up after the first month of denials or the second or the tenth; and if, now, the press should stop telling the country about each new twist and turn in the arguments and investigations.

Would the country be better off if we had never learned about the secret funds, the burglary of Dr. Fielding's office, the enemies' list, the tapes, and all the other dispiriting facts of Watergate?

This is not just a question the president's supporters ask. I hear it often, from troubled citizens who look at all of the national urgencies that face us, and look at the cost of Watergate in terms of national unity and governmental strength, and wonder whether it is worth the price for these particular offenses to be exposed.

This is a serious question, and one which we at the *Post* have thought about a great deal. But finally, I think, one can only accept the implied answer if one is willing to concede too much about the strength and resiliency of this country—things that I, for one, am not willing to concede.

I am not willing to concede, for instance, that we can and should tolerate serious breaches of the Constitution and the laws, because disclosure would be disruptive. I am not willing to concede that the American people can only stand a limited number of shocks and a measured amount of disillusionment. Or that we can best serve ourselves and our heritage by running away from our troubles. Or that national stability rests on national ignorance.

This is hardly the faith of a free people. For to say that the press ought to suppress some news, if we deem it too bad or too unsettling, is to make the press into the censor or the nursemaid of a weak and immature society. And to argue that the press ought to be censored or suppressed, or limited in its inquiries, is to shred the First Amendment and dam up the flow of ideas and information.

Writing of federalism and the separation of powers in the *Federalist Papers*, James Madison said, "In framing a government which is to be administered by men over men, the great difficulty lies in this: you must first enable the government to control the governed; and in the next place oblige it to control itself."

For all the safeguards built into our system of government, each branch cannot properly exercise its controls without knowing what the others are doing; and the people cannot properly exert their will without the knowledge on which to base their decisions.

Precisely because it is *not* a fourth branch of government, the press plays an essential role in "obliging the government to control itself." And if we do not serve in this way, the rest of the rights guaranteed by our Constitution cannot be sustained.

PART 8

POLITICAL
SPEECHES

Anna Howard Shaw
Parodies Emotionalism in Politics

*"I saw men jump up in their seats and jump
down again, and run around in a ring."*

As a young girl eager to preach, Anna Howard Shaw (1847–1919) often stood atop tree stumps and sermonized alone in the quiet of the Michigan wilderness. Ordained a Methodist minister in 1880, she later earned a medical degree from Boston University. She could treat "body and soul," but became famous as an orator, preaching women's rights and temperance.

Shaw was, by some press accounts in her day, "queen of the platform," the woman of rich contralto voice who crafted eloquent speeches and inescapably logical arguments. She was especially well-known for her humor—her talent for wit, sarcasm, and gentle cajoling. "Why does the Scripture say that there shall be no marriages in heaven?" she asked in a speech. "Ah, my dear friends (she drew a long sigh) because there will be no men there." When an anti-suffragist claimed that she controlled the way her husband voted, Shaw said she doubted it, since no woman would publicly admit a fool for a husband. Audiences cheered, applauded, and lapped it up—as did some of her toughest opponents.

Shaw's flair for the sarcastic comes through in this brief speech, delivered in 1913 at a convention of the National American Woman Suffrage Association; Shaw was president of the NAWSA for eleven years. Here, in good jest, she finds irony in the male claim that women are too emotional for the rational world of politics.

———————

B y some objectors, women are supposed to be unfit to vote because they are hysterical and emotional and, of course, men would not like to have emotion enter into a political campaign. They want to cut out all emotionalism, and so they would like to cut us out.

I had heard so much about our emotionalism that I went to the last Democratic National Convention held in Baltimore to observe the calm repose of the male politicians. I saw some men take a picture of one gentleman whom they wanted elected, and it was so big they had to walk sideways as they carried it forward. And they were followed by hundreds of other men, screaming and yelling, shouting and singing the "Houn' Dawg"; then, when there was a lull, another set of men would start forward under another man's picture, not to be outdone by the "Houn' Dawg" melody, whooping and howling still louder. I saw men jump up on the seats and throw their hats in the air and shout, "What's the matter with Champ Clark?" Then, when those hats came down, other men would kick them back into the air, shouting at the top of their voices: "He's all right!" Then I heard others howling for "Underwood, Underwood, first, last and all the time!"

No hysteria about it—just patriotic loyalty, splendid manly devotion to principle. And so they went on and on until five o'clock in the morning—the whole night long. I saw men jump up in their seats and jump down again and run around in a ring. I saw two men run towards another man to hug him both at once, and they split his coat up the middle of his back and sent him spinning around like a wheel. All this with the perfect poise of the legal male mind in politics!

Now, I have been to many women's conventions in my day, but I never saw a woman leap up on a chair and take off her bonnet and toss it in the air and shout: "What's the matter with" somebody. I never saw a woman knock another woman's bonnet off her head as she screamed: "She's all right!" I never heard a body of women, whooping and yelling for five minutes when somebody's name was mentioned in a convention. But we are willing to admit that we are emotional. I have actually seen women stand up and wave their handkerchiefs. I have even seen them take hold hands and sing, "Blessed Be the Tie That Binds."

Nobody denies that women are excitable. Still, when I hear how emotional and excitable we are, I cannot help seeing in my mind's eye the fine repose and dignity of this Baltimore and other political conventions I have attended!

Lady Astor
Reflects on Women in Politics

"I can conceive of nothing worse than a man-governed world except a woman-governed world . . ."

Lady Nancy Astor (1879–1964) was told she was too rich to win the workingman's vote. So, with her critics ever in mind, she teased her audiences: "And now my dears, I'm going back to one of my beautiful palaces to sit down in my tiara and do nothing and when I roll out in my car I will splash you all with mud and look the other way." The drolleries came fast and thick—as did the laughter and applause.

Born in Virginia, Nancy Langhorne married the wealthy Waldorf Astor in 1906, after a first and brief failed marriage. When her husband rose from Tory MP to Viscount in 1919, the Viscountess—hostess of the grand Cliveden Estate in Buckinghamshire, England—took to the hustings and quickly endeared herself to his constituency in Plymouth. That year, the people's "Our Nancy" became the first woman elected to the British House of Commons.

She promised not "to pull members' legs more often than necessary" and no long-winded, long-reasoned speeches. "I'm no orator and don't want to be. I've heard too many fine phrases from the emptiest heads in Europe." She spoke without reserve and without apology, which she suffered for in the 1930s. Winston Churchill, joined by a suspicious public, railed against the

Astors, Neville Chamberlain, and others who advocated dialogue with Hitler over force. Lady Astor denied any sympathy toward "Hitler or Hitlerism," prevailed over the crisis, but bore the label of "appeaser" for many years.

On April 9, 1922, less three years after assuming her seat in Parliament, she delivered this speech at New York's Town Hall. The woman who wanted to leave "fine phrases" to others has many of them here—not for show but for substance. Directly, rhetorically, pithily, she exhorts women to use their political ambitions wisely and in joint effort with men.

I know that this welcome has nothing to do with me. Ever since I entered the "Mother of Parliaments" I realized that I ceased to be a person and had become a symbol. The safe thing about being a symbol is this—you realize that you, of yourself, can do nothing, but what you symbolize gives you courage and strength, and should give you wisdom. I certainly have been given courage and strength. I won't say too much about wisdom.

My entrance into the House of Commons was not, as some thought, in the nature of a revolution. It was an evolution. It is interesting how it came about. My husband was the one who started me off on this downward path—from the fireside to public life. If I have helped the cause of women he is the one to thank, not me. He is a strange and remarkable man.

First, it was strange to urge your wife to take up public life, especially as he is a most domesticated man; but the truth is that he is a born social reformer. He has avoided the pitfalls which so many well-to-do men fall into. He doesn't think that you can right wrongs with philanthropy. He realizes that one must go to the bottom of the causes of wrongs and not simply gild them up.

For eleven years, I helped my husband with his work at Ply-

mouth—I found out the wrongs and he tried to right them—
and this contribution of work was a wonderful and happy combination and I often wish that it was still going on.

However, I am not here to tell you of his work, but it is
interesting in so far that it shows you how it came about that I
stood for Parliament at all. Unless he had been the kind of a
man he was, I don't believe that the first woman member of the
oldest Parliament in the world would have come from Plymouth, and that would have been a pity. Plymouth is an ideal
port to sail from or to. It has been bidding Godspeed to so many
voyages. I felt that I was embarking on a voyage of faith, but
when I arrived at my destination some of the honorable members looked upon me more as a pirate than a pilgrim.

A woman in the House of Commons! It was almost
enough to have broken up the House. I don't blame them—it
was equally hard on the woman as it was on them. A pioneer
may be a picturesque figure, but they are often rather lonely
ones. I must say for the House of Commons, they bore their
shock with dauntless decency. No body of men could have
been kinder and fairer to a "pirate" than they were. When you
hear people over here trying to run down England, please
remember that England was the first large country to give the
vote to women and that the men of England welcomed an
American-born woman in the House with a fairness and a justice which, at least, this woman will never forget.

The different ones received me in different ways. I shall
never forget a Scotch labor leader coming up to me, after I had
been in the House a little while, and telling me that I wasn't a bit
the sort of woman he thought I would be—"I'll not tell you
that, but I know now that you are an ordinary, homely, kindly
body," and he has proved it since by often asking my advice on
domestic questions.

Then there was an Irish member who said to me, "I don't

know what you are going to speak about, but I am here to back you." And the last was from a regular Noah's Ark man, a typical squire type. After two and a half years of never agreeing on any point with him, he remarked to someone that I was a very stupid woman but he must add that I was a "very attractive one," and he feared I was a thoroughly honest social reformer. I might add that being the first woman, I had to take up many causes which no one would call exactly popular. I also had to go up against a prejudice of generations, but I must say their decency has never failed, though my manners must have been somewhat of a trial.

Now I must leave the more personal side and get to what it is all about and why we are here. Women and politics—some women have always been in politics, and have not done badly, either. It was when we had the Lancastrian kings that it was said that the kings were made kings by act of Parliament—they did rule by means of Parliament. Then Henry VIII, that old scalawag, accepted the principles of the Lancastrians to rule by Parliament, but he wanted the principle in an entirely different way. He made Parliament the engine of his will: he pressed or frightened it into doing anything he wished. Under his guidance Parliament defied and crushed all other powers, spiritually and temporally, and he did things which no king or Parliament ever attempted to do—things unheard of and terrible.

Then Elizabeth came along. It is true she scolded her Parliaments for meddling with matter with which, in her opinion, they had no concern, and more than once soundly rated the Speaker of her Commons, but she never carried her quarrels too far, and was able to end her disputes by some clever compromise; in other words, she never let Parliament down, and that is what I don't believe any wise woman will do in spite of the fears of some of the men.

Now, why are we in politics? What is it all about? Something much bigger than ourselves. Schopenhauer was wrong in nearly everything he wrote about women—and he wrote a lot—but he was right in one thing. He said, in speaking of women, "the race is to her more than the individual," and I believe that it is true. I feel somehow we do care about the race as a whole, our very nature makes us take a forward vision; there is no reason why women should look back—mercifully we have no political past; we have all the mistakes of sex legislation with its appalling failures to guide us.

We should know what to avoid, it is no use blaming the men—we made them what they are—and now it is up to us to try and make ourselves—the makers of men—a little more responsible in the future. We realize that no one sex can govern alone. I believe that one of the reasons why civilization has failed so lamentably is that it has had a one-sided government. Don't let us make the mistake of ever allowing that to happen again.

I can conceive of nothing worse than a man-governed world except a woman-governed world—but I can see the combination of the two going forward and making civilization more worthy of the name of civilization based on Christianity, not force. A civilization based on justice and mercy. I feel men have a greater sense of justice and we of mercy. They must borrow our mercy and we must use their justice. We are new brooms; let us see that we sweep the right rooms.

Personally, I feel that every woman should take an active part in local politics. I don't mean by that that every woman should go in for a political career—that, of course, is absurd—but you can take an active part in local government without going in for a political career. You can be certain when casting your vote you are casting it for what seems nearest right—for what seems more likely to help the majority and not bolster up an organized minority. There is a lot to be done in local politics, and it is a fine apprenticeship to central government; it is very practical, and I think that, although practical, it is too near to be attractive. The things that are far away are more apt to catch our eye than the ones which are just under our noses; then, too, they are less disagreeable.

Political development is like all other developments. We must begin with ourselves, our own consciences, and clean out our own hearts before we take on the job of putting others straight. So with politics if we women put our hands to local politics, we begin the foundations. After all, central governments only echo local ones; the politician in Washington, if he is a wise man, will always have one eye on his constituency, making that constituency so clean, so straight, so high in its purpose, that the man from home will not dare to take a small, limited view about any question, be it national or an international one. You must remember that what women are up against is not what they see, but the unseen forces.

We are up against generations and generations of prejudice. Ever since Eve ate the apple—but I would like to remind you, and all men, why she ate the apple. It was not simply because it was good for food or pleasant to the eyes; it was a tree to be desired to make one wise. "She took of the fruit thereof, and did eat; and she gave also unto her husband with her, and he did eat." We have no record of Adam murmuring against the fruit—of his doing anything but eat it with docility. In passing, I would like to say that the first time Adam had a chance he laid the blame on woman—however, we will leave Adam.

Ever since woman's consciousness looked beyond the material, man's consciousness has feared her vaguely; he has gone to her for inspiration, he has relied on her for al that is best and most ideal in his life, yet by sheer material force he has limited her. He has, without knowing it, westernized the harem mind of the East. I don't believe he knows it yet so we must break it to him gently. We must go on being his guide, his mother, and his better half. But we must prove to him that we are a necessary half not only in private but in political life.

The best way that we can do that is to show them our ambitions are not personal. Let them see that we desire a better, safer, and cleaner world for our children and their children and we realize that only by doing our bit by facing unclean things with cleanliness, by facing wrongs with right, by going fearlessly into all things that may be disagreeable, that we will somehow make it a little better world.

I don't know that we are going to do this—I don't say that women will change the world but I do say that they can if they want and I, coming in from the Old World which has seen a devastating war, cannot face the future without this hope—that the women of all countries will do their duty and raise a generation of men and women who will look upon war and all that leads to it with as much horror as we now look upon a cold-blooded murder. All of the women of England want to do away with war.

If we want this new world, we can only get it by striving for it; the real struggle will be within ourselves, to put out of our consciousness, of our hearts and of our thoughts, all that makes for war, hate, envy, greed, pride, force, and material ambition.

Clare Boothe Luce
Delivers Her "G.I. Joe and G.I. Jim" Speech

"Jim was the heroic heir of the unheroic Roosevelt Decade . . ."

Clare Boothe Luce was a Republican congresswoman from Connecticut when she said that Franklin Roosevelt had "lied us into war." Bright, talented, attractive, way too witty for any one person's good, Luce had a flair for the incendiary. "Globaloney"—she called Henry Wallace's proposal for postwar freedom of the skies. "Ram-squaddled, do-gooding, New Deal bureaucrats" she tagged FDR and his cabinet. Of her enemies, Roosevelt was a particular favorite. Luce, a New Dealer turned conservative, had gone to Washington "to help the President think" but instead found him frequently condescending, uninterested in the views of a "young, pretty thing."

On June 27, 1944, all that was anti-Roosevelt about Clare Boothe Luce culminated in this speech—her famous "G.I. Joe and G.I Jim" address to the Republican National Convention in Chicago. Joe was the fellow who comes home to parades and brass bands; Jim lies "immobilized for all eternity," resting in an unmarked grave. "His young bones bleach on the tropical roads of Bataan. A white cross marks his narrow grave on some Pacific island," she says in a paragraph packed with vivid imagery. The "terrible truth that cannot be denied" she argues, is that Roosevelt's promises for peace "lie quite as dead as young Jim lies now."

The speech, impassioned and fluent, was not without risk. FDR was a popular president, and the country saw glory in his war. The "Republican hatchet" was calling him a warmonger, with the blood of America's sons on his hands. What her admirers saw as brilliant her opponents saw as mean, and Democrats, including Roosevelt, quickly swarmed into Connecticut to denounce her. When the campaign dust settled, Luce narrowly won reelection, and FDR succeeded to a fourth term.

We have been called together in a time of historic crisis to choose the next president of the United States. Plainly the honor of speaking to you in this hour so fraught with consequence has come to me because I am a woman. Through one woman's voice our party seeks to honor the millions of American women in war-supporting industries, the millions in Red Cross work, and the thousands upon thousands in Civil Service, in hospital and canteen and volunteer work. Our party honors the women in the armed services and our truly noble army nurses. . . . Above all we honor the wives and sisters and sweethearts and mothers of our fighting men. . . .

And yet, I know and you know that American women do not wish their praises sung as women any more than they wish political pleas made to them as women. They feel no differently from men about doing their patriotic jobs. They feel no differently from men about the ever-growing threats to good government. They feel no differently about the inefficiency, abusiveness, evasion, self-seeking, and personal whim in the management of the nation's business, which are little by little distorting our democracy into a dictatorial bumbledom. And certainly they feel no differently about pressing this war to the enemy's innermost gates, or creating from the sick havocs of war itself, a fair and healthy peace.

But there is one thing that women feel, not differently but more deeply about than men. That is the welfare of their sons and brothers and husbands in the service.

In this crowded convention hall, it is rare to see a woman without the little red and white pin whose blue star shows that somewhere on land, in the air, at sea, there is a man in uniform who is very dear to her. It is no more than the truth to say that he is dearer to her than all else in the world. To speak of what is closest to the mind and heart of an American woman today is inevitably to speak of the man who is known affectionately at home, and fearsomely on every battle front, as G.I. Joe.

American women want these minutes and, yes, every minute of our thought and concern to turn on this fighting man. His hopes, his aspirations, his dangerous present, and his still uncertain future, are uppermost in their minds.

Now, G.I. Joe's last name is Legion, because there are about 12 million of him. What his immediate wants are today, his generals know best. Mostly they are more tools, and better tools, which will increase his margin of safety and multiply his chances of victory. To the filling of these wants, all Americans are pledged to the limit of their capacity.

But this convention is gathered together to consider not so much G.I. Joe's immediate wants, as to clarify what his wants are likely to be in the next four years, and to plan to meet those wants. . . .

We know that Joe himself is not thinking of his future wants at this hour. He is too busy engaging a desperate enemy. If you asked him today what he wants of the future, he would probably say, "I want to go home, of course. But I want to go home by way of Berlin and Tokyo."

And this tremendous and heroic want of Joe's to sail into the roadsteads of Yokohama, and march by the waters of the Rhine is alone a greater guarantee of the future security of our nation, than any guarantee we can offer.

This is Joe's gift, beyond price, to America.

We have come together here to nominate a president who will jealously and prayerfully guard that gift all his years in office. . . .

We are come together here to nominate the kind of president who in the years ahead will keep Joe's America—America: that is to say, a country in which a man and woman have everything to live for.

But wait. If today you asked Joe, in the heat of the battle, why he wanted to get to Berlin and Tokyo, why he wanted to keep America, America, you might get a very unexpected and sobering answer. He'd say that the biggest reason was that he wanted to vindicate and avenge G.I. Jim. And because G.I. Jim is the biggest reason today that Joe is fighting like a man possessed of devils and guarded by angels, we had better talk of him in the time that remains to us.

Who is G.I. Jim? Ask rather, who *was* G.I. Jim? He was Joe's pal, his buddy, his brother. Jim was the fellow who lived next door to you. But "he shall return no more to his house, neither shall his place know him any more." Jim was, you see, immobilized by enemy gunfire, immobilized for all eternity.

But Jim's last name was *not* Legion. You read casualty lists. You have seen Jim's last name there: Smith, Martof, Johnson, Chang, Novak, LeBlanc, Konstantakis, Yanada, O'Toole, Svendson, Sanchez, Potavin, Goldstein, Rossi, Nordal, Wroblewski, McGregor, Schneider, Jones. . . . You see, Jim was the grandson and great grandson of many nations. But he was the son of the United States of America. He was the defender of the republic, and the lover of liberty. And he died as his father died in 1918, and their fathers in 1898, 1861, in 1846 and in 1812, in 1776. He died to make a more perfect union, "that government of the people, by the people and for the people shall not perish from the earth."

His young bones bleach on the tropical roads of Bataan. A white cross marks his narrow grave on some Pacific island. His dust dulls the crimson of the roses that bloom in the ruins of an Italian village. The deserts of Africa, the jungles of Burma, the rice fields of China, the plains of Assam, the jagged hills of Attu, the cold depths of the Seven Seas, the very snows of the Arctic, are the richer for mingling with the mortal part of him. Today his blood flecks the foam of the waves that fall on the Normandy beachheads. He drops again and again amid the thunder of shells, while silently down on the tragic soil of France the white apple blossoms drift over him. Yes, even as it was in 1918. Or, nameless phrase, tantalizing and inscrutable as the misty black and bottomless pit of time, Jim is just "missing in action." Then all that marks him anywhere is a gold star in the window, and the tears that are silently shed for him.

There are many gold stars on the women sitting in these halls. To all who loved Jim, even more than to those who love Joe, everything we do and say here must be helpful and inspiring.

We are come together here to nominate a president who will make sure that Jim's sacrifice shall not prove useless in the years that lie ahead.

For a fighting man dies for the future as well as the past; to keep all that was fine of his country's yesterday, and to give it a chance for a finer tomorrow.

Do we here in this convention dare ask if Jim's heroic death in battle was historically inevitable? If this war might not have been averted? We know that this war was in the making everywhere in the world after 1918. In the making here, too. Might not skillful and determined American statesmanship have helped to unmake it all through the thirties? Or, when it was clear to our government that it was too late to avert war, might not truthful and fearless leadership have prepared us better for it in material and in morale, in arms and in aims?

These are bitter questions. And the answers to bitter questions belong to time's perspective. Being human, we Republicans are partisan. But being partisan, we risk being unjust if we try to answer these questions in days so fateful. But this, even as partisans, we dare say: the last twelve years have not been Republican years. Maybe Republican presidents during the twenties were overconfident that prosperity would last at home, and that sanity would prevail abroad. But it was not a Republican president who dealt with the visibly rising menaces of Hitler and Mussolini and Hirohito. Ours was not the administration that promised young Jim's mother and father and neighbors and friends economic security and peace. Yes, peace. No Republican president gave these promises which were kept to their ears, but broken in their hearts. For this terrible truth cannot be denied: these promises, which were given by a government that was elected again and again and again because it made them, lie quite as dead as young Jim lies now. Jim was the heroic heir of the unheroic Roosevelt decade: a decade of confusion and conflict that ended in war.

In war itself, Jim learned hard and challenging truths that his government was too soft and cynical, in peace, to tell him. In battle he learned that all life is risk; that a fellow has first to rely on himself, before his comrades can rely on him; he learned that perfect teamwork is possible only after a man is willing to stand up to the worst alone. Jim found out that a large part of his security lay in his own willingness to take a lot of responsibility for it. That being the case, he asked no more than the best tools, a chance to use his own brains in the pinches, and the kind of leaders who were willing to risk their skins a little, too, when the pinches came. Of course, all this knowledge, born in the struggle to survive, will be of more use to Joe, the veteran, than to Jim. For in the end Jim also learned that the only perfect democracy is the democracy of the dead.

But Jim did not complain too much about his government. Sure, mistakes, awful mistakes, had been made by his government. But Jim figured that anybody can make mistakes. Maybe his friends and neighbors had made them, too. How could his friends and neighbors tell that they had been going for some promises that could not, or should not, be kept? How could they tell that some of them were never spoken to be kept? Maybe they'd have talked differently, acted differently, voted differently, if they'd known all the facts. But maybe they wouldn't. Anyway, Jim has taken the rap for everyone, from the man in the White House, down to the man in the house around the corner. And it was O.K. with him. Jim was ready to pay with his life for his countrymen's mistakes, anytime, if it gave the homefolks and good old Joe and his family a fresh start on life, liberty, and the pursuit of happiness, in a world wiped clean of the Nazi marauders and Japanese spoilers.

If Jim could stand here and talk to you he'd say, "Listen, folks, the past wasn't perfect. But skip it. Get on with the business of making this old world better. . . . Take your hats off to the past, but take your coats off to the future. I didn't look back when I struck the beaches. Is it tougher at home for you fellows?"

This is what Jim would say if he could stand here and talk to you. Well, I suspect Jim is at this convention, although he is no longer, you understand, a republican or a democrat. But a man who dies to keep America America just might like to stay on a bit to see whether or not he's really succeeded. So if Jim were here, it might be the most natural thing in the other-world. Maybe he was brought here by some friend who knows his way around American presidential conventions. Yes, maybe he was brought here by General George Washington. All Americans know that the General's spirit has watched over every gathering where presidents have been picked for 147 years. . . .

Jim always knew that Washington so loved his country and the institutions that he helped to author, that he refused more than two terms. That was a tradition Washington's spirit never saw broken at any president-making gathering until it was broken by the man who promised in this very city twelve years ago that "happy days are here again," who promised peace, yes peace, to Jim's mother and father. . . .

Oh, yes, Jim and his friend, the father of his country, want us to choose well, as well as we know how here: they want us to choose a man who would rather tell the truth than be president; to choose a man who loves his country and its institutions more than he loves power. But they do not want us to pretend that any one republican, more than any one democrat is indispensable. They want us to think as Americans. And as Americans, they want us to raise here a "standard to which the wise and honest can repair." They know that the event, today as yesterday, is in the hands of God.

And this we will do, for Jim's sake. And then we can say, before all our fellow citizens, that his spirit and Washington's spirit will be happier here than at the Democratic Convention.

Then Jim can exultantly say:

I am the Risen Soldier, I have come
From a thousand towns, the city blocks
The factories, the fields of this fair land. . . .
Many am I,
Yet truly one, the Son of many streams
That poured their wealth into the common cup
The wide and golden cup of Liberty. . . .

I am the Risen Soldier; though I die
I shall live on and, living, still achieve
My country's mission—Liberty in Truth . . .

Lord, it is sweet to die—as as it were good
To Live, to strive for these United States,

Which, in Your wisdom, You have willed should be
A beacon to the world, a living shrine
Of Liberty and Charity and Peace.

It is as Americans that we are gathered here. We come to choose a president who need not apologize for the mistakes of the past but who will redeem them, who need not explain G.I. Jim's death but who will justify it. Apology and explanation must suffice for the next convention that meets in this city.

We Republicans are here to build a greater and freer America, not only for, but *with* millions of young, triumphant, boastful G.I. Joes, who are fighting their way home to us.

Let the next convention that meets here point to Joe's homecoming with foreboding. Let another party call Joe, who has saved us, "the terrible problem of the returned veteran." Another candidate, not ours, can hold his return as an economic club over the heads of the people. We are Americans! We say, "Joe, we welcome you. So hurry home, Joe, by way of Berlin and Tokyo. We need you to build this greater America!"

Eleanor Roosevelt
Defends the United Nations

"I warn you against the short-sighted and selfish men who are trying to distort the vision of the American people."

On the eve of Franklin Roosevelt's election as president in 1932, his wife was found weeping alone in a room far from celebrators. "Now I'll have no identity," she said. Of course, the future held just the opposite for this first lady, writer, lecturer, and, later, U.S. delegate to the United Nations.

An American emblem for women's independence, Eleanor Roosevelt (1884–1962) was a precedent breaker—dismaying and delighting political observers with her press conferences for women reporters, frequent travels around the country, and a penchant for speaking her mind, particularly on behalf of child welfare, civil rights, and other areas of social reform.

In this addres, delivered on July 23, 1952, seven years after FDR's death, she spoke in support of the United Nations before the Democratic National Convention in Chicago. Her remarks aimed squarely at "a small articulate minority"—those both in and outside her late husband's party—who advocated withdrawal from the peace-keeping organization. These "men who lack vision," she warns here, would lead the country "not to peace but to chaos."

The speech, widely cheered, widely circulated, loses some force on the printed page, yet offers an interesting glimpse into one of this first lady's most passionate causes. Her arguments for U.S. membership in the UN, drawn here against the backdrop of the Korean War, still resonate in American political circles, where the debate on U.S./UN relations goes unresolved.

———

I remember well, even though it seems a long time ago, hearing for the first time a statement and the reasons why, when the war ended, we must make another try to create another world organization to help us keep the peace of the world. This talk took place in my husband's study in the White House one evening during the bitter days of the last war when victory was not yet in sight.

My husband, discussing what would happen after the war, turned to a friend and said in effect "When this war is over and we have won it, as we will, we must apply the hard lessons learned in the war and in the failure of the League of Nations to the task of building a society of nations dedicated to enduring peace. There will be sacrifices and discouragements but we must not fail for we may never have another chance."

There have been sacrifices and discouragements, triumphs and setbacks. The United Nations is attempting to convert this last chance, carrying mankind's best hope, into an effective instrument that will enable our children and our children's children to maintain peace in their time. The path upon which we have set our course is not an easy one. The trail is often difficult to find. We must make our maps as we go along but we travel in good company with men and women of goodwill in the free countries of the world.

Without the United Nations our country would walk alone, ruled by fear, instead of confidence and hope. To weaken or hamstring the United Nations now, through lack of faith and lack of vision, would be to condemn ourselves to endless struggle for survival in a jungle world.

In examining what the UN has done, and what it is striving to do, it must be remembered that peace, like freedom, is elusive, hard to come by, harder to keep. It cannot be put into a purse or hip pocket and buttoned there to stay. To achieve peace we must recognize the historic truth that we can no longer live apart from the rest of the world. We must also recognize the fact that peace, like freedom, is not won once and for all. It is fought for daily, in many small acts, and is the result of many individual efforts.

These are days of shrinking horizons, a "neighborhood of nations though unhappily all of us are not as yet good neighbors."

We should remember that the UN is not a cure-all. It is only an instrument capable of effective action when its members have a will to make it work. It cannot be any better than the individual nations are. You often ask what can I, as an individual, do to help the U.S., to help in the struggle for a peaceful world.

I answer—make your country the best possible country for all its citizens to live in, and it will become a valuable member of the Neighborhood of Nations. This can only be done with home, community, representatives.

The UN is the machinery through which peace may be achieved and it is the responsibility of sixty nations and their delegations to make that machinery work. Yet you and I may carry the greatest responsibility because our national strength has given us opportunities for leadership among the nations of the free world.

The UN is the only machinery for the furtherance of peace that exists today. There is a small articulate minority in this country which advocates changing our national symbol which is the eagle to that of the ostrich and withdrawing from the UN. This minority reminds me of a story of a shortsighted and selfish man who put green goggles on his cow and fed her sawdust. The cow became sick and died. I warn you against the shortsighted and selfish men who are trying to distort the vision of the American people. We must have eagle eyes. These men who lack vision are poor in hope. They turn their back on the future and live in the past. They seek to weaken and destroy this world organization through their attacks on the UN. They are expressing a selfish, destructive approach which leads not to peace but to chaos and might eventually lead to World War Three. . . .

This brings us to the action taken by the UN which has brought sorrow into many American homes. The communist attack on Korea and the brilliant fight put up by our armies is a matter of history. When the attack occurred we had two choices. We could meet it or let aggression triumph by default and thereby invite further piecemeal conquests all over the globe. This inevitably would have led to World War Three just as the appeasement of Munich and the seizure of Czechoslovakia led to World War Two, the most destructive war in history.

Great sacrifices have been made in Korea by our soldiers, and at home by our mothers, wives, and sweethearts in support of this UN action. To a more limited extent the same sacrifices have been made by other member nations. There is torment and anguished waiting in many homes this very night, but at the same time there must be gratitude that our own land has been preserved from attack, and for all of us there must be pride in the proof of the staunchness and heroism of American men.

We pray for a just and lasting peace in Korea for the sake of the people of that land and for our own men and those soldiers of the United Nations fighting with them. We cannot hurry this peace until the communists agree to honest terms. If you ask the reason why our men are in Korea, I think it was perhaps best summed up by an American flying Ace, Major James Jabara, who upon returning to his home in Wichita, Kansas, in an interview was asked what his feelings were while fighting in Korea. Major Jabara said, "I fought in Korea so I would not have to fight on Main Street in Wichita."

Korea was not only the first successful application of collective security on the part of the UN to stop aggression, without provoking general war, but it has stimulated a free world to build up its defenses. It has not been as quick in the achievement of results as it would have been if the UN had been fully organized to put down any aggression. It has been impossible to organize that machinery as yet because two nations, the U.S. and USSR, haven't been able to come to an agreement as to how this collective security within the UN may be organized. We think the fault lies with the USSR because she will not see that without a planned method of disarmament and control of all weapons, adequately verified through inspection, we and many other nations in the world cannot feel safe. But at least through the UN we can go on with negotiations and pray for a pure heart and clean hands, which may eventually bring us the confidence even of the Soviet Union and lead us to the desired results.

In the UN we meet with the communists and it is fortunate this meeting place exists. We know we cannot relax our vigilance or stop our efforts to control the spread of communism. Their attacks on us in the UN have one great value—they keep us from forgetting our shortcomings or becoming apathetic in our efforts to improve democracy.

The UN has helped to keep the peace in many areas of the world, notably in Iran and Greece and Palestine and Indonesia, and Pakistan and India. These disputes might have spread into a general war and torn the free world apart and opened the way for communist expansion and another world war.

While the UN came into being under the present administration, and President Truman has been steadfast in his support of the organization, the UN would not be in existence today if it were not for strong bipartisan support in the beginning.

. . . I beg you to keep an open mind, never to forget the interests of your own country but to remember your own country may be able to make a contribution, which is valuable in the area of human rights and freedoms, in joining with other nations not merely in declarations but in covenants.

I returned not long ago from parts of the world where our attitude on human rights and freedoms affects greatly our leadership.

Some of you will probably be thinking that once upon a time the old lady speaking to you now did a tremendous amount of traveling around the United States. In fact, you may remember a cartoon showing two men down in a coal mine, one man saying to the other: "Gosh, here comes Eleanor. Now what is she doing—traveling around the world just making more trouble?"

In World War Two, when I visited so many hospitals in the Pacific, I was glad I had traveled so much through my own country and could say to a lonely boy far from home: "You came from Lubbock, Texas?" The boy's face would light up. "Yes ma'am. I remember when you were there." I can only hope that in the future there may be some little unexpected values which will come out of these latest travels, too.

I hope all our travels may serve the great common hope that through the United Nations peace may come to the world. . . .

Barbara Jordan
Argues for the Impeachment of Richard Nixon

"My faith in the Constitution is whole, it is complete, it is total."

A lawyer and the first black woman elected to the Texas state senate, Barbara Jordan (1936–1996) came to her country's attention on July 25, 1974, when she delivered this speech as a member of the U.S. House Judiciary Committee weighing impeachment of President Richard Nixon.

At the televised hearings, the thirty-eight-year-old Texas congresswoman read from notes, laying the Constitution—and the words of its framers—like a yardstick against the actions of Nixon and his aides. Schooled in debate, gifted with a sonorous voice, she spoke methodically, as was her style, overenunciating long words and phrases for emphasis ("We"—"the"—"people").

The speech, one of the most gripping and indelible moments of the Watergate years, led to Jordan's selection as keynote speaker of the Democratic National Convention in 1976—and again in 1992.

M r. Chairman, I join my colleague Mr. Rangel in thanking you for giving the junior members of this committee the glorious opportunity of sharing the pain of this inquiry.

Mr. Chairman, you are a strong man, and it has not been easy but we have tried as best we can to give you as much assistance as possible.

Earlier today we heard the beginning of the Preamble to the Constitution of the United States, "We, the people." It is a very eloquent beginning. But when that document was completed, on the seventeenth of September in 1787, I was not included in that "We, the people." I felt somehow for many years that George Washington and Alexander Hamilton just left me out by mistake. But through the process of amendment, interpretation, and court decision I have finally been included in "We, the people."

Today, I am an inquisitor. I believe hyperbole would not be fictional and would not overstate the solemnness that I feel right now. My faith in the Constitution is whole, it is complete, it is total. I am not going to sit here and be an idle spectator to the diminution, the subversion, the destruction of the Constitution.

"Who can so properly be the inquisitors for the nation as the representatives of the nation themselves?" (*Federalist*, no. 65.) The subject of its jurisdiction are those offenses which proceed from the misconduct of public men. That is what we are talking about. In other words, the jurisdiction comes from the abuse of violation of some public trust. It is wrong, I suggest, it is a misreading of the Constitution for any member here to assert that for a member to vote for an article of impeachment means that that member must be convinced that the president should be removed from office. The Constitution doesn't say that. The powers relating to impeachment are an essential check in the hands of this body, the legislature, against and upon the encroachment of the executive. In establishing the division between the two branches of the legislature, the House and the Senate, assigning to the one the right to accuse and to the other the right to judge, the framers of this Constitution were very astute. They did not make the accusers and the judges the same person.

We know the nature of impeachment. We have been talking about it awhile now. "It is chiefly designed for the president and his high ministers" to somehow be called into account. It is designed to "bridle" the executive if he engages in excesses. "It is designed as a method of national inquest into the conduct of public men." (Hamilton, *Federalist*, no. 65.) The framers confined in the Congress the power, if need be, to remove the president in order to strike a delicate balance between a president swollen with power and grown tyrannical, and preservation of the independence of the executive. The nature of impeachment is a narrowly channeled exception to the separation-of-powers maxim; the federal convention of 1787 said that. It limited impeachment to high crimes and misdemeanors and discounted and opposed the term "maladministration." "It is to be used only for great misdemeanors," so it was said in the North Carolina ratification convention. And in the Virginia ratification convention: "We do not trust our liberty to a particular branch. We need one branch to check the others."

The North Carolina ratification convention: "No one need be afraid that officers who commit oppression will pass with immunity."

"Prosecutions of impeachments will seldom fail to agitate the passions of the whole community," said Hamilton in the *Federalist Papers*, no. 65. "And to divide it into parties more or less friendly or inimical to the accused." I do not mean political parties in that sense.

The drawing of political lines goes to the motivation behind impeachment; but impeachment must proceed within the confines of the constitutional term "high crimes and misdemeanors."

Of the impeachment process, it was Woodrow Wilson who said that "nothing short of the grossest offenses against the plain law of the land will suffice to give them speed and effectiveness. Indignation so great as to overgrow party interest may secure a conviction; but nothing else can."

Common sense would be revolted if we engaged upon this process for insurance, campaign finance reform, housing, environmental protection, energy sufficiency, mass transportation. Pettiness cannot be allowed to stand in the face of such overwhelming problems. So today we are not being petty. We are trying to be big because the task we have before us is a big one.

This morning, in a discussion of the evidence, we were told that the evidence which purports to support the allegations of misuse of the CIA by the president is thin. We are told that that evidence is insufficient. What that recital of the evidence this morning did not include is what the president did know on June 23, 1972. The president did know that it was Republican money, that it was money from the Committee for the Re-Election of the President, which was found in the possession of one of the burglars arrested on June 17.

What the president did know on June 23 was the prior activities of E. Howard Hunt, which included his participation in the break-in of Daniel Ellsberg's psychiatrist, which included Howard Hunt's participation in the Dita Beard ITT affair, which included Howard Hunt's fabrication of cables designed to discredit the Kennedy administration.

We were further cautioned today that perhaps these proceedings ought to be delayed because certainly there would be new evidence forthcoming from the president. The committee subpoena is outstanding, and if the president wants to supply that material, the committee sits here.

The fact is that yesterday, the American people waited with great anxiety for eight hours, not knowing whether their president would obey an order of the Supreme Court of the United States.

At this point I would like to juxtapose a few of the impeachment criteria with some of the president's actions.

Impeachment criteria: James Madison, from the Virginia ratification convention. "If the president be connected in any suspicious manner with any person and there be grounds to believe that he will shelter him, he may be impeached."

We have heard time and time again that the evidence reflects payment to the defendants of money. The president had knowledge that these funds were being paid and that these were funds collected for the 1972 presidential campaign.

We know that the president met with Mr. Henry Petersen twenty-seven times to discuss matters related to Watergate and immediately thereafter met with the very persons who were implicated in the information Mr. Petersen was receiving and transmitting to the president. The words are "if the president be connected in any suspicious manner with any person and there be grounds to believe that he will shelter that person, he may be impeached."

Justice Story: "Impeachment is intended for occasional and extraordinary cases where a superior power acting for the whole people is put into operation to protect their rights and rescue their liberties from violations."

We know about the Huston plan. We know about the break-in of the psychiatrist's office. We know that there was absolute complete direction in August 1971 when the president instructed Ehrlichman to "do whatever is necessary." This instruction led to a surreptitious entry into Dr. Fielding's office.

"Protect their rights." "Rescue their liberties from violation."

The South Carolina ratification convention impeachment criteria: those are impeachable "who behave amiss or betray their public trust."

Beginning shortly after the Watergate break-in and continuing to the present time, the president has engaged in a series of public statements and actions designed to thwart the lawful investigation by government prosecutors. Moreover, the president has made public announcements and assertions bearing on the Watergate case which the evidence will show he knew to be false.

These assertions, false assertions, impeachable, those who misbehave. Those who "behave amiss or betray their public trust."

James Madison again at the Constitutional Convention: "A president is impeachable if he attempts to subvert the Constitution."

The Constitution charges the president with the task of taking care that the laws be faithfully executed, and yet the president has counseled his aides to commit perjury, willfully disregarded the secrecy of grand jury proceedings, concealed surreptitious entry, attempted to compromise a federal judge while publicly displaying his cooperation with the processes of criminal justice.

"A president is impeachable if he attempts to subvert the Constitution."

If the impeachment provision in the Constitution of the United States will not reach the offenses charged here, then perhaps that eighteenth-century Constitution should be abandoned to a twentieth-century paper shredder. Has the president committed offenses and planned and directed and acquiesced in a course of conduct which the Constitution will not tolerate? That is the question. We know that. We know the question. We should now forthwith proceed to answer the question. It is reason, and not passion, which must guide our deliberations, guide our debate, and guide our decision.

Margaret Thatcher
Takes Up the Leadership of Her Party

"Let me give you my vision . . ."

Born in Lincolnshire, England, Margaret Hilda Roberts Thatcher became the first woman to lead Britain's Conservative Party after she defeated Edward Heath in 1975. "I am a conviction politician," said the stalwart conservative, fervently opposed to the "consensus policies" of moderate and liberal Tories that had long dominated her party. Soon, Thatcherism—an admixture of tax cuts, monetarism, privatization, and an unapologetic assertion of Victorian values—began to take shape.

On October 10, 1975, at the Conservative Party Conference in Blackpool, the free-enterprise enthusiast laid out the Thatcherite vision in her first speech as Party leader. The Socialist Labour government was her villain: socialism, she says in these excerpts, is an encumbrance to progress and economic recovery; conservatism, a wide-open path to free markets and personal independence.

The speech was emphatic, effective, and interrupted throughout by cheers, shouts, and foot-stamping. The new leader gave her party hope, and became prime minister in 1979 when Conservatives returned to power.

. . . W henever I visit communist countries their politicians never hesitate to boast about their achievements. They know them all by heart; they reel off the facts and figures, claiming this is the rich harvest of the communist system. Yet they are not prosperous as we in the West are prosperous, and they are not free as we in the West are free.

Our capitalist system produces a far higher standard of prosperity and happiness because it believes in incentive and opportunity, and because it is founded on human dignity and freedom. Even the Russians have to go to a capitalist country— America—to buy enough wheat to feed their people—and that after more than fifty years of a State-controlled economy. Yet they boast incessantly, while we, who have so much more to boast about, forever criticize and decry.

Is it not time we spoke up for our way of life? After all, no Western nation has to build a wall round itself to keep its people in.

So let us have no truck with those who say the free enterprise system has failed. What we face today is not a crisis of capitalism but of socialism. No country can flourish if its economic and social life is dominated by nationalization and State control.

The cause of our shortcomings does not, therefore, lie in private enterprise. Our problem is not that we have too little socialism. It is that we have too much. If only the Labour Party in this country would act like Social Democrats in West Germany! If only they would stop trying to prove their socialist virility by relentlessly nationalizing one industry after another!

Of course, a halt to further State control will not on its own restore our beliefs in ourselves, because something else is happening to this country. We are witnessing a deliberate attack on our values, a deliberate attack on those who wish to promote merit and excellence, a deliberate attack on our heritage and our great past, and there are those who gnaw away at our national self-respect, rewriting British history as centuries of unrelieved gloom, oppression, and failure—as days of hopelessness, not days of hope. And others, under the shelter of our education system, are ruthlessly attacking the minds of the young. Everyone who believes in freedom must be appalled at the tactics employed by the Far Left in the systematic destruction of the North London Polytechnic: blatant tactics of intimidation designed to undermine the fundamental beliefs and values of every student, tactics pursued by people who are the first to insist on their own civil rights while seeking to deny them to the rest of us.

We must not be bullied or brainwashed out of our beliefs. No wonder so many of our people, some of the best and the brightest, are depressed and talking of emigrating. Even so, I think they are wrong. They are giving up too soon. Many of the things we hold dear are threatened as never before, but none has yet been lost, so stay here, stay and help us defeat socialism so that the Britain you have known may be the Britain your children will know.

These are the two great challenges of our time—the moral and political challenge, and the economic challenge. They have to be faced together and we have to master them both.

What are our chances of success? It depends on what kind of people we are. What kind of people are we? We are the people that in the past made Great Britain the workshop of the world, the people who persuaded others to buy British, not by begging them to do so but because it was best.

We are a people who have received more Nobel Prizes than any other nation except America, and head for head we have done better than America, twice as well in fact.

We are the people who, among other things, invented the computer, the refrigerator, the electric motor, the stethoscope, rayon, steam turbine, stainless steel, the tank, television, penicillin, radar, the jet engine, hovercraft, float glass and carbon fibers, et cetera—and the best half of Concorde.

We export more of what we produce than either West Germany, France, Japan, or the United States, and well over ninety percent of these exports come from private enterprise. It is a triumph for the private sector and all who work in it, and let us say so loud and clear.

With achievements like that who can doubt that Britain can have a great future, and what our friends abroad want to know is whether that future is going to happen.

Well, how can we Conservatives make it happen? Many of the details have already been dealt with in the Conference debates. But policies and programs should not just be a list of unrelated items. They are part of a total vision of the kind of life we want for our country and our children.

Let me give you my vision: a man's right to work as he will, to spend what he earns, to own property, to have the State as servant and not as master—these are the British inheritance. They are the essence of a free country and on that freedom all our other freedoms depend.

But we want a free economy, not only because it guarantees our liberties, but also because it is the best way of creating wealth and prosperity for the whole country, and it is this prosperity alone which can give us the resources for better services for the community, better services for those in need.

By their attack on private enterprise, this Labour Government has made certain that there will be next to nothing available for improvements in our social services over the next few years. We must get private enterprise back on the road to recovery, not merely to give people more of their own money to spend as they choose, but to have more money to help the old and the sick and the handicapped. And the way to recovery is through profits, good profits today leading to high investment, leading to well-paid jobs, leading to a better standard of living tomorrow. No profits mean no investment and that means a dying industry geared to yesterday's world, and that means fewer jobs tomorrow. . . .

We are now seeing the full consequences of nearly twenty months of Labour Government. They have done the wrong things at the wrong time in the wrong way, and they have been a disaster for this country. . . .

Some socialists seem to believe that people should be numbers in a State computer. We believe they should be individuals. We are all unequal. No one, thank heaven, is quite like anyone else, however much the socialists may pretend otherwise. We believe that everyone has the right to be unequal. But to us, every human being is equally important. Engineers, miners, manual workers, shop assistants, farmworkers, postmen, house-wives—these are the essential foundations of our society, and without them there would be no nation. But there are others with special gifts who should also have their chance, because if the adventurers who strike out in new directions in science, technology, medicine, commerce, and industry are hobbled, there can be no advance. The spirit of envy can destroy; it can never build. Everyone must be allowed to develop the abilities he knows he has within him, and she knows she has within her, in the way they choose.

Freedom to choose is something we take for granted until it is in danger of being taken away. Socialist Governments set out perpetually to restrict the area of choice, and Conservative Governments to increase it. We believe that you become a responsible citizen by making decisions for yourself, not by having them made for you. But they are made for you by Labour all right!

Shirley Chisholm
Says Vote for the Individual, Not the Party

---

*"We are looking for any party and any person
who will work to meet our needs."*

In 1968, "Fighting Shirley Chisholm" (b. 1924), a Democrat from Brooklyn, became the first black woman elected to Congress and, four years later, the first to campaign for America's highest office. "I ran for the presidency, despite hopeless odds, to demonstrate sheer will and refusal to accept the status quo," she later wrote. George McGovern became her party's nominee.

Throughout Chisholm's congressional tenure—she retired in 1983—she described her politics as "unbought and unbossed" (the title she gave her 1970 autobiography) and rejected party label as a dictate for how she or anyone else should vote. That was the theme of this speech, delivered on June 24, 1978, in New York, to the Independent Black Women's Caucus.

Chisholm's style is trenchant, unabashedly direct—"we've been taken for granted by one party and written off by another." The minority vote has power, she argues; "the time has come" to exercise it.

While I am a Democrat, most of the time—as you all know quite well—I act, think, and vote independently. And though I am a Democrat, I will no longer ask my brothers and sisters to vote for any man or any woman because of the party designation that attaches to their name.

In view of the current status of black folks in this country, we need to reevaluate into which basket we put our eggs—and how many. For we have found—do I need to say it?—we have found that the fox gets into the henhouse whenever we look away.

Now we've been taken—for granted and otherwise—far too often. We've been drawn in by big words, promises, and more promises. Yet the only time we see many of our elected officials is when they come around at election time.

Ever since the demise of Herbert Hoover and the rise of Franklin Delano Roosevelt and his New Deal, we've been taken for granted by one party and written off by the other.

Well, it's taken us some time to catch up, because as Benjamin Mays said: "He who starts behind in the race for life must run faster or forever remain behind."

Black has become a beautiful color not because it is loved, as James Baldwin says, but because it is feared.

And this urgency on the part of blacks is not to be forgotten.

We are feared because we have demonstrated the political power we possess. We have the ability by our sheer numbers to elect or defeat candidates.

This fact scares the more insecure members of our society. New realities always upset the apple cart, the status quo. And it is precisely this new reality which is responsible for the courting of the minority vote.

In many ways, this knowledge, this sophistication of the political process is a recent development.

In fact, the presidential election of 1976 stands as a crisp, clear symbol of our emerging influence. Just as the oil-producing countries of the world were not fully aware of their power until they cut off their exports of energy products in

1973–1974, the black American could not see clearly the inherent power of the ballot to influence *national* elections until the 1976 results were analyzed.

Well, my friends, the results are in, and we now see a concerted effort on the part of the Republican party to bring black Americans into their ranks.

Why? *Because they need us.*

The competition between parties for the minority vote is healthy competition which can only benefit our two-party system.

And in view of the current status of blacks in this society, with unemployment among our young people running above 40 percent, I can see no situation to preclude the support by blacks for candidates—be they Democrat or Republican—*who have something to offer us* in return for our votes.

When there is economic recession—as there is in the minority communities—there is protest. And protest is an important characteristic of voting behavior.

In 1892 and again during the panic of World War I reactions helped the Republicans gain power. But the Great Depression following the Hoover Administration brought a violent reaction against Republicans and revived the Democratic party.

In fact, that development has been seen as the most far-reaching realignment since the Civil War: It gave the Democrats an opportunity to become the majority party . . . and the Republicans so far have not recovered.

More recently we have witnessed the debacles of the past ten years or so in the public and private sectors, bribes, payoffs, world scandals, causing governments to fall.

We have witnessed the benign neglect of our young people through an education system that doesn't educate and a justice system that doesn't mete out justice fairly.

And what has happened to us since the 1976 election? Well, the administration just last week issued a report of presidential appointments which says that some ten percent of the jobs went to blacks and eighteen percent went to women. I suppose that's some progress.

But what I also know is this: eighteen months ago the campaign cry was jobs for the unemployed. Economic justice. But at some point someone decided that we no longer had an unemployment problem in this country—we have an inflation problem. Well, I don't know where these folks have been looking, but if they could come up to Brooklyn to my district I could show them that nothing has changed . . . At least nothing has changed for the better. None of the folks where I live are any better off than they were in November of 1976.

I guess we better ask ourselves whether our souls are on ice. That is, since we put a Democrat in the White House, are we now to be written off, to be again taken for granted?

My friends, we must not accept the notion that we are "better off."

Can anyone say today in 1978 that eleven o'clock on Sunday morning is still not the most segregated hour in America.

But we are not seeking to get into a church. We no longer desire to sit at lunch counters. We are seeking our economic freedom.

It has been suggested that blacks should stay with the Democratic party because, historically, Democrats have embodied an ideology, a philosophy, of tolerance, acceptance and understanding.

Ideology implies some coherence of attitudes, beliefs, which can give meaning to a spectrum of matters, social, political or otherwise. The assumption is one of a set of relationships which allows a person to make sense out of events.

By that definition, no contemporary political party ideology is acceptable en toto.

So what is it that we must do? To whom or to what organization or institution shall we appeal?

Now I know very well after ten years of experience in the Congress that battles in politics are never won on the merits of the case. What may begin as a discussion of the right and wrong, the good and evil, the moral and immoral, soon deteriorates into a bottom line: are your ducks lined up? To put it more accurately, have you got the votes?

And let us tell it like it really is. Let us be straight and up front.

We want from the Republicans and the Democrats attention and a commitment to our problems. We will give our votes and support to individuals—not political parties—*in return for* their support of programs which benefit *us*. Can I make it any clearer?

The events of the past two weeks within the state of New York are telling. Where are we in 1978? We have only to look at the state nominating convention.

What does it mean when the party of the people, which says it seeks an ethnically balanced state ticket, leaves out the most visible ethnic group?

What does it mean when a black state senator receives a standing ovation at the convention—and nothing else—from the party of the people?

What does it mean when the party of the people nominates a state ticket which includes no black and no woman?

Let me share with you some thoughts of Dr. Benjamin Mays:

If you are ignorant, the world is going to cheat you.
If you are weak, the world is going to kick you.
If you are a coward, the world is going to keep you
running.

My friends, let the word go forth to all who must seek our votes:

We are not ignorant, we are not weak, and we are not cowardly. We will no longer be cheated or kicked around. And the only running we are going to do is running toward the power that must be seized and held to control our destinies.

Not failure, but low aim, is sin.

We now have to push ourselves, drive ourselves to work for those people who commit to us. And we must work against those who deny us.

Let the word go forth that we know what we must do. We are at a critical juncture and we dare not let it pass. The black political leadership looks at the Democratic leadership at state levels in the nation because the state party machinery usually has a stranglehold on the potential destinies of minority citizens.

And as the competition between parties becomes sharper, we must continue to recognize that the day-to-day happenings in the lives of minority citizens will be enhanced or sublimated dependent on the support that is given or withheld. . . .

And those of us in this room know all too well that whatever is given to us is almost always a trap.

My friends . . . the time has come for people of color in America to recognize that the political parties which remain in power are those that adapt themselves to change and whose programs are pragmatic and flexible.

The time has come for us to turn away from the packaging and labeling and sloganisms which have been thrust upon us.

The time has come for us to deal with the political fact that there are no longer any substitutes for success and fulfillment in this life. Because it is no longer comforting to believe that failure down here below will be rewarded somehow above.

The time has come . . . and let the word go forth . . . that the sleeping giant has awakened . . . that we are going to flex our muscles . . . that people of color, be they Republicans, Democrats, or independent thinkers . . . that we will no longer look only to the label or party designation.

We are looking for any party and any person who will work to meet our needs.

Because, my friends, for all too many Americans, *freedom is just another word for nothing left to lose.**

---

*A phrase from the popular sixties folk song "Me and Bobby McGee."

Jeane Kirkpatrick
Excoriates the San Francisco Democrats

"The election of Ronald Reagan marked an end to the dismal period of retreat and decline."

In 1979, a Georgetown University political science professor came to the attention of Ronald Reagan when she published a *Commentary* magazine article titled "Dictatorships and Double Standards," a critical review of foreign policy under Jimmy Carter. A year later, the newly elected Reagan appointed Jeane Kirkpatrick (b. 1926) U.S. ambassador to the United Nations.

On August 20, 1984, Ambassador Kirkpatrick, a Democrat, spoke before the Republican National Convention in Dallas— spiriting the Grand Old Party with this commanding keynote in support of Reagan's reelection. "Lean on 'em, Jeane!" read signs from the convention floor as she railed against her fellow Democrats, chiefly those who had dominated the rostrum at the Democratic convention in San Francisco. "San Francisco Democrats," were those who "did not seem to notice much, care much, or do much" about foreign policy—not at their convention, not during their last turn at the White House.

Pointing to a litany of Reagan first-term accomplishments (restoration of American pride, of "economic and military strength"), Kirkpatrick sought to draw Democrats away from nominee Walter Mondale and a party that, in her view, was soft on defense, rife with desultory policies, and eager to "blame

America first"; "but then they always blame America first," she says here in a skillfully repeated phrase. The speech roused the convention—its themes resonated for the remainder of the campaign—and Ronald Reagan swept to a landslide victory.

———•—•———

T his is the first Republican convention I have ever attended. I am grateful that you should invite me, a lifelong Democrat; on the other hand, I realize you are today inviting many lifelong Democrats to join our common cause. . . .

I shall speak tonight of foreign affairs, even though the other party's convention barely touched the subject. When the San Francisco Democrats treat foreign affairs as an afterthought, as they did, they behaved less like a dove or a hawk than like an ostrich—convinced it could shut out the world by hiding its head in the sand.

Today, foreign policy is central to the security, to the freedom, to the prosperity, even to the survival of the United States. And *our* strength, for which we make many sacrifices, is essential to the independence and freedom of our allies and of our friends.

Ask yourself, what would become of Europe if the United States withdrew? What would become of Africa if Europe fell under Soviet domination? What would become of Europe if the Middle East came under Soviet control? What would become of Israel, if surrounded by Soviet client states? What would become of Asia if the Philippines or Japan fell under Soviet domination? What would become of Mexico if Central America became a Soviet satellite? What then could the United States do?

These are questions the San Francisco Democrats have not answered. These are questions they have not even *asked*.

The United States cannot remain an open, democratic society if we are left alone—a garrison state in a hostile world. We need independent nations with which to trade, to consult, and cooperate. We need friends and allies with whom to share the pleasures and protection of our civilization. We cannot, therefore, be indifferent to the subversion of others' independence or to the development of new weapons by our adversaries or of new vulnerabilities by our friends.

The last Democratic administration did not seem to notice much, care much, or do much about these matters. And at home and abroad, our country slid into deep trouble. North and South, East and West, our relations deteriorated.

The Carter administration's motives were good, but their policies were inadequate, uninformed, and mistaken. They made things worse, not better. Those who had least, suffered most. Poor countries grew poorer. Rich countries grew poorer, too. The United States grew weaker.

Meanwhile, the Soviet Union grew stronger. The Carter administration's unilateral "restraint" in developing and deploying new weapon systems was accompanied by an unprecedented Soviet buildup, military and political.

The Soviets, working on the margins and through the loopholes of SALT I, developed missiles of stunning speed and accuracy and targeted the cities of our friends in Europe. They produced weapons capable of wiping out our land-based missiles. And then, feeling strong, Soviet leaders moved with boldness and skill to exploit their new advantages. Facilities were completed in Cuba during those years that permit Soviet nuclear submarines to roam our coasts, that permit Soviet planes to fly reconnaissance missions over the eastern United States, and permit Soviet electronic surveillance to monitor our telephone calls and telegrams.

Those were the years the Ayatollah Khomeini came to power in Iran, while in Nicaragua the Sandinistas developed a one-party dictatorship based on the Cuban model.

From the fall of Saigon in 1975 until January 1981, Soviet influence expanded dramatically—into Laos, Cambodia, Afghanistan, Angola, Ethiopia, Mozambique, South Yemen, Libya, Syria, Aden, Congo, Madagascar, Seychelles, and Grenada. Soviet bloc forces sought to guarantee what they call the "irreversibility" of their newfound influence and to stimulate insurgencies in a dozen other places. During this period, the Soviet Union invaded Afghanistan, murdered its president, and began a ghastly war against the Afghan people.

The American people were shocked by these events. We were greatly surprised to learn of our diminished economic and military strength; we were demoralized by the treatment of our hostages in Iran, and we were outraged by harsh attacks on the United States in the United Nations. As a result, we lost confidence in ourselves and in our government.

Jimmy Carter looked for an explanation for all these problems and thought he found it in the American people. But the people knew better. It was not malaise we suffered from, it was Jimmy Carter—and Walter Mondale.

And so in 1980 the American people elected a very different president. The election of Ronald Reagan marked an end to the dismal period of retreat and decline. His inauguration, blessed by the simultaneous release of our hostages, signaled an end to the most humiliating episode in our national history.

The inauguration of President Reagan signaled a reaffirmation of historic American ideals. Ronald Reagan brought to the presidency confidence in the American experience confidence in the legitimacy and success of American institutions; confidence in the decency of the American people, and confidence in the relevance of our experience to the rest of the world.

That confidence has proved contagious. Our nation's subsequent recovery in domestic and foreign affairs, the restoration of our economic and military strength, has silenced talk of inevitable American decline and reminded the world of the advantages of freedom.

President Reagan faced a stunning challenge, and he met it. In the three and one-half years since his inauguration, the United States has grown stronger, safer, more confident, *and we are at peace.* . . .

And at each step of the way, the same people who were responsible for America's decline have insisted that the president's policies would fail.

They said we could never deploy missiles to protect Europe's cities. But today Europe's cities enjoy that protection.

They said it would never be possible to hold elections in El Salvador, because the people were too frightened and the country too disorganized. But the people of El Salvador proved them wrong, and today President Napoléon Duarte has impressed the democratic world with his skillful, principled leadership.

They said we could not use America's strength to help others—Sudan, Chad, Central America, the Gulf states, the Caribbean nations—without being drawn into war. But we have helped others resist Soviet, Libyan, and Cuban subversion, *and we are at peace.*

They said that saving Grenada from totalitarianism and terror was the wrong thing to do—they didn't blame Cuba or the Communists for threatening American students and murdering Grenadans—they blamed the United States instead. But then, somehow, they always blame America first.

When our marines, sent to Lebanon on a multinational peacekeeping mission with the consent of the United States Congress, were murdered in their sleep, the "blame America first crowd" did not blame the terrorists who murdered the marines, they blamed the United States. But then, they always blame America first.

When the Soviet Union walked out of arms control negotiations, and refused even to discuss the issues, the San Francisco Democrats did not blame Soviet intransigence. They blamed the United States. But then, they always blame America first.

When Marxists dictators shoot their way to power in Central America, the San Francisco Democrats do not blame the guerrillas and their Soviet allies, they blame United States policies of one hundred years ago. But then, they always blame America first.

The American people know better. They know that Ronald Reagan and the United States did not cause the Marxist dictatorship in Nicaragua, or the repression of Poland, or the brutal new offensives in Afghanistan, or the destruction of the Korean airliner, or new attacks on religious and ethnic groups in the Soviet Union, or the jamming of Western broadcasts, or the denial of Jewish emigration, or the brutal imprisonment of Anatoly Shcharansky and Ida Nudel, or the obscene treatment of Andrei Sakharov and Elena Bonner, or the re-Stalinization of the Soviet Union.

The American people also know that it is dangerous to blame ourselves for terrible problems we did not cause. They understand just as the distinguished French writer Jean-François Revel understands the danger of endless self-criticism and self-denigration. He wrote, "Clearly, a civilization that feels guilty for everything it is and does will lack the energy and conviction to defend itself."

With the election of Ronald Reagan, the American people declared to the world that we *have* the necessary energy and conviction to defend ourselves as well as a deep commitment to peace.

And now, the American people, proud of our country, proud of our freedom, proud of ourselves, will reject the San Francisco Democrats and send Ronald Reagan back to the White House.

PART 9

COMMENCEMENTS

Gloria Steinem
Defines a New Kind of Humanism

*"We have had five thousand years of patriarchy
and racism. Perhaps we have a chance for five
thousand years of humanism . . ."*

Gloria Steinem (b. 1934) had a busy year in 1971: she co-founded the National Women's Political Caucus; helped ready the launch of *Ms.* magazine; and spoke deliberately and prolifically on behalf of women's rights, Democratic politics, and racial justice. She also delivered this address on May 30, 1971, to the graduating class of Smith College, in Northampton, Massachusetts.

Steinem graduated from Smith in 1956, after a difficult childhood spent caring for an emotionally ill mother, and gained fame as a journalist in 1963 after going undercover as a Playboy Bunny to expose the objectification of women. She regretted the decision, convinced it had cost her more serious assignments; but soon her political journalism flourished—as did her activism. By the 1970s, Steinem had emerged as a leading spokesperson of the feminist movement—despite a gripping fear of public speaking.

In her Smith speech, Steinem is reflective but direct. She wants, she says, to "say to you some of the things I wish so desperately someone had said to me." Those "things" come wrapped in a theme—that life's miscreant, she tells them, is "the patriarchal and racist system under which we continue to live," and women must assert themselves against it.

Only the fifth woman commencement speaker since the college opened in 1875, Steinem sees reason to admonish her alma mater, but also reason to praise the class of 1971—because "in honoring a female commencement speaker," she says, "you are really honoring yourselves."

Friends and sisters: It's strange to come back to my own college as a commencement speaker; a little unsettling for me. At our graduation ceremonies in 1956, when I sat before this platform in cap and gown exactly as you sit before me now, I had no ambitions nor even such dreams.

Had I been asked why not, I would not have known the answer. "Because speaking at commencements is for other people," I might have said, providing I took the question seriously at all. And in my head, I would have pictured a man behind this podium, a man probably old and definitely white. I had internalized, without conscious thought and without formal instruction, the racist and sexist values around me.

The non-white men and female human beings I had seen in everyday life were usually dependent on acceptance by white men in some overt or subtle way. I didn't look like the ruling class; I was maybe even biologically and therefore immutably inferior to it (unlike black men whom one insisted, if only intellectually, were just as good). And that was that.

Of course, no one asked me why my imagination couldn't stretch to commencement speaking, any more than they asked me why I didn't consider being a politician, a business executive, an engineer, or even a writer. The dark fifties, I am afraid, were not brightened by much encouragement of women to be ambitious or autonomous or to dream unfeminine dreams. A more representative question was asked me by a vocational adviser when I brought up the subject of law school. "Why study three extra years and end up in the back room of some law firm doing research and typing," she said, with great good sense, "when you can graduate from Smith College and do research and typing right away?"

Smith did not invent the fifties any more than it invented the patriarchal and racist system under which we continue to live. There have been many foresighted and courageous individuals who have worked to make this campus a more human place than the world around it. In my day, for instance, there was not one black woman in the class, even though two-thirds of the applicants from the area around Washington, D.C., where I lived, were black.

When I asked a professor here why the black women had not been accepted, he explained that one had to accept only the strongest and the most outstanding, because it was going to be so hard for them in later life because there were not enough educated black men to go around. It's interesting, isn't it, how often racist arguments are used to support sexist standards and vice versa. In fact, there was not one black or nonwhite human being on the faculty or in the administration, and Smith, a college with feminist beginnings, was so lost to them that the administration offered, as a supposed inducement to prospective students, that the faculty was 75 percent male. The main excuse for educating us at all was that we would then educate our children. Indeed, the assumption was that we ourselves were children; creatures who were rarely encouraged to use in the real world all the knowledge being stuffed into our heads; creatures who were punished if they were not in their houses every week night by 10:15 P.M.

As you can see, much has changed. Through scholarship and recruitment programs, we white women are less ghettoized here now. Black women are joining us in growing numbers and may even eventually represent at least the percentage that black

Americans do, at least that percentage in the overall population. Some restitution is being made for the fact that here, as at most American institutions, we have been studying white history, a history written for, by, and about white men. There is a Black Studies program, and I understand that Smith is now the only women's college to offer a Black Studies major. I am very proud of that.

We are even beginning to learn something about ourselves as women. I didn't know until last year, for instance, that the library had a fine collection of feminist literature. I believe women even use it now. There are a few Women's Studies courses, though still far short of the potential major and full department that Women's Studies should be. We are even beginning to recognize that women come here as adults, that if they chose not to enter college, they would be voting for a president, working for a living, and becoming parents at the same age. Women students have many fewer rules now, and hopefully soon they will be totally in charge of their own lives. College, after all, should be the beginning of adulthood, not an artificial prolongation of life as a child.

But there has been a larger change of consciousness in the last few years, a change in which Smith, as a women's college, should have been taking a lead. We have been discovering, in all areas of academic study and personal experience, that the so-called masculine-feminine differences are largely societal, not biological at all; that those differences have application only to reproduction (supposing one chooses to reproduce), and that they have no meaning for education, job selection, or lifestyle; indeed, that the myths of feminine inferiority have been used largely to suppress the talents and strengths of half the human race. . . .

I thought before I came here, that Smith, with its feminist beginnings, would be turning out whole human beings; that this would be a free place where repressive myths were being examined. The myth, for instance, that men need fulfilling work in addition to marriage and children, but that women, for some mysterious reason, do not. I had written a whole Utopian speech about new social and political forms that would grow from this change. I thought we had understood the ultimate truth: that our inferior position all these hundreds of years had not been ordained by God or by biology, but was and is, in the purest sense, political.

For two days, I have been talking here to women students, and to women faculty, and to faculty wives, and I've discovered that women here are still sometimes trapped into so-called feminine occupations; that the vocational office still routinely asks how many words per minute you can type, though the vocational office of Amherst or Harvard does not; that the male supremacist teachings of Freud may be dead, I hope, but that some professors are still condescending to us out of minds that Freud and other male supremacists have formed; that the faculty is still 70 percent male and that some of the females on it have doubts about the way in which tenure is awarded or part-time female teachers are used; that encouragement of women's studies has often had to come from students or faculty wives and not from the College itself; that there is little emphasis on informing women of the real prejudice that they will meet, much less giving them philosophical and tactical tools to fight; that there is still fear of so-called abnormal sexual behavior, whatever that means, whether it is too heterosexual or not heterosexual enough; that women students are still made to feel they have to worry more about combining marriage and a career than men do. The sense of a wide range of alternatives for women has increased, but not enough. We are still being given skills and knowledge, but not encouraged to use those skills and knowledge in the world as whole human beings.

So let me say to you some of the things that I wish so desperately someone had said to me. It would have saved me so much time and heartache.

First of all, we have been reading, for the most part, white male history. As Virginia Woolf once said, bitterly, "Anonymous was a woman." It seems to me in both high school and college, we generally started the study of history about the time of Charlemagne, right smack in a period of patriarchy and racism. In that period, so graciously dismissed as prehistory, however, it turns out that we had such a thing as a gynocracy. Indeed, for an earlier part of human history, more or less from perhaps 12,000 to 8,000 B.C., there's a lot of reason to believe that women were certainly equal and possibly superior; that women were worshiped *because* we had the children. We somehow have allowed ourselves to be talked into the notion that the bearing of children is an inferior function, but in those earlier days it was worshiped. Men's ceremonies imitated it. . . . And this continued until the discovery of paternity, a day I like to imagine as a big light bulb over somebody's head, and they sang, "Oh, that's why!" Scholars, in fact, are now beginning to believe that women discovered paternity several years before they told anybody about it because they wanted to preserve their independence.

With the discovery of paternity, with the end of the notion that women bore fruit like trees until they were ripe, came a whole lot of institutions we will readily recognize: the idea of ownership, for instance, of property and of children; the origin of marriage, which was really locking women up long enough to make sure who the father was; and the subjugation of women as the primary political subjugation. We were the means of production—the original means of production. And we were locked up in the institution of marriage and for the bearing of children as the notion that the state owns the body of a woman, a notion we still see in our abortion laws. As that grew, women became the first subjugated group and the group which all others were to follow in pattern. We were given the jobs to do that the men did not want to do. . . . That is still the definition of feminine work—jobs which men do not want to do.

As other tribes and races were brought into this situation, they were, as captured peoples, given the role of women. So there has always been a very close parallel between all second-class groups, and it is especially visible in this country with females and the largest second-class group, which is blacks. I don't mean to compare the suffering. No one would compare the suffering, and Gunnar Myrdal, who made this parallel thirty years ago, did not do that. Black people lose their lives and white women more often lose their identities. But there are many, many parallels when it comes to myths. We are both supposed to have smaller brains, passive natures—childlike natures, to be unable to govern ourselves—God forbid we should try to govern a white male; to have special job skills—we are awfully good at detail work as long as it is poorly paid detail work—when it's brain surgery, we are suddenly not so good anymore. . . .

If we are to change this society in the deepest kind of way, then all of us who have been marked for cheap labor, all of us must stand up together and say, "No more." We must resist those efforts that are made to turn us against each other. . . . In many parts of the country, for instance, there are political slates of the outs—white women, black women, black men, Puerto Ricans, Chicanos—who are forming slates together to try to break the hold of the white males on the state legislatures and on other political bodies.

We must realize something that we haven't up to now . . . that women are sisters, that we have many of the same problems; that the class divisions that the men have made for themselves apply to men but don't apply to us. The wife of a rich man is not usually a powerful person; she is often kept as an ornament and a child. She often comes to realize in the middle of the Movement that she may have more in common with her maid than she does with her husband. There are housewives who are suffering from a system designed to give the employer two for the price of one. . . . Housewives and domestics are organizing together for a decent wage so that they don't have to end up begging or asking for alimony—which in our system is more like war reparations. . . .

It is a common cause clearly with black women because . . . most of the women who are poor are members of some minority group, and they suffer even more from the policies that deny them legal abortions; that send them to their deaths in botched abortions at a rate greater each year than American men die in Vietnam. Abortion is our number one health problem . . .

I think black women are often an example to white women; they have had to be stronger and more courageous than we, and also black men tend to understand this desire for freedom and equality on the part of all women better than white men. As Bobby Seale says, "In a Panther house everybody does the dishes and everybody sweeps the floor, and everybody makes the revolutionary policy, because real manhood does not depend on the subjugation of anybody. . . ."

Women in prisons also have special problems. First of all, they are often given longer sentences for the same crimes. They are often arrested in situations where men are not. Prostitutes are arrested; their customers are not. . . .

There are beautiful women who have their own kind of problems because they are objects much more than anyone else. It's a kind of "you get the liquor; we'll get the girls" psychology, which means that women are interchangeable moving parts; that a beautiful woman is much less likely to be taken seriously as a human being than a less attractive one. And the unattractive ones have fundamentally the same problem because all that they are, all that they try to do, is written off with the argument, "Well, they are only doing it because they can't get a man. . . ."

It's the older women who are often more radical than young ones. Perhaps you can see that here today in the alumnae classes. My own class, which is in the heart of its nesting period, is perhaps more conservative (and of course we grew up in the dark fifties) than the women here who are forty or fifty years out. They have been through the system; they know. The women who are young sometimes say radical things but don't act upon them, because secretly they are preserving their ability to marry a rich man and be a parasite and not upset the system too much. Look to our older sisters who have done that and who know that that is not a human or possible solution, no matter how rich he is. We must have work of our own. . . .

Of course men and women need each other and love each other and will continue to, but we do not need men any *more* than they need us.

Love has almost been politicized out of existence. It really is only possible between equals. And as soon in a relationship as you need him more than he needs you, a lot of other things begin to happen; a lot of not very attractive things; a lot of Uncle Toming and giggling and pretending you don't know what you really know, and saying, "How clever of you to know it's Tuesday." A lot of men don't know whether they are loved for themselves or for their social identity and their wall-to-wall carpeting.

Sex is probably the same kind of situation. . . . Men have come to be so dependent on the idea of superiority that they think they cannot get along without it. I assure them that they can and that however used they may have got to submission, cooperation is better. . . .

Now you have become alumnae . . . I hope that you will place your own energies and any pressures at your disposal to making this college a women's college, and not a school for girls. Women need to know that there are all the choices of life available to them.

Couldn't there be a freshman orientation course . . . that does something to enlarge the idea that we have in our heads that somehow it's a job or it's marriage, and there's nothing in between?

Couldn't we be concerned with the education of older women and of poor women—of ways to get them into this institution—to give them its benefits and to give us the benefit of their presence?

Couldn't we discuss in our political science courses and elsewhere the problem of the masculine mystique? How much that has influenced our foreign policy, how much of the reason that we are in Vietnam is because of the notion that masculinity depends upon the subjugation of other people, that it depends upon saving face after all possible national interests have disappeared . . . ?

Shouldn't we talk about the politics of marriage? That in a real partnership, the wife's work is just as important . . . that it is truly a partnership, both responsible for the house and both responsible for the children? That now we have a kind of situation in which the children suffer from too much mother and too little father and that, for a while at least, we should start to talk about parenthood and not about motherhood?

The politics of religion—why is it that God always looks so exactly like the ruling class? As the position of the priesthood goes up, you find in all great religions, whether it's Hinduism or Catholicism, that the position of women goes down. . . . I'm happy to say that the situation is reversing itself. The position of the priesthood is going down and the position of women is going up. Radical nuns are taking over the pulpits from priests because we now know there is no reason why a woman should be a nun and a man a priest (or a woman a nurse and a man a doctor, or a woman a typist and a man a boss). Perhaps a whole generation of us should fail to learn how to type. Protestant women are now voting in the church (that's a great revolution, you know); Jewish women are rewriting the prayers (especially those in which Orthodox Jews thank God every morning for not having been born women). . . .

Isn't it interesting that motherhood becomes sacred—that the Madonna image is prevalent—whenever the state needs workers and the state needs soldiers? Motherhood is not an instinct. . . . So perhaps God, perhaps she, had something else in mind for us. . . . Not everyone should be a parent any more than everyone with vocal cords should be an opera singer. . . .

I think one of the questions before us now is the integration, the sexual integration of Smith College. I think perhaps the truth is, as we know in our hearts, that we are not ready for it yet. Our heads are not together enough yet as women to be integrated with male students. This college has to turn into a real college for all women . . . that it has to become again a feminist institution, a radicalizing institution. . . .

So, because I think that my presence here today is a small part, a very small part, of a change in the heads of students, I am happy to be here. I am not happy to be one of five women commencement speakers in the history of this College. . . .

I am honored to be here today as a beginning. Because I believe in honoring a female commencement speaker, you are really honoring yourselves. So perhaps if we live this revolution every day—and it is a revolution we live every day—which stretches all the way from thinking about calling ourselves Ms. (which is pronounced m-i-z I understand, instead of Miss or Mrs.—after all Mr. is enough to identify a man. Why should we always be identified by our role?). It stretches all the way from that, to the demand for justice and equality in all areas of life . . . it would revolutionize the economy. . . . By standing up, by refusing to be cheap labor pools any more—whether it's in the kitchen or in the office or in the factory or on the campus—we will revolutionize this system. We will humanize it for more compassionate distribution of goods and services and of human opportunities.

If we do, perhaps we have a chance for a third kind of period. After all, we have had at least five thousand years of the superiority of women. We have had five thousand years of patriarchy and racism. Perhaps we have a chance for five thousand years of humanism. And perhaps, if we really live this revolution every day, historians will look back at this time and say that, for the first time, the human animal stopped dividing itself up according to visible difference—according to race, according to sex—and started to look for the real, the human potential inside.

Ayn Rand
Makes the Case for Philosophy

*"As a human being, you have no choice about
the fact that you need a philosophy."*

At odds with the dictatorial constraints of her life in communist Russia, twenty-one-year-old Alice Rosenbaum emigrated to the United States and chose her pen name: Ayn Rand (1905–1982).

She wanted to be a writer, a famous one she told friends, and after a brief stint in Hollywood—working as an extra in Cecille B. DeMille's *The King of Kings*—she found success in 1935 with her Broadway-produced play *The Night of January 16th*. Rand published her first novel, *We the Living,* the following year, but she is best known as the author of *The Fountainhead* and *Atlas Shrugged,* two mammoth works that convey heroic characters infused with the spirit of individualism. Individualism was her "theme song," she said, and a crucial tenet of the philosophy she called Objectivism, which embraces a code of morality based on reason.

An ardent anticommunist, Rand believed that capitalism was the basis for all political freedom and deplored big government, making her a frequent target of the liberal left. While speaking at Yale Law School in 1960, a shout from a young socialist came from the balcony: "Under your system, who will take care of the janitors?" "Young man," she countered, "the janitors!"

Rand never liked formal speechmaking; it was a nervous chore, she said, "a duty I perform to advance the spread of my ideas." Still, onstage, she was a dramatic figure—often dressed in a black cape pinned with a gold dollar sign, reading from a script in her heavy Russian accent. Among her better-known speeches is this one, delivered before rows of gray-uniformed cadets at West Point on March 6, 1974. All human beings need a philosophy, she argues; without one, there is only "self-doubt, like a ball and chain in the place where your mind's wings should have grown." The conclusion is effusive—a salute to the Point and its "glorious tradition"—words spoken by Rand but perhaps made louder by Rosenbaum, the woman, she says, who "came from a country of the worst tyranny on earth."

———

Since I am a fiction writer, let us start with a short short story. Suppose that you are an astronaut whose spaceship gets out of control and crashes on an unknown planet. When you regain consciousness and find that you are not hurt badly, the first three questions in your mind would be: Where am I? How can I discover it? What should I do?

You see unfamiliar vegetation outside, and there is air to breathe; the sunlight seems paler than you remember it and colder. You turn to look at the sky, but stop. You are struck by a sudden feeling: if you don't look, you won't have to know that you are, perhaps, too far from the earth and no return is possible; so long as you don't know it, you are free to believe what you wish—and you experience a foggy, pleasant, but somehow guilty, kind of hope.

You turn to your instruments: they may be damaged, you don't know how seriously. But you stop, struck by a sudden fear: how can you trust these instruments? How can you be sure that they won't mislead you? How can you know whether they will work in a different world? You turn away from the instruments.

Now you begin to wonder why you have no desire to do anything. It seems so much safer just to wait for something to turn up somehow; it is better, you tell yourself, not to rock the spaceship. Far in the distance, you see some sort of living creatures approaching; you don't know whether they are human, but they walk on two feet. *They,* you decide, will tell you what to do.

You are never heard from again.

This is fantasy, you say? You would not act like that and no astronaut ever would? Perhaps not. But this is the way most men live their lives, here, on earth.

Most men spend their days struggling to evade three questions, the answers to which underlie man's every thought, feeling, and action, whether he is consciously aware of it or not: Where am I? How do I know it? What should I do?

By the time they are old enough to understand these questions, men believe that they know the answers. Where am I? Say, in New York City. How do I know it? It's self-evident. What should I do? Here, they are not too sure—but the usual answer is: whatever everybody does. The only trouble seems to be that they are not very active, not very confident, not very happy—and they experience, at times, a causeless fear and an undefined guilt, which they cannot explain or get rid of.

They have never discovered the fact that the trouble comes from the three unanswered questions—and that there is only one science that can answer them: *philosophy*.

Philosophy studies the *fundamental* nature of existence, of man, and of man's relationship to existence. . . .

Now some of you might say, as many people do: "Aw, I never think in such abstract terms—I want to deal with concrete, particular, real-life problems—what do I need philosophy for?" My answer is: In order to be able to deal with concrete, particular, real-life problems—i.e., in order to be able to live on earth.

You might claim—as most people do—that you have never been influenced by philosophy. I will ask you to check that claim. Have you ever thought or said the following? "Don't be so sure—nobody can be certain of anything." You got that notion from David Hume (and many, many others), even though you might never have heard of him. Or: "This may be good in theory, but it doesn't work in practice." You got that from Plato. Or: "That was a rotten thing to do, but it's only human, nobody is perfect in this world." You got it from Augustine. Or: "It may be true for you, but it's not true for me." You got it from William James. Or: "I couldn't help it! Nobody can help anything he does." You got it from Hegel. Or: "I can't prove it, but I *feel* that it's true." You got it from Kant. Or: "It's logical, but logic has nothing to do with reality." You got it from Kant. Or: "It's evil, because it's selfish." You got it from Kant. Have you heard the modern activists say: "Act first, think afterward"? They got it from John Dewey.

Some people might answer: "Sure, I've said those things at different times, but I don't have to believe that stuff *all* of the time. It may have been true yesterday, but it's not true today." They got it from Hegel. They might say: "Consistency is the hobgoblin of little minds." They got it from a very little mind, Emerson. They might say: "But can't one compromise and borrow different ideas from different philosophies according to the expediency of the moment?" They got it from Richard Nixon—who got it from William James.

Now ask yourself: if you are not interested in abstract ideas, why do you (and all men) feel compelled to use them? . . .

You have no choice about the necessity to integrate your observations, your experiences, your knowledge into abstract ideas, i.e., into principles. Your only choice is whether these principles are true or false, whether they represent your conscious, rational convictions—or a grab bag of notions snatched at random, whose sources, validity, context, and consequences you do not know, notions which, more often than not, you would drop like a hot potato if you knew.

But the principles you accept (consciously or subconsciously) may clash with or contradict one another; they, too, have to be integrated. What integrates them? Philosophy. A philosophic system is an integrated view of existence. As a human being, you have no choice about the fact that you need a philosophy. Your only choice is whether you define your philosophy by a conscious, rational, disciplined process of thought and scrupulously logical deliberation—or let your subconscious accumulate a junk heap of unwarranted conclusions, false generalizations, undefined contradictions, undigested slogans, unidentified wishes, doubts, and fears, thrown together by chance, but integrated by your subconscious into a kind of mongrel philosophy and fused into a single, solid weight: *self-doubt* like a ball and chain in the place where your mind's wings should have grown.

You might say, as many people do, that it is not easy always to act on abstract principles. No, it is not easy. But how much harder is it, to have to act on them without knowing what they are?

Your subconscious is like a computer—more complex a computer than men can build—and its main function is the integration of your ideas. Who programs it? Your conscious mind. If you default, if you don't reach any firm convictions, your subconscious is programmed by chance—and you deliver yourself into the power of ideas you do not know you have accepted. But one way or the other, your computer gives you printouts, daily and hourly, in the form of *emotions*—which are lightning-like estimates of the things around you, calculated according to your values. If you programmed your computer by conscious thinking, you know the nature of your values and emotions. If you didn't, you don't.

Many people, particularly today, claim that man cannot live by logic alone, that there's the emotional element of his nature to consider, and that they rely on the guidance of their emotions. Well, so did the astronaut in my story. The joke is on him—and on them: man's values and emotions are determined by his fundamental view of life. The ultimate programmer of his subconscious is *philosophy*—the science which, according to the emotionalists, is impotent to affect or penetrate the murky mysteries of their feelings. . . .

When men abandon reason, they find not only that their emotions cannot guide them, but that they can experience no emotions save one: terror. The spread of drug addiction among young people brought up on today's intellectual fashions demonstrates the unbearable inner state of men who are deprived of their means of cognition and who seek escape from reality—from the terror of their impotence to deal with existence. . . . One of the most dangerous things a man can do is to surrender his *moral* autonomy to others: like the astronaut in my story, he does not know whether they are human, even though they walk on two feet.

Now you may ask: If philosophy can be that evil, why should one study it? Particularly, why should one study the philosophical theories which are blatantly false, make no sense, and bear no relation to real life?

My answer is: In self-protection—and in defense of truth, justice, freedom, and any value you ever held or may ever hold.

Not all philosophies are evil, though too many of them are, particularly in modern history. On the other hand, at the root of every civilized achievement, such as science, technology, progress, freedom—at the root of every value we enjoy today, including the birth of this country—you will find the achievement of *one man,* who lived over two thousand years ago: Aristotle.

If you feel nothing but boredom when reading the virtually unintelligible theories of *some* philosophers, you have my deepest sympathy. But if you brush them aside, saying: "Why should I study that stuff when I *know* it's nonsense?"—you are mistaken. It *is* nonsense, but you *don't* know it—not so long as you go on accepting all their conclusions, all the vicious catch phrases generated by those philosophers. And not so long as you are unable to *refute* them. . . .

There is a special reason why you, the future leaders of the United States Army, need to be philosophically armed today. You are the target of a special attack by the Kantian-Hegelian-collectivist establishment that dominates our cultural institutions at present. You are the army of the last semi-free country left on earth, yet you are accused of being a tool of imperialism—and "imperialism" is the name given to the foreign policy of this country, which has never engaged in military conquest and has never profited from the two world wars, which she did not initiate, but entered and won. (It was, incidentally, a foolishly over-generous policy, which made this country waste her wealth on helping both her allies and her former enemies.)

Something called "the military-industrial complex"—which is a myth or worse—is being blamed for all of this country's troubles. Bloody college hoodlums scream demands that ROTC units be banned from college campuses. Our defense budget is being attacked, denounced, and undercut by people who claim that financial priority should be given to ecological rose gardens and to classes in esthetic self-expression for the residents of the slums.

Some of you may be bewildered by this campaign and may be wondering, in good faith, what errors you committed to bring it about. If so, it is urgently important for you to understand the nature of the enemy. You are attacked, not for any errors or flaws, but for your virtues. You are denounced, not for any weaknesses, but for your strength and your competence. You are penalized for being the protectors of the United States. . . .

Today's mawkish concern with and compassion for the feeble, the flawed, the suffering, the guilty, is a cover for the profoundly Kantian hatred of the innocent, the strong, the able, the successful, the virtuous, the confident, the happy. A philosophy out to destroy man's mind is necessarily a philosophy of hatred for man, for man's life, and for every human value. Hatred of the good for being the good is the hallmark of the twentieth century. *This* is the enemy you are facing.

A battle of this kind requires special weapons. It has to be fought with a full understanding of your cause, a full confidence in yourself, and the fullest certainty of the *moral* rightness of both. Only philosophy can provide you with these weapons.

The assignment I gave myself for tonight is not to sell you on *my* philosophy, but on philosophy as such. I have, however, been speaking implicitly of my philosophy in every sentence— since none of us and no statement can escape from philosophical premises. What is my *selfish* interest in the matter? I am confident enough to think that if you accept the importance of philosophy and the task of examining it critically, it is *my* philosophy that you will come to accept. Formally, I call it Objectivism, but informally I call it a philosophy for living on earth. You will find an explicit presentation of it in my books, particularly in *Atlas Shrugged*.

In conclusion, allow me to speak in personal terms. This evening means a great deal to me. I feel deeply honored by the opportunity to address you. I can say—not as a patriotic bromide, but with full knowledge of the necessary metaphysical, epistemological, ethical, political, and esthetic roots, that the United States of America is the greatest, the noblest, and, in its original founding principles, the *only* moral country in the history of the world. There is a kind of quiet radiance associated in my mind with the name West Point—because you have preserved the spirit of those original founding principles and you are their symbol. . . .

The army of a free country has a great responsibility: the right to use force, but not as an instrument of compulsion and brute conquest—as the armies of other countries have done in their histories—only as an instrument of a free nation's self-defense, which means: the defense of a man's individual rights. The principle of using force only in retaliation against those who initiate its use is the principle of subordinating might to right. The highest integrity and sense of honor are required for such a task. No other army in the world has achieved it. You have.

West Point has given America a long line of heroes, known and unknown. You, this year's graduates, have a glorious tradition to carry on—which I admire profoundly, not because it is a tradition, but because it *is* glorious.

Since I came from a country guilty of the worst tyranny on earth, I am particularly able to appreciate the meaning, the greatness, and the supreme value of that which you are defending. So, in my own name and in the name of many people who think as I do, I want to say, to all the men of West Point, past, present, and future: Thank you.

Barbara Bush
Triumphs at Wellesley

"The controversy ends here. But our conversation is only beginning."

On June 1, 1990, Barbara Bush (b. 1925) delivered the commencement day address at Wellesley College in Massachusetts. Weeks of controversy preceded her speech, spurred by a petition signed by 150 of the school's graduating seniors, who protested the participation of "a woman who has gained recognition through the achievements of her husband"; Wellesley, they said, "teaches us that we will be rewarded on the basis of our own merit, not on that of a spouse." "In my day, they would have been considered different. In their day, I'm considered different. *Vive la différence*," Bush responded graciously.

Born Barbara Pierce in Rye, New York, this great-great-grand niece of American's fourteenth president left Smith College in 1945 to marry George Bush, who became America's forty-first president in 1989. As first lady, she earned both respect and high approval ratings for her compassionate crusade for literacy as well as for her candor, wit, and self-effacing style: "Why would he tell me secrets," she told a reporter of her husband, "when he says I begin every sentence with 'Don't tell George I told you this, but . . . ' "

Raisa Gorbachev, wife of glasnost architect Mikhail Gorbachev, joined Bush on the Wellesley podium—which faced an audience of more than five thousand people inside the school's grand commencement tent, five thousand outside, and millions more watching on television as networks broadcast the much-anticipated moment live to the nation.

For a woman once so timid she cried when she had to speak to the Houston Garden Club, Barbara Bush exuded confidence. She knew that she "did not want to complain, explain, or apologize in any way," she later wrote. Instead, here, she voices themes: "believe in something larger than yourself"; enjoy life; "cherish your human connections," she says as she couples point with humor. Throughout the speech, the audience is animated—applauding, cheering—soon leaping to their feet as she marches to a close with a wry well wish.

———————

More than ten years ago when I was invited here to talk about our experiences in the People's Republic of China, I was struck by both the natural beauty of your campus . . . and the spirit of this place.

Wellesley, you see, is not just a place . . . but an idea . . . an experiment in excellence in which diversity is not just tolerated, but is embraced.

The essence of this spirit was captured in a moving speech about tolerance given last year by the student body president of one of your sister colleges. She related the story by Robert Fulghum about a young pastor who, finding himself in charge of some very energetic children, hit upon a game called "Giants, Wizards, and Dwarfs." "You have to decide now," the pastor instructed the children, "which you are . . . a giant, a wizard, or a dwarf?" At that, a small girl tugging on his pants leg, asked, "But where do the mermaids stand?"

The pastor told her there are *no* mermaids. "Oh yes there are," she said. "I am a mermaid."

This little girl knew what she was and she was not about to

give up on either her identity *or* the game. She intended to take her place wherever mermaids fit into the scheme of things. Where *do* the mermaids stand . . . all those who are different, those who do not fit the boxes and the pigeonholes? "Answer that question," wrote Fulghum, "and you can build a school, a nation, or a whole world on it."

As that very wise young woman said, "Diversity . . . like anything worth having . . . requires *effort*." Effort to learn about and respect difference, to be compassionate with one another, to cherish our own identity . . . and to accept unconditionally the same in all others.

You should all be very proud that this is the Wellesley spirit. Now I know your first choice for today was Alice Walker, known for *The Color Purple*. Instead you got me—known for . . . the color of my hair! Of course, Alice Walker's book has a special resonance here. At Wellesley, each class is known by a special color . . . and for four years the class of '90 has worn the color purple. Today you meet on Severance Green to say good-bye to all that . . . to begin a new and very personal journey . . . a search for your own true colors.

In the world that awaits you beyond the shores of Lake Waban, no one can say what your true colors will be. But this I know: You have a first-class education from a first-class school. And so you need not, probably cannot, live a "paint-by-numbers" life. Decisions are not irrevocable. Choices do come back. As you set off from Wellesley, I hope that many of you will consider making three very special choices.

The first is to believe in something larger than yourself . . . to get involved in some of the big ideas of your time. I chose literacy because I honestly believe that if more people could read, write, and comprehend, we would be that much closer to solving so many of the problems plaguing our society.

Early on I made another choice which I hope you will

make as well. Whether you are talking about education, career, or service, you are talking about life . . . and life must have joy. It's supposed to be fun!

One of the reasons I made the most important decision of my life . . . to marry George Bush . . . is because he made me laugh. It's true, sometimes we've laughed through our tears . . . but that shared laughter has been one of our strongest bonds. Find the joy in life, because as Ferris Bueller said on his day off . . . "Life moves pretty fast. Ya don't stop and look around once in a while, ya gonna miss it!"

The third choice that must not be missed is to cherish your human connections: your relationships with friends and family. For several years, you've had impressed upon you the importance to your career of dedication and hard work. This is true, but as important as your obligations as a doctor, lawyer, or business leader will be, you are a human being first, and those human connections—with spouses, with children, with friends—are the most important investments you will ever make.

At the end of your life, you will never regret not having passed one more test, not winning one more verdict, or not closing one more deal. You will regret time not spent with a husband, a friend, a child, or a parent.

We are in a transitional period right now . . . fascinating and exhilarating times . . . learning to adjust to the changes and the choices we . . . men and women . . . are facing. I remember what a friend said, on hearing her husband lament to his buddies that he had to baby-sit. Quickly setting him straight my friend told her husband that when it's your own kids . . . it's not called baby-sitting!

Maybe we should adjust faster, maybe slower. But whatever the era . . . whatever the times, one thing will never change: fathers and mothers, if you have children . . . they must come first. Your success as a family . . . our success as a society . . .

depends *not* on what happens at the White House, but on what happens inside your house.

For over fifty years, it was said that the winner of Wellesley's Annual Hoop Race would be the first to get married. Now they say the winner will be the first to become a CEO. Both of these stereotypes show too little tolerance for those who want to know where the mermaids stand. So I offer you today a new legend: the winner of the Hoop Race will be the first to realize her dream . . . not society's dream . . . her own personal dream. And who knows? Somewhere out in this audience may even be someone who will one day follow my footsteps, and preside over the White House as the president's spouse. I wish him well!

The controversy ends here. But our conversation is only beginning. And a worthwhile conversation it is. So as you leave Wellesley today, take with you deep thanks for the courtesy and honor you have shared with Mrs. Gorbachev and me. Thank you. God bless you. And may your future be worthy of your dreams.

Madeleine Albright
Speaks to the Nationalist Impulse

*"We can think of Auschwitz and despair; or
we can contemplate Auschwitz and vow never
to allow despair to excuse inaction."*

The child "Madlenka" was two years old when her parents fled
Czechoslovakia in 1939, ten days after the Nazi occupation, and
eleven years old when her family sought political asylum in the
United States. "She knows what it means when the powerful
decide about the less powerful," Czech Republic president
Vaclev Havel said of his friend, Madeleine Albright (b.1937),
"and that when they decide spheres of interest among themselves, this always leads to wars and misfortune."

Daughter of a diplomat, student of international politics, a
"hawk" among Clinton foreign policy advisers, Albright served
as U.S. ambassador to the United Nations before becoming the
country's first female secretary of state in 1997. It was as ambassador that she gave this address—delivered on June 7, 1994, at
Harvard University's Phi Beta Kappa Literary Exercises.

Her theme is nationalism—what happens when its "rabid
edge" rises up among race and creed and ethnic group like a
Berlin Wall. National pride is one thing, she tells graduates, but
"when pride in 'us' curdles into hatred of 'them,' the result is a
narrowing of vision and a compulsion to violence." The speech,
articulate in style and dramatic in content, includes references to
Adolf Hitler and Auschwitz, which became are all the more

poignant well after delivery. Albright, raised a Roman Catholic, learned later that her parents were born Jewish and that three of her grandparents perished in the Holocaust.

———✦———

As a native of Czechoslovakia, I grew up highly conscious of language and other symbols that distinguish one nation from all others. And I learned the history of a people that had maintained its identity, its culture, and its language despite three centuries of foreign domination.

Today, what has been referred to historically as the "nationalities problem" has reemerged. The accommodation of legitimate grievances and the prevention or containment of ethnic violence are among the imperatives of our time.

As any veteran of the Harvard-Yale game can tell you, we all have a tendency to identify with and express ourselves as members of groups, whether the group is a family, tribe, community, religion, or nation.

The roots of such groupings run as deep as human history, but the rise of the nation-state is a phenomenon of the last two centuries. That is when citizens began to replace monarchs as the embodiment of national identity; and central governments began levying taxes to finance armies, administer education, regulate commerce, and enforce laws.

The nationalist impulse is now embedded in modern culture, the glue provided by emblems of patriotic fervor—from *The Iliad* to Joan of Arc to the "Star-Spangled Banner," and from charismatic leaders from Prince Sihanouk to Haile Selassie to Simon Bolívar. "Patriotism," said Daniel Webster, "produces an elevation of soul"; Hegel called the state "divine and perpetual"; and Kipling asked "who dies, if the country lives?"

During his diplomatic career, my father served as ambassador from what is now the former Czechoslovakia to what is now the former Yugoslavia. He understood the depth of nationalist passions, calling them "a permanent, vital influential force for good *and* evil."

It was his experience, as it is ours, that national pride can be the custodian of rich cultural legacies; it can unite people in defense of a common good; it can provide a sense of identity and belonging that stretches across territory and time.

But as we are now reminded daily, when pride in "us" curdles into hatred of "them," the result is a narrowing of vision and a compulsion to violence.

There is a radio station in Rwanda that urges the murder of little children; Tutsi orphans there have been separated by ethnicity and slaughtered; older victims have been allowed to choose between being shot to death and hacked to death, but only if they can afford bullets.

Earlier this year, I visited a mass grave near Vukovar, in the Former Yugoslavia. What I saw there was a garbage dump; a field of rusted refrigerators and scraps of farm equipment beneath which two to three hundred human beings are buried. There are no flowers, no signs or markers, and no excavation has yet been allowed.

A Serb soldier, drunk with nationalism, actually said recently that "all the world should know (that what) we are defending (here is) Christian Europe."

Today, we have but to scan the horizon to see the passions of nationalism and ethnic pride not elevating, but degrading, the human soul. Conflict threatens to engulf not only Bosnia and Rwanda, but whole areas of the globe. We see the terrible price of intolerance and chaos—the savagery of ethnic cleansing, the terror of rape used as a weapon of war, millions of refugees trudging down dangerous roads to live not in homes, but in camps.

Most of the victims of these conflicts are not soldiers. They are not those who have wandered into a crossfire, or found themselves too close to a military target. They are not—in the terminology of war—collateral damage. They are men and women like you and me; boys and girls like those we know; murdered not because of what they had done, but for who they were.

Throughout history, when great multiethnic empires have broken up, nationalist movements have emerged. That happened after World War I; it happened during the collapse of colonialism; it is happening today.

The Soviet empire sought to destroy the separate ethnic identities of its subject peoples—to rewrite history, to manipulate provincial borders, to discourage religion, to create what Vaclav Havel has called the "monstrous illusion that we are all the same."

But now, as Havel has observed: "after decades of falsified history . . . nothing has been forgotten. Nations are now remembering their ancient achievements . . . their ancient suppressors . . . their ancient statehoods and their former borders."

There are thousands of self-defined ethnic groups in the world, more than one hundred in the former Soviet Union alone. It would be neither right nor reasonable for each to have its own flag, currency, airline, army, and state.

The world is not infinitely divisible; intermingled populations can only rarely be unmingled without wrenching violence; and neither blood, nor language, nor history, nor national characteristics are as distinctive and pure as apostles of separatism would have us believe.

We are not, after all, prize-winning collies or biogenetic tomatoes. We are *people* living in an age when even hermits and Eskimos get CNN, and where the forces shaping our lives are increasingly the same.

But still the world is a living, not a stagnant place. The status quo is always changing. And to deny the possibility of peaceful chance is to invite violence among the desperate and honestly aggrieved. The shield of sovereignty no longer bars appropriate international interest in the treatment of ethnic and other subnational groups.

Today, violent separatist movements are gaining strength. History from Sarajevo to Sarejevo warns us that when small powers fight, big powers are often drawn in. We all have a profound stake in seeing that the embers of ethnic conflict are cooled, and models for easing fear, reconciling ambition, and clarifying principle are established.

That is why the Clinton administration supports the work of the CSCE* and others to enhance respect for the rights of minorities. It is why we stress that *individuals* are entitled to basic human rights irrespective of group identity. It is why we are working to strengthen the UN and regional peacekeeping so that we will be better able to prevent and respond to situations like we now see in Rwanda.

It is also why we are determined to make the War Crimes Tribunal for the Former Yugoslavia an effective instrument of truth. Real peace will not be possible in that land until collective guilt for past atrocities is expunged and individual responsibility is assigned.

Finally, it is why we will continue to view with deadly seriousness the rise of ultranationalist groups in strategic parts of the globe.

Let us never forget that the extreme views of Adolf Hitler caused many to ridicule him when they should have opposed him. Today, we may want to agree with the Russian Foreign Minister that Vladimir Zhirinovsky is less a political problem

*Commission on Security and Cooperation in Europe.

than a medical one. But when Zhirinovsky talks about Russian soldiers washing "their boots in the warm waters of the Indian Ocean," or about current borders resulting in "the slow murder of the Russian nation," he cannot be ignored. The rabid edge of nationalism has enduring appeal to the desperate and embittered, and to the ambitious who would exploit such feelings to enhance their own power.

In Bosnia, the battle there is not among three competing nationalities. That is a myth that has undermined the international response. We should not accept it; and I ask you—do not accept it. This is a war between violent separatists and the government of an internationally recognized multiethnic state. As Americans, we have a stake in the survival and viability of that state. For we derive our very identity from the conviction that those of different races, creeds, and ethnic origins can live together productively, freely, and in peace.

The Harvard dictionary of American ethnic groups is 1,076 pages long, from the Acadians to the Zoroastrians. We are all proud of groups to which we belong. But we also believe that loyalty to group does not justify the betrayal of more universal values. Although we have our fair share of demagogues and xenophobes, we find our real bearings in a broader and more uplifting tradition.

The founders of America did not view the nation simply as an end in itself, but as an instrument of law, justice, liberty, and tolerance. They believed with Goethe that "above the nations is humanity"; and with Diderot that there can be no real citizenship and therefore no real nation "under the yoke of despotism." In this view, nationalism is *in*clusionary, not *ex*clusionary, the difference between the true nation of South Africa today and the mutant South Africa of decades past.

As our own history attests, a government that allocates the privileges of citizenship according to ethnicity or race or tribe invites division and risks civil war. Aggrieved minorities within free nations will find little sympathy if they go beyond the assertion of rights to the promotion of violence. But peoples repressed by dictators and despots will warrant the continued attention and concern of all civilized people.

In respecting the distinctions of physiology, culture, and history that separate us, let us never forget the common humanity that binds us. We are different peoples, but one species—a species distinguished not only by our ability to manipulate our thumbs, but by our ability to think conceptually, create great civilizations, compose masterpieces of art and ponder the mysteries of life.

Within our species, like all species, variations occur. But today, more than ever, the fates of all peoples are intertwined.

There are those who say that we are the prisoners of history; and that we can do little to contain ethnic violence because the scars of past grievances are too often too deep.

There are those who feel unaffected by crimes committed against others because the victims are far away, and because other problems—and other crimes—demand our attention at home.

There are those who view human tragedies elsewhere against a broad geopolitical canvas and say it would be "unrealistic" for us to care; it is God's problem, not our own.

There is much within our experience to support each of these attitudes. We cannot escape what David Broder has called "the damnable duality of human nature." We cannot base our lives or our policies on illusions about human character.

But we can understand that there will be limits on what we can accomplish without ourselves limiting what we attempt. We can accept the reality of cruelty without accepting cruelty. We can think of Auschwitz and despair; or we can contemplate Auschwitz and vow never to allow despair to excuse inaction.

We are the same species as Adolf Hitler, but also Lincoln, Gandhi, Mandela, and Anne Frank.

We are the same species as the stranglers of Sarajevo, and of its defenders; the same as the butchers of Rwanda and the same as the many, including many Rwandans and Bosnian Serbs, who have risked their lives to save others.

We are the inheritors of a nation that did too little, too late to stop the Holocaust, and that stormed the beaches of Normandy and liberated Buchenwald.

This morning, in this beautiful setting, tradition and memory blend with promise and hope. This college is a monument to the noblest aspirations of humankind. Each of you have demonstrated at a young age ambition and skill.

But the future will ask something more of you. It will ask you to choose. To settle for an America or a world crippled by faction, prejudice, and unreasoning hate; or to help build a future informed by the better angels of our nature, where allegiance to group cements, not unravels, our understanding of each other.

Let us all vow to do what we can in this life not to be imprisoned by history, but to shape it; to build a world not without conflict, but in which conflict is effectively contained; a world, not without repression, but in which the sway of freedom is enlarged; a world not without lawless behavior, but in which the interests of the law-abiding are progressively more secure.

That is our mission in this new era. That is your assignment in your new life.

PART 10

RELIGIOUS
SPEECHES

Mary Baker Eddy
Preaches the Doctrine of Christian Science

"May God enable my students to take up the cross as I have done . . ."

Mary Baker Eddy (1821–1910) and her teachings so agitated Mark Twain that he wrote a book about her and attacked: "A marvelous woman; with a hunger for power such as has never been seen before." "She could draft a set of rules that Satan himself would say could not be improved on—for devilish effectiveness—by his staff." Yet, the founder of Christian Science was not dismayed: "Christian Science is my only ideal; and the individual and his ideal can never be severed."

Raised a Congregationalist in New Hampshire, emotionally and physically frail since childhood, Eddy sought help for her sufferings (a possible spinal illness) in 1862 from Phineaus J. Quimby, a physician who advanced the science of mental and spiritual healing. Eddy's illness subsided but then returned after Quimby's death and a later fall on the ice. In despair, she turned to the New Testament and claimed herself healed by "all a thing or state of my mental consciousness." God had intervened with "His healing truth," she said. That same year, Eddy pioneered the Christian Science movement and, in 1875, published *Science and Health*, her religion's principal "textbook and scripture." She launched the *Christian Science Monitor* in 1908.

At her death, some critics dismissed her life's work as

"largely one of sunshine and mental uplift." Yet her obituaries, as obituaries do, spilled with plaudits: "the leading woman of her time," "of great executive ability and judgment."

In this speech, delivered on June 3, 1895, at her home in Concord, New Hampshire, Eddy speaks to alumni of the Massachusetts Metaphysical College, a teaching institution she founded in 1881. Replete with analogy and evangelical tone, she exhorts her audience to "take up the cross as I have done" and "practice, teach and live Christian Science!"

My Beloved Students: Weeks have passed into months, and months into years, since last we met; but time and space, when encompassed by divine presence, do not separate us. Our hearts have kept time together, and our hands have wrought steadfastly at the same object-lesson, while leagues have lain between us.

We may well unite in thanksgiving for the continued progress and unprecedented prosperity of our cause. It is already obvious that the world's acceptance and the momentum of Christian Science increase rapidly as years glide on.

As Christian Scientists, you have dared the perilous defense of Truth, and have succeeded. You have learned how fleeting is that which men call great; and how permanent that which God calls good.

You have proven that the greatest piety is scarcely sufficient to demonstrate what you have adopted and taught; that your work, well done, would dignify angels.

Faithfully, as meekly, you have toiled all night; and at break of day caught much. At times, your net has been so full that it broke: human pride, creeping into its meshes, extended it beyond safe expansion; then, losing hold of divine Love, you lost your fishes, and possibly blamed others more than yourself. But those whom God makes "fishers of men" will not pull for the shore; like Peter, they launch into the depths, cast their nets on the right side, compensate loss, and gain a higher sense of the true idea. Nothing is lost that God gives: had He filled the net, it would not have broken.

Leaving the seed of Truth to its own vitality, it propagates: the tares cannot hinder it. Our Master said, "Heaven and earth shall pass away, but my words shall not pass away"; and Jesus' faith in Truth must not exceed that of Christian Scientists who prove its power to be immortal.

The Christianity that is merely of sects, the pulpit, and fashionable society is brief; but the Word of God abideth. Plato was a pagan; but no greater difference existed between his doctrines and those of Jesus, than today exists between the Catholic and Protestant sects. I love the orthodox church; and in time, that church will love Christian Science. Let me specially call the attention of this Association to the following false beliefs inclining mortal mind more deviously:

The belief in anti-Christ: that somebody in the flesh is the son of God, or is another Christ, or is a spiritually adopted child, or is an incarnated babe, is the evil one in other words, the one evil—disporting itself with the subtleties of sin!

Even honest thinkers, not knowing whence they come, may deem these delusions verities, before they know it, or really look the illusions in the face. The ages are burdened with material modes. Hypnotism, microbes, x-rays, and ex-common sense occupy time and thought; and error, given new opportunities, will improve them. The most just man can neither defend the innocent nor detect the guilty, unless he knows how to be just; and this knowledge demands our time and attention.

The mental stages of crime, which seem to belong to the latter days, are strictly classified in metaphysics as some of the many features and forms of what is properly denominated, in extreme cases, moral idiocy. I visited in his cell the assassin of President Garfield, and found him in the mental state called moral idiocy. He had no sense of his crime; but regarded his act as one of simple justice, and himself as the victim. My few words touched him; he sank back in his chair, limp and pale; his flippancy had fled. The jailer thanked me, and said, "Other visitors have brought to him bouquets, but you have brought what will do him good."

This mental disease at first shows itself in extreme sensitiveness; then, in a loss of self-knowledge and of self-condemnation—a shocking inability to see one's own faults, but an exaggerating sense of other people's. Unless this mental condition be overcome, it ends in a total loss of moral, intellectual, and spiritual discernment, and is characterized in this Scripture: "The fool hath said in his heart, There is no God." This state of mind is the exemplification of total depravity, and the result of sensuous mind in matter. Mind that is God is not in matter; and God's presence gives spiritual light, wherein is no darkness.

If, as is indisputably true, "God is Spirit," and Spirit is our Father and Mother, and that which it includes is all that is real and eternal, when evil seems to predominate and divine light to be obscured, free moral agency is lost; and the Revelator's vision, that "no man might buy or sell, save he that had the mark, or the name of the beast, or the number of his name," is imminent.

Whoever is mentally manipulating human mind, and is not gaining a higher sense of Truth by it, is losing in the scale of moral and spiritual being, and may be carried to the depths of perdition by his own consent. He who refuses to be influenced by any but the divine Mind, commits his way to God, and rises superior to suggestions from an evil source. Christian Science shows that there is a way of escape from the latter-day ultimatum of evil, through scientific truth; so that all are without excuse.

Already I clearly recognize that mental malpractice, if persisted in, will end in insanity, dementia, or moral idiocy. Thank God! this evil can be resisted by true Christianity. Divine Love is our hope, strength, and shield. We have nothing to fear when Love is at the helm of thought, but everything to enjoy on earth and in heaven.

The systematized centers of Christian Science are life, giving fountains of truth. Our churches, The *Christian Science Journal and the Christian Science Quarterly,* are prolific sources of spiritual power whose intellectual, moral, and spiritual animus is felt throughout the land. . . .

The teachers of Christian Science need to watch incessantly the trend of their own thoughts; watch that these be not secretly robbed, and themselves misguided, and so made to misteach others. Teachers must conform strictly to the rules of divine Science announced in the Bible and their textbook, *Science and Health with Key to the Scriptures.* They must themselves practice, and teach others to practice, the Hebrew Decalogue, the Sermon on the Mount, and the understanding and enunciation of these according to Christ.

They must always have on armor, and resist the foe within and without. They cannot arm too thoroughly against original sin, appearing in its myriad forms: passion, appetites, hatred, revenge, and all the et cetera of evil. Christian Scientists cannot watch too sedulously, or bar their doors too closely, or pray to God too fervently, for deliverance from the claims of evil. Thus doing, Scientists will silence evil suggestions, uncover their methods, and stop their hidden influence upon the lives of mortals. Rest assured that God in His wisdom will test all mankind on all questions; and then, if found faithful, He will deliver us from temptation and show us the powerlessness of evil—even its utter nothingness.

The teacher in Christian Science who does not specially instruct his pupils how to guard against evil and its silent modes, and to be able, through Christ, the living Truth, to protect themselves therefrom, is committing an offense against God and humanity. With *Science and Health* for their textbook, I am astounded at the apathy of some students on the subject of sin and mental malpractice, and their culpable ignorance of the workings of these—and even the teacher's own deficiency in this department. I can account for this state of mind in the teacher only as the result of sin; otherwise, his own guilt as a mental malpractitioner, and fear of being found out.

The helpless ignorance of the community on this subject is pitiable, and plain to be seen. May God enable my students to take up the cross as I have done and meet the pressing need of a proper preparation of heart to practice, teach, and live Christian Science! Your means of protection and defense from sin are constant watchfulness and prayer that you enter not into temptation and are delivered from every claim of evil, till you intelligently know and demonstrate, in Science, that evil has neither prestige, power, nor existence, since God, good, is All-in-all.

The increasing necessity for relying on God to defend us against the subtler forms of evil, turns us more unreservedly to Him for help, and thus becomes a means of grace. If one lives rightly, every effort to hurt one will only help that one; for God will give the ability to overcome whatever tends to impede progress. Know this: that you cannot overcome the baneful effects of sin on yourself, if you in any way indulge in sin; for, sooner or later, you will fall the victim of your own as well as of others' sins. Using mental power in the right direction only, doing to others as you would have them do to you, will overcome evil with good, and destroy our own sensitiveness to the power of evil.

The God of all grace be with you, and save you from "spiritual wickedness in high places."

Maude Royden
Preaches to the Newly Enfranchised

*"Let us make ourselves one for all time with
those who are oppressed, exploited, betrayed."*

"When you have nothing left but God," said England's first woman preacher, "then you become aware that God is enough." Suffragist, pacifist, and "England's greatest woman," as Jane Addams dubbed her, Maude Royden (1876–1956) rose to the pulpit in 1917. A devoted member of the Church of England (her "soul naturally Anglican," she said), Royden believed that "hard thinking" was a Christian duty and, for nearly four decades, fused religious doctrine with the moral, social, and political problems of the early twentieth century.

In "Thanksgiving and Consecration," a sermon delivered at London's City Temple on February 10, 1918, Royden celebrates the "essential" resolution of one of those problems—votes for women, which came in January 1918 under the terms of England's Fourth Franchise Bill.

Suffrage, for this pastor, was "a great moral and human question"—one of many battles in the "great campaign" against human suffering. Here, echoing "do not forget" in a persuasive litany, she cautions celebrants from forgetting "what the world is like to those who have neither position nor wealth." Should they forget, then their fight was in vain—

"though every woman in the country had a vote." This is the closing half of her sermon which ends in the words of Hebrews 12:1.

———•·•———

Ours is only one battle in a great campaign. Let us now forget the bitterness of hope deferred, resentment, betrayal, and disappointment, but let us not forget what it is to be defeated, disappointed, betrayed. Of all that we have learned from our great fight, let us forget what might make us bitter or rebellious, but let us forever remember what links us to all the struggling causes of freedom.

Some of you who have stood at street corners to plead with men for what seemed to you the barest justice, *do not forget* what it is like to be a beggar. Those who have been deprived of opportunity, given perhaps too little education, set down to work that is uncongenial because the traditional work it was convenient for society that women should do, *do not forget* what it is like to be exploited, to be poor, solitary, betrayed. You who have worked long and remember when the fight went against you, *do not forget* what it is like to meet great odds.

Some of us in this great fight could not easily have understood the suffering of the world. Women rich, protected, respected, went out where they were not known, where wealth and position were no protection to them, and learned for the first time how the world looks to those who have no wealth, no position, what it is like to be received with insult, derision, contempt, indifference. All this is nothing, my sisters, tonight, but *do not forget* what the world is like to those who have neither position nor wealth. Some of you who have undergone the unnameable brutalities of our prison system, forget your terrible experience, only *do not forget* that there are prisoners still, that that detestable desecration of the human body that was prac-

ticed against some of you goes very near to poison the soul.
Nothing that you have suffered will be in vain, you will grudge
none of it, far less resent any of it, if it has given you the key to
the suffering of the world.

But if it has not, if women should ever forget what it was
like to be oppressed, laughed at, derided, scorned, insulted, then
our fight would indeed have been in vain, though every woman
in the country had a vote. It is the fellowship of all who are
oppressed that we have won.

> From all that terror teaches,
>   From lies of speech and pen,
> From all the easy speeches
>   That comfort cruel men,
> From sale and profanation
>   Of honor and the sword
> From sleep and from damnation
>   Deliver us, good Lord!

Do not be comforted by easy speeches, you who were fed
with them so long; none of it matters now so long as you do not
forget.

What shall women bring to the civilization of the world?
For one thing, a greater sense of the sacredness of human life. I
sometimes think that the true harvest of our civilization in
future shall be this. Men shall say, as they have said in the past,
that life itself may be sacrificed to a great ideal. They are proving that today on the battlefield and in prison. Women say amen
to that—but for nothing less shall human life be sacrificed; not
for the convenience of society, for cheap labor, for the lusts of
men; not to heap up wealth or to increase the material riches of
Empire; not for the convenience of one class, sex, or nation. By
human life we mean life that is human, not mere existence. To
die is not the worst of tragedies, but life that is made inhuman—

shall not women everywhere strive against that sacrifice? That children should be born in slums, that girls and boys of thirteen should be put into factories, because you want the rents of slums and the cheap labor of industrialism—shall women submit to that kind of exploitation? No; we are citizens of a great Empire, and we have to consider lives not only here, but abroad. From India, from Egypt, yes, and from Ireland, comes the plea to which we cannot ever be deaf. No race any more than a class exists for the convenience or glorification of another. You who as a sex so long have been exploited for another sex, will you submit to the exploitation of a race or a class for another race or class, even if it be your own?

Rather let us pledge ourselves that none shall be exploited for the convenience of another. It is a great ideal, a tremendous task; we have so much leeway to make up; but it is a task which shall make us feel that the struggles of those who went before us have not been in vain, that we have indeed found the work to which to set our hand.

Nothing is too great to hope for tonight. Do you realize that it is in face of the greatest display of material force the world has ever seen that we make this great affirmation of the supremacy of spiritual force? We used to be told that the only argument against the enfranchisement of women was the greater physical strength of men, and it is during a war when physical strength is glorified that our country has affirmed that it believes that freedom belongs to all who are spiritually equal, and that it is spiritual, not physical, power which in the last resort governs the world. The enfranchisement of women means nothing less than that. The bill that has brought us freedom is not a very logical one, certainly not entirely just,* but the principle that women shall have a share in the government of the country means nothing else than the sealing of our faith

*The bill gave the vote to women over age thirty but to all men over age twenty-one.

in the greatness of spiritual power. No task to which we can set ourselves is too great for us. Even in the midst of this tragic war, it is possible for us to cry to the world, "Lift up your hearts," and to get the answer, "We lift them up unto the Lord."

In great humility, with the consciousness that we are unworthy of all that has been done and sacrificed for us, let us consecrate ourselves to the service of God, of our country, and through our country, of all the world. Let us make ourselves one for all time with those who are oppressed, exploited, betrayed. Let us remember, as our great American international president reminded us, that while there are any oppressed, disenfranchised, unfree, no one of us is altogether enfranchised or wholly free. And "seeing we also are compassed about with so great a cloud of witnesses, let us lay aside every weight, and the sin which doth so easily beset us; and let us run with patience the race that is set before us."

Elizabeth Dole
Finds Lessons in the Story of Esther

---

*"While the particulars of her challenge may
differ greatly from the challenges that you and I
face, the forces at work are as real as the moral
is relevant."*

Mary Hanford worried when her daughter showed no ability
for sewing, and again, when she chose political science as her
major over home economics, and again, when she announced
she wanted to go to law school. "Don't you want to be a wife,
a mother, and a hostess for your husband?" the anxious Mrs.
Hanford asked. But all concerns eventually quieted as young
Elizabeth, raised a Methodist in Salisbury, North Carolina,
forged a resume that grew to include a law degree from Harvard, cabinet posts in the Reagan and Bush administrations, the
presidency of the American Red Cross, and though, cut short
by a lack of funds, a run for the Republican presidential nomination in 2000.

Married to former Senator Robert Dole in 1975—much to
Mrs. Hanford's delight—Elizabeth Dole (b. 1935) gained distinction as the most viable female candidate ever to seek the
White House. On the campaign trail, her speeches often mir-
rored her performance style at the 1996 Republican National
Convention, where she left the podium to move among the delegates on the convention floor—as she spoke in support of her
husband, the GOP presidential nominee.

Dole was at the podium for this address—a speech of faith

delivered at the National Prayer Breakfast in Washington, D.C., on February 5, 1987. Then Secretary of Transportation under Ronald Reagan, Dole spoke before an audience of nearly four thousand people—politicians and dignitaries—who gather annually to abandon differences in favor of prayer and personal reflection.

Every president beginning with Dwight Eisenhower has attended the ecumenical event; this time, it was Reagan, who Dole singles out with a timely nod. Her speech, a compelling composite of storytelling and retrospection, draws from the Book of Esther as Dole teams the challenges of the Persian queen with effective and inspirational testimony of her own spiritual journey. The speech follows in full—closing with a forceful summation of its principal theme: "dependence on God."

I consider it one of the greatest possible privileges to be invited to share this morning a little of my own spiritual journey with fellow travelers. Like most of us, I'm just one person struggling to relate faith to life, but I am grateful that members of the congressional prayer groups have asked me to speak from the heart about the difference that Jesus Christ has made in my life.

But first, I must mention a political crisis, a crisis from which I have learned some very important lessons.

Now this is a political crisis involving high stakes, intrigue, behind-the-scenes negotiations, influence in high places, and even a little romance.

Where have I learned of this crisis? On the front page of the newspapers?

No, the newspapers haven't carried this story.

No, the political crisis I'm talking about occurred around 2,450 years ago.

And we learn about it in the Bible, in the Book of Esther.

Esther is the saga of a woman forced to make a decision concerning the total commitment of her life, a decision she was reluctant to make. She had to be vigorously challenged. And it is this part of her story to which I can so easily relate in my own spiritual journey. For while the particulars of her challenge may differ greatly from the challenges that you and I face, the forces at work are as real as the moral is relevant. The basic lessons Esther had to learn are lessons I needed to learn. Thus, the story of Esther, over the years, has taken on great significance for me. Indeed, it reflects an individual's discovery of the true meaning of life.

The story takes place in the ancient kingdom of Persia, where there lived a particularly faithful man of God named Mordecai. Now Mordecai, a Jew, had a young cousin named Esther, whom he had adopted after the death of her parents and raised as if she were his own daughter. In fact, Mordecai had raised a young woman literally fit for a king, for Esther grew into a woman of extraordinary grace and beauty.

Then one day Xerxes, the King of Persia, commanded that a search be made throughout all the provinces for the most beautiful women, so that he could choose a new queen—a sort of "Miss Persia pageant." (*Laughter.*)

Esther, above all others, found favor in the eyes of the king, and this young orphan girl was crowned Queen of Persia.

The king was so delighted with his new queen that he threw a magnificent banquet and even went so far as to lower all the taxes.

Mr. President—(*Laughter.*)

I thought you would particularly like that part of the story. (*Laughter.*)

Meanwhile, Mordecai, out amongst the people, learned to

his horror that one of the top men in government had developed a very careful plan to put to death all of God's people, the Jews, throughout the entire kingdom.

Of course, Mordecai immediately thought of Esther, and he sent an urgent message saying, "Esther, you must do something. You may be the only person who can persuade the king to call off this terrible plan."

But Esther wants no part of this. Her response to Mordecai: "All the king's officials and the people of the royal provinces know that for any man or woman who approaches the king in the inner court without being summoned, the king has set but one law, that he be put to death. The only exception to this is for the king to extend the golden scepter to him and spare his life. But thirty days have passed since I was called to go to the king."

In other words, Esther is saying, "Mordecai, you don't understand protocol. I have to follow standard operating procedures. Chances are that if I go to the king, I just might lose my head!" Well, Mordecai has no sympathy with Esther's refusal to help. Tens of thousands of her own people stand to lose their heads. Mordecai feels compelled to send a second message to Esther.

I once heard a very insightful pastor, Gordon MacDonald, highlight three distinct parts to this second appeal, three profound challenges which strike at the heart of Esther's reluctance.

First. Esther think not that you'll escape this predicament any more than other Jews. You'll lose everything you have if this plan is carried out, all the comforts, all the fringe benefits. It seems that Mordecai is saying: if the thing that stops you from being a servant to thousands of people is your comfort and security, forget it, lady, for you are no more secure in there than we are out here. Esther shares the predicament.

The second theme is privilege. If you keep silent, Esther, at a time like this, deliverance and relief will arise from some other place.

God has given you, Esther, the privilege to perform. If you don't use that privilege, he may permit you to be pushed aside and give your role to someone else.

The third theme is providence. Mordecai says, Esther, who knows but that God had placed you where you are for such a time as this.

Finally, Mordecai's appeal struck home. Esther's response: "Go, gather up all the Jews and fast for me. Do not eat or drink for three days, night or day. I and my maids will fast as you do. When this is done, I will go to the king, even though it is against the law. And if perish, I perish."

That's total commitment. Indeed, the story of Esther is for me a very challenging and humbling one. For there came a time in my life when I had to confront what commitment to God is all about.

My witness contains no road to Damascus experience.

My spiritual journey began many years ago in a Carolina home, where Sunday was the Lord's day, reserved for acts of mercy and necessity, and this was as much a part of our lives as fried chicken and azaleas in the spring.

My grandmother, Mom Cathey, who lived within two weeks of her one hundredth birthday, was my role model.

I remember many Sunday afternoons with other neighborhood children in her home—the lemonade and cookies—I think that's what enticed us—the Bible games, listening to Mom Cathey as she read from this Bible, which is now one of my most cherished possessions.

She practiced what she preached and lived her life for others. In a tragic accident, Mom Cathey lost a son at the hands of a drunk driver. The insurance policy on his life built a hospital wing in a far-off church mission in Pakistan. Although Mom was not at all a wealthy woman, almost anything she could spare went to ministers at home and missions abroad. When it became necessary, in her nineties, to go into a nursing home, she welcomed the opportunity. I can still hear her saying, "Elizabeth, there might be some people there who don't know the Lord, and I can read the Bible to them."

I love to find the notes in the margin of her Bible, notes written in the middle of the night when she couldn't sleep. For example, I find by Psalm 139, this notation. "May 22, 1952, 1:00 A.M.—my prayer 'Search me, O God, and know my heart—try me, and know my thoughts and see if there be any wicked way in me and lead me in the way everlasting.' "

I can't remember an unkind word escaping Mom's lips in all the years I knew her or an ungracious deed marring her path. My grandmother was an almost perfect role model.

And I wanted to be like her. From an early age, I had an active church life. But as we move along, how often in our busy lives something becomes a barrier to total commitment of one's life to the Lord! In some cases, it may be money, power, prestige.

In my case, my career became of paramount importance. I worked very hard, to excel, to achieve. My goal was to do my best, which is all fine and well. But I'm inclined to be a perfectionist. And it's very hard, you know, to try to control everything, surmount every difficulty, foresee every problem, realize every opportunity. That can be pretty tough on your family, your friends, your fellow workers, and on yourself. In my case, it began crowding out what Mom Cathey had taught me were life's most important priorities.

I was blessed with a beautiful marriage, challenging career, and yet, only gradually over many years did I realize what was missing. My life was threatened with spiritual starvation.

I prayed about this, and I believe, no faster than I was ready, God led me to people and circumstances that made a real difference in my life.

I found Ed Bauman of Foundry Methodist Church, a

tremendously sensitive, caring pastor, who helped me see what joy there can be when God is the center of life and all else flows from that center.

A spiritual growth group gave me renewed strength, as I began to meet each Monday night with others who shared my need to stretch and grow spiritually, and I was strengthened through Bible study with other Senate wives. I learned that Sunday can be set aside for spiritual and personal rejuvenation without disastrous effects on one's work week.

And suddenly, the story of Esther took on new meaning.

I finally realized I needed to hear and to heed those challenges Mordecai so clearly stated.

Mordecai's first challenge: Predicament. "Don't think your life will be spared from the slaughter, Esther. If you try to save your life, you'll lose it all!"

It's a call to total commitment, to literally lay her life on the line.

But I can sympathize with Esther's dilemma. She had all the comforts, a cushy life. And when you get all those things around you, it can build up a resistance to anything which might threaten that comfort and security they seem to provide.

I know all too well how she felt. Perhaps you do, too. I enjoy the comfortable life. I had built up my own little self-sufficient world. I had God neatly compartmentalized, crammed into a crowded file drawer of my life, somewhere between "gardening" and "government."

That is, until it dawned on me that I share the predicament, that the call to commitment Mordecai gave to Esther is like the call which Jesus Christ presents to me.

"If anyone would come after me," Jesus tells us, "He must deny himself and take up his cross and follow me. For whomever wants to save his life will lose it, but whomever loses his life for me and for the gospel will save it. What good is it for a man to gain the whole world, yet forfeit his soul?"

Hard words to swallow, when you are busy doing your own thing, but the most compelling logic I've ever heard. For if Christ is who he says he is—our savior, the central figure in all of history, who gives meaning to a world of confusing, conflicting priorities, then I had to realize Christ could not be compartmentalized.

It would be different if I had believed that Christ was just a man, as some do. Then I could easily have compartmentalized him, or if I had believed he was just a good teacher of morals, then perhaps I could have just put his book away on my shelf, or if I had thought he was just a prophet, even then, I might have been tempted to file him away.

But I knew that Jesus Christ was my Lord and savior, the risen Lord who lives today, sovereign over all. And I knew it was time to cease living life backwards, time to strive to put Christ first, preeminent, with no competition, at the very center of my life. It was time to submit my resignation as master of my own little universe.

And God accepted my resignation.

Mordecai's second challenge was privilege "If you don't take this privilege seriously, Esther, God will give it to another."

This, too, was a challenge I needed to hear.

What God had to teach me was this. It is not what I do that matters, but what a sovereign God chooses to do through me. God doesn't want worldly successes. He wants me. He wants my heart in submission to him. Life is not just a few years to spend on self-indulgence and career advancement. It is a privilege, responsibility, a stewardship to be lived according to a much higher calling.

This alone gives true meaning to life.

Mordecai's warning to Esther is sobering. God forbid that someday I look back and realize that I was too distracted by things of this world, too busy, too driven, and my work was given to another.

The third challenge: providence. "Esther, who knows, but

that God in his providence has brought you to such a time as this."

What Mordecai's words say to me is that each one of us has a unique assignment in this world given to us by a sovereign God, to love and to serve those within our own sphere of influence.

We have been blessed to be a blessing; we've received that we might give.

The challenges Esther needed to hear were challenges I needed to hear and continually need to hear: the call to total commitment.

But there is one last lesson I had to learn from Esther—the way in which her heart responded.

Esther called on her fellow believers to pray and to fast, and then she cast herself—indeed, her very life—upon God in dependence on him: "If I perish, I perish."

And how did God work in this situation? What was the outcome of Esther's commitment and dependence on God? Scripture tells us that the king extended the golden scepter, sparing Esther's life, that his heart went out to her cause and that God's people were gloriously rescued!

Esther could have played it on her own wits and charm and just left God out of the picture, but she knew her cause would only succeed if God were with her, and she rallied others to join her in a spirit of humble dependence through prayer.

It has struck me that this is really our purpose in gathering together this morning at this, the annual National Prayer Breakfast. We have come to humbly acknowledge our dependence on God. We have come, as our invitations to this event state, to seek the Lord's guidance and strength in our individual lives and in the governing of our nation, with the hope that the power of Christ may deepen our fellowship with one another.

But in this city accustomed to giving directions, it's not easy to seek them instead. Dependence on God is not an easy thing for Washington-type achievers, and it has not been easy for me.

Often, I find myself faced with tasks demanding wisdom and courage beyond my own, and not just on the big decisions. I am constantly in need of God's grace to perform life's routine duties with the love for others, the peace, the joy inherent in God's call.

I've had to learn that dependence is a good thing, that when I have used up my own resources, when I can't control things and make them come out my way, when I'm willing to trust God with the outcome, when I'm weak—then, I'm strong. Then I'm in the best position to feel the power of Christ rest upon me, encourage me, replenish my energy and deepen my faith.

Power from God, not from me.

Yes, the story of Esther is actually a story of dependence. It's not a story about the triumph of a man or a woman, but the triumph of God. He is the real hero of this story.

And in the same way, I've come to realize there can be only one hero in my story, too: God in Jesus Christ.

Total commitment to Christ is a high and difficult calling. And one I will struggle with the rest of my days. But I know that for me, it's the only life worthy of our Lord.

The world is ripe and ready, I believe, for men and women who will accept this calling, men and women who recognize they are not immune from the predicaments of the day, men and women who are willing to accept the privilege of serving, and who are ready to see that the providence of God may have brought them to such a time as this.

Benazir Bhutto
Labels Discrimination and Intolerance as Betrayers of Islam

"It offends my religion."

"We are proud of the fact that Islam is the religion of tolerance, but does the world know that we are a religion of tolerance?" Benazir Bhutto (b. 1953) asked her Parliament in 1991. "No! They think that we are a religion that discriminates against women, which discriminates against minorities and that I believe . . . is a great disservice to a great religion which came to liberate mankind."

Bhutto was speaking as Opposition Leader in the National Assembly—less than a year after serving as Pakistan's first woman prime minister, the first woman prime minister of the Muslim faith, and, at thirty-five years old, the youngest chief executive in the world. Her government had been dismissed in what the press called an "extraconstitutional coup" and, though she rose to the post a second time in 1993, she was ousted again, this time by a military-backed leader who assailed her with charges of corruption.

As a young woman, Bhutto traveled abroad, studying at Harvard and Oxford before returning to Pakistan in 1977 to champion democracy and human rights. It would be a torturous struggle. Two years into her fight, she saw her father, former prime minister Zulfikar Ali Bhutto, hanged by the regime that overthrew him. Suffering imprisonment and later exile, she continued to speak out in defiance: "As the daughter of a martyr, I know how to fight for the right of an oppressed people," she told Pakistanis.

On September 4, 1995, at the Fourth Women's Conference in Beijing, Bhutto again took issue with those she saw attempting to interpret Islam for their own purposes, and in the process, degrading the tenets of her faith. Speaking with candid, measured phrases, an expressiveness drawn from her own struggles, she assures her audience that true Islam embraces equality for women.

My dear sisters, ladies and gentlemen . . . As the first woman ever elected to head an Islamic nation, I feel a special responsibility about issues that relate to women.

In addressing the new exigencies of the new century, we must translate dynamic religion into a living reality. We must live by the true spirit of Islam, not only by its rituals. And for those of you who may be ignorant of Islam, cast aside your preconceptions about the role of women in our religion.

Contrary to what many of you may have come to believe, Islam embraces a rich variety of political, social, and cultural traditions. The fundamental ethos of Islam is tolerance, dialogue, and democracy.

Just as in Christianity and Judaism, we must always be on guard for those who will exploit and manipulate the Holy Book for their own narrow political ends, who will distort the essence of pluralism and tolerance for their own extremist agendas.

To those who claim to speak for Islam but who would deny to women our place in society, I say:

The ethos of Islam is equality, equality between the sexes.

There is no religion on earth that, in its writing and teachings, is more respectful of the role of women in society than Islam.

My presence here, as the elected woman prime minister of a great Muslim country, is testament to the commitment of Islam to the role of women in society.

It is this tradition of Islam that has empowered me, has strengthened me, has emboldened me.

It was this heritage that sustained me during the most difficult points in my life, for Islam forbids injustice; injustice against people, against nations, against women.

It denounces inequality as the gravest form of injustice.

It enjoins its followers to combat oppression and tyranny.

It enshrines piety as the sole criteria for judging humankind.

It shuns race, color, and gender as a basis of distinction amongst fellow men.

When the human spirit was immersed in the darkness of the Middle Ages, Islam proclaimed equality between men and women. When women were viewed as inferior members of the human family, Islam gave them respect and dignity.

When women were treated as chattels, the Prophet of Islam (*Peace Be Upon Him*) accepted them as equal partners.

Islam codified the rights of women. *The Koran* elevated their status to that of men. It guaranteed their civic, economic, and political rights. It recognized their participative role in nation building.

Sadly, the Islamic tenets regarding women were soon discarded. In Islamic society, as in other parts of the world, their rights were denied. Women were maltreated, discriminated against, and subjected to violence and oppression, their dignity injured and their role denied.

Women became the victims of a culture of exclusion and male dominance. Today more women than men suffer from poverty, deprivation, and discrimination. Half a billion women are illiterate. Seventy percent of the children who are denied elementary education are girls.

The plight of women in the developing countries is unspeakable. Hunger, disease, and unremitting toil is their fate. Weak economic growth and inadequate social support systems affect them most seriously and directly.

They are the primary victims of structural adjustment processes which necessitate reduced state funding for health, education, medical care, and nutrition. Curtailed resource flows to these vital areas impact most severely on the vulnerable groups, particularly women and children.

This, Madam Chairperson, is not acceptable. It offends my religion. It offends my sense of justice and equity. Above all, it offends common sense.

That is why Pakistan, the women of Pakistan, and I personally have been fully engaged in recent international efforts to uphold women's rights. *The Universal Declaration of Human Rights* enjoins the elimination of discrimination against women.

The *Nairobi Forward Looking Strategies* provide a solid framework for advancing women's rights around the world. But the goal of equality, development, and peace still eludes us.

Sporadic efforts in this direction have failed. We are satisfied that the *Beijing Platform of Action* encompasses a comprehensive approach toward the empowerment of women. This is the right approach and should be fully supported.

Women cannot be expected to struggle alone against the forces of discrimination and exploitation. I recall the words of Dante, who reminded us that "The hottest place in Hell is reserved for those who remain neutral in times of moral crisis."

Today in this world, in the fight for the liberation of women, there can be no neutrality.

My spirit carries many a scar of a long and lonely battle against dictatorship and tyranny. I witnessed, at a young age, the overthrow of democracy, the assassination of an elected prime minister, and a systematic assault against the very foundations of a free society.

But our faith in democracy was not broken. The great Pakistani poet and philosopher Dr. Allama Iqbal says, "Tyranny cannot endure forever." It did not. The will of our people prevailed against the forces of dictatorship.

But, my dear sisters, we have learned that democracy alone is not enough.

Freedom of choice alone does not guarantee justice.

Equal rights are not defined only by political values.

Social justice is a triad of freedom, an equation of liberty:

Justice is political liberty.
Justice is economic independence.
Justice is social equality.

Delegates, sisters, the child who is starving has no human rights.

The girl who is illiterate has no future.

The woman who cannot plan her life, plan her family, plan a career, is fundamentally not free. . . .

Ladies and gentlemen, I am determined to change the plight of women in my country. More than sixty million of our women are largely sidelined.

It is a personal tragedy for them. It is a national catastrophe for my nation. I am determined to harness their potential to the gigantic task of nation building. . . .

I dream of a Pakistan in which women contribute to their full potential. I am conscious of the struggle that lies ahead. But, with your help, we shall persevere. Allah willing, we shall succeed.

PART 11

FAREWELLS

AND

TRANSITIONS

Elizabeth Woodville Grey
Entrusts Her Son to the Archbishop
of Canterbury

"And may the nephews be sure of their uncle?"

On June 16, 1483, while holding the hand of her nine-year-old son, Elizabeth Woodville Grey (1437–1492), queen consort of Edward IV, delivered this brief speech in Westminster Abbey before the Archbishop of Canterbury and members of the Privy Council of England. The king was dead; Elizabeth and her daughters were in sanctuary at the abbey; and at the direction of the Council, the boy was to join his twelve-year-old brother, Edward V, in the Tower of London— merely for safekeeping, she was told, until Edward's coronation.

The two young princes were never seen again. Soon after Elizabeth's speech, the Council, claiming the late king was a bigamist, declared her marriage illegal, her children illegitimate, and her brother-in-law, Richard of Gloucester, the rightful heir to the throne. Some historians contend that Richard sought the crown for himself, usurped Edward's throne, and had his nephews murdered. Other experts cast blame on Henry VII, who defeated Richard III in battle in 1485. Still others contend that the boys were never murdered at all, but rather escaped and lead secret lives. In 1674, the skeletons of two children were found buried at the foot of a staircase within the Tower—leading to speculation but little agreement about what happened to the "Little Princes."

Sixteenth-century historian Raphael Holinshed reconstructed the speech—revealing a dark moment in the life of this anguished queen.

———•+•———

My lords and all my lords, I neither am so unwise to mistrust your wits, nor so suspicious to mistrust your truths . . . as if either of both in you, might turn both you and me to great sorrow, the realm to much harm and you to great reproach.

For lo, here is this gentleman, whom I doubt not but I could here keep safe, if I would, whatever any man say. I doubt not also, but there be some abroad so deadly enemies unto my blood, that if they knew where any of it lay in their own body, they would let it out.

We have also experience that desire of a kingdom knows no kindred. The brother has been the brother's bane. And may the nephews be sure of their uncle? Each of these children is the other's defense while they be asunder, and each of their lives lie in the other's body. Keep one safe and both be sure, and nothing for them both more perilous, than to be both in one place. For what wise merchant adventures all his goods in one ship?

All this notwithstanding, here I deliver him and his brother in him, to keep, into your hands, of whom I shall ask them both before God and the world. Faithful you be that know I well, and I know well you be wise. Power and strength to keep him (if you must) lack you not of yourself, nor can lack help in this cause. And if you cannot elsewhere, then may you leave him here. But only one thing I beseech you, for the trust which his father put in you ever, and for the trust that I put in you now, that as far as you think that I fear too much, be you well ware that you fear not as far too little.

Farewell mine own sweet son. God send you good keeping. Let me kiss you yet once before you go, for God knows when we shall kiss together again. (*She kissed him and blessed him, turned her back, wept and went her way, leaving the child weeping.*)

Lady Jane Grey
Speaks from the Gallows

"I die a true Christian woman . . ."

In 1553, a beautiful and reluctant Lady Jane Grey (1537–1554) married Guildford Dudley, son of the Duke of Northumberland. The Duke, conspiring with Jane's father, the Duke of Suffolk, persuaded King Edward VI, dying of tuberculosis, to name Grey as his successor; four days after the king's death, the fifteen-year-old was proclaimed queen of England. Her reign, however, lasted just nine days—after the people revolted against the scheming Northumberland in favor of Edward's sister, Mary.

The "nine days queen," an innocent victim of her relatives' ambitions, was confined to the Tower of London, convicted of high treason, and ordered beheaded. On February 12, 1554, she gave this brief speech upon the scaffold, demonstrating a young girl's calm repose in the face of death and a firm attachment to the Protestant religion.

———

G ood people, I am come hither to die, and by a law I am condemned to do the same. The fact against the queen's highness was unlawful and the consenting thereunto by me, but touching the procurement and desire thereof by me or on my behalf, I do wash my hands thereof in innocence before God, and the face of you, good Christian people, this day. (*Wrings her hands as if to wash away sin.*)

I pray you all, good Christian people, to bear me witness that I die a true Christian woman, and that I do look to be saved by no other means, but only by the mercy of God, in the blood of his only son, Jesus Christ; and I confess that when I did know the word of God, I neglected the same, loved myself and the world, and therefore this plague and punishment is happily and worthily happened unto me for my sins; and yet I thank God that, of his goodness and mercy, he hath given me a time and respite to repent.

And now, good Christian people, while I am alive, I pray you assist me with your prayers. (*The crowd kneels.*)

In English, Grey then recites the psalm, Miserere mei Deus, while the priest intones it in Latin. Seeing the distress on his face, she kisses him on the cheek—then hands her gloves and handkerchief to her attendants and her prayer book to Sir John Brydges, saying "You asked for a parting memory of me. . . ." After the young girl removes her outerdress, the executioner falls at her feet and begs forgiveness, which she gives willingly. "I pray you dispatch me quickly," she says as she kneels. "Will you take it off before I lay me down?" "No madam." She wraps a handkerchief about her eyes, and feels for the block: "What shall I do? Where is it? Where is it?" A standerby takes pity, climbs the scaffold, and guides Grey's hands to the block. Whereupon she lays down her head, stretches forth her body, and utters her final words: "Lord, into thy hands I commend my spirit."

Queen Elizabeth I
Presents Her Golden Speech

*"To be a king and wear a crown is a thing
more glorious to them that see it, than it is
pleasant to them that bear it."*

Elizabeth I was sixty-eight years old and in the final years of her reign when 140 members of the House of Commons gathered at Whitehall to thank and hear their queen, who had, with good nudging, agreed to rescind several unpopular monopolies. As she entered the Council chamber, members fell to their knees.

What followed has since become known as the "Golden Speech"—the "golden words" of Elizabeth's last major address to the Commons, delivered the afternoon of November 30, 1601. With all the pomp of great occasion heightening the moment, Elizabeth spoke of devotion, a theme woven with references to her love for her people and her duty to her crown.

She was, as usual, eloquent and stirring—moreso in the eyes of her subjects, who sensed their declining queen's unspoken farewell.

M r. Speaker: We have heard your declaration and perceive your care of our estate, by falling into the consideration of a grateful acknowledgment of such benefits as you have received; and that your coming is to present thanks unto us, which I accept with no less joy than your loves can have desire to offer such a present.

I do assure you there is no prince that loves his subjects better, or whose love can countervail our love. There is no jewel, be it of never so rich a prize, which I set before this jewel: I mean your love. For I do esteem it more than any treasure or riches; for that we know how to prize, but love and thanks I count invaluable. And, though God hath raised me high, yet this I count the glory of my crown, that I have reigned with your loves. This makes me that I do not so much rejoice that God hath made me to be a queen, as to be a queen over so thankful a people. Therefore I have cause to wish nothing more than to content the subject and that is a duty which I owe. Neither do I desire to live longer days than that I may see your prosperity and that is my only desire. And as I am that person that still, yet under God, hath delivered you, so I trust, by the almighty power of God, that I shall be his instrument to preserve you from every peril, dishonor, shame, tyranny, and oppression, partly by means of your intended helps, which we take very acceptably, because it manifesteth the largeness of your good loves and loyalties unto your sovereign.

Of myself I must say this: I never was any greedy, scraping grasper, nor a strait fast-holding prince, nor yet a waster. My heart was never set on any worldly goods, but only for my subjects' good. What you do bestow on me, I will not hoard it up, but receive it to bestow on you again. Yea, mine own properties I account yours, to be expended for your good. Therefore render unto them, I beseech you, Mr. Speaker, such thanks as you imagine my heart yieldeth, but my tongue cannot express.

Mr. Speaker, I would wish you and the rest to stand up for I shall yet trouble you with longer speech.

Mr. Speaker, you give me thanks, but I doubt me I have more cause to thank you all than you me; and I charge you to thank them of the House of Commons from me, for had I not received a knowledge from you, I might have fallen into the lap of an error only for lack of true information.

Since I was queen, yet did I never put my pen to any grant, but that upon pretext and semblance made unto me that it was both good and beneficial to the subjects in general, though a private profit to some of my ancient servants, who had deserved well at my hands. But the contrary being found by experience, I am exceedingly beholden to such subjects as would move the same at first. And I am not so simple to suppose but that there be some of the Lower House whom these grievances never touched, and for them I think they speak out of zeal to their countries and not out of spleen or malevolent affection, as being parties grieved. And I take it exceeding grateful from them because it gives us to know that no respects or interests had moved them, other than the minds they bear to suffer no diminution of our honor and our subjects' love unto us. The zeal of which affection, tending to ease my people and knit their hearts unto me, I embrace with a princely care. Far above all earthly treasure, I esteem my people's love, more than which I desire not to merit.

That my grants should be grievous to my people and oppressions to be privileged under color of our patents, our kingly dignity shall not suffer it. Yea, when I heard it, I could give no rest to my thoughts until I had reformed it. Shall they, think to escape unpunished, that have oppressed you, and have been respectless of their duty and regardless our honor? No. Mr. Speaker, I assure you, were it not more for conscience' sake than for any glory or increase of love that I desire these errors, troubles, vexations, and oppressions done by these varlets and lewd persons, not worthy of the name of subjects, should not escape without condign punishment. But I perceive they dealt with me like physicians who, ministering a drug, make it more acceptable by giving it a good aromatical savour, or when they give pills, do gild them all over.

I have ever used to set the last judgment day before mine eyes and so to rule as I shall be judged to answer before a higher judge. To whose judgment seat I do appeal, that never thought was cherished in my heart that tended not to my people's good. And now, if my kingly bounty have been abused, and my grants turned to the hurt of my people, contrary to my will and meaning, or if any in authority under me have neglected or perverted what I have committed to them, I hope God will not lay their culps and offenses to my charge. And though there were danger in repealing our grants, yet what danger would not I rather incur for your good, than I would suffer them still to continue?

I know the title of a king is a glorious title, but assure yourself that the shining glory of princely authority hath not so dazzled the eyes of our understanding, but that we well know and remember that we also are to yield an account of our actions before the Great Judge. To be a king and wear a crown is a thing more glorious to them that see it, than it is pleasant to them that bear it. For myself, I was never so much enticed with the glorious name of a king or royal authority of a queen, as delighted that God hath made me his instrument to maintain his truth and glory and to defend this kingdom, as I said, from peril, dishonor, tyranny, and oppression.

There will never queen sit in my seat with more zeal to my country or care to my subjects, and that will sooner with willingness yield and venture her life for your good and safety, than myself. And though you have had and may have many princes more mighty and wise sitting in this seat, yet you never had nor shall have any that will be more careful and loving.

Should I ascribe anything to myself and my sexly weakness, I were not worthy to live then, and of all most unworthy of the mercies I have had from God, who hath ever yet given me a heart which never yet feared foreign or home enemy. I speak it to give God the praise, as a testimony before you, and not to attribute anything unto myself.

For I, O Lord, what am I, whom practices and perils past should not fear! O what can I do that I should speak for any glory! God forbid.

This, Mr. Speaker, I pray you deliver unto the House, to whom heartily recommend me. And so I commit you all to your best fortunes and further councils. And I pray you, Mr. Comptroller, Mr. Secretary, and you of my council, that before these gentlemen depart into their countries, you bring them all to kiss my hand.

Maria Stewart
Bids Farewell to the Podium

"God has tried me as by fire."

The first woman to speak before a mixed audience of men, women, blacks, and whites, Maria Stewart gave just four public lectures during a speaking career that lasted less than two years. Her brief time at the podium had been difficult because while progressiveness accepted her message—education, empowerment, and godliness—an increasingly hostile public could not accept the messenger. As a woman and an African American, she was not to speak in public.

This is Stewart's final address, delivered in Boston on September 21, 1833. Soon afterward, she headed to New York and later Washington, D.C., where she continued her education and led a distinguished career as a teacher and hospital matron.

In this closing excerpt of her speech—a valedictory to public life—we find her eloquent and pious—especially and defiantly pious.

I am about to leave you, perhaps never more to return. For I find it is no use for me as an individual to try to make myself useful among my color in this city. It was contempt for my moral and religious opinions in private that drove me thus before a public. Had experience more plainly shown me that it was the nature of man to crush his fellow, I should not have thought it so hard. Wherefore, my respected friends, let us no longer talk of prejudice, till prejudice becomes extinct at home. Let us no longer talk of opposition, till we cease to oppose our own. For while these evils exist, to talk is like giving breath to the air, and labor to the wind.

Though wealth is far more highly prized than humble merit, yet none of these things move me. Having God for my friend and portion, what have I to fear? Promotion cometh neither from the East nor West, and as long as it is the will of God, I rejoice that I am as I am; for man in his best estate is altogether vanity. Men of eminence have mostly risen from obscurity; nor will I, although a female of a darker hue, and far more obscure then they, bend my head or hand my harp upon willows; for though poor, I will virtuous prove. And if it is the will of my heavenly Father to reduce me to penury and want, I am ready to say, amen, even so be it. "The foxes have holes, and the birds of the air have nests, but the Son of man hath not where to lay his head."

During the short period of my Christian warfare, I have indeed had to contend against the fiery darts of the devil. And was it not that the righteous are kept by the mighty power of God through faith unto salvation, long before this I should have proved to be like the seed by the wayside. For it has actually appeared to me at different periods as though the powers of the earth and hell had combined against me to prove my overthrow. Yet amidst their dire attempts, I have found the Almighty to be "a friend that sticketh closer than a brother." He never will forsake the soul that leans on him; though he chastens and corrects it, it is for the soul's best interest. "And as a Father pitieth his children, so the Lord pitieth them that fear him."

But some of you have said, "Do not talk so much about religion, the people do not wish to hear you. We know these things, tell us something we do not know." If you know these things, my dear friends, and have performed them, far happier, and more prosperous would you now have been. "He that knoweth the Lord's will and obeyeth it not, shall be beaten with many stripes." Sensible of this, I have regardless of the frowns and scoffs of a guilty world, plead up religion, and the pure principles of morality among you. Religion is the most glorious theme that mortals can converse upon. . . .

Finally my brethren, let us follow after godliness, and the things which make for peace. Cultivate your own minds and morals; real merit will elevate you. Pure religion will burst your fetters. Turn your attention to industry. Strive to please your employers. Lay up what you can. And remember, that in the grave, distinction withers, and the high and low are alike renowned.

But I draw to a conclusion. Long will the kind sympathy of some much loved friend be written on the tablet of my memory, especially those kind individuals who have stood by me like pitying angels, and befriended me when in the midst of difficulty; many blessings rest on them. Gratitude is all the tribute I can offer. A rich reward awaits them.

To my uncoverted friends, one and all, I would say, shortly this frail tenement of mine will be dissolved and lie mouldering in ruins. O, solemn thought! Yet why should I revolt, for it is the glorious hope of a blessed immortality, beyond the grave, that has supported thus far through this vale of tears. Who among you will strive to meet me at the right hand of Christ? For the great day of retribution is fast approaching, and who shall be able to abide his coming? You are forming characters for eternity. As you live so will you die; as death leaves you, so judgment will find you. Then shall we receive the glorious welcome,

"Come ye blessed of my Father, inherit the kingdom prepared for you from before the foundation of the world." Or hear the heart-rending sentence, "Depart ye cursed into everlasting fire prepared for the devil and his angels." When thrice ten thousand years have rolled away, eternity will be but just begun. Your ideas will but just begin to expand. O, eternity, who can unfathom thine end, or comprehend thy beginning.

Dearly beloved, I have made myself contemptible in the eyes of man, that I might win some. But it has been like labor in vain. "Paul may plant, and Apollos water, but God alone giveth the increase."

To my brethren and sisters in the church, I would say, be ye clothed with the breast-plate of righteousness, having your loins girt about with truth, prepared to meet the Bridegroom at his coming; for blessed are those servants that are found watching.

Farewell. In a few short years from now, we shall meet in those upper regions where parting will be no more. There we shall sing and shout, and shout and sing, and make heaven's high arches ring. There we shall range in rich pastures, and partake of those living streams that never dry. O, blissful thought! Hatred and contention shall cease, and we shall join with redeemed millions in ascribing glory and honor, and riches, and power and blessing to the Lamb that was slain, and to him that sitteth upon the throne. Nor eye hath seen, nor ear heard, neither hath it entered into the heart of man to conceive of the joys that are prepared for them that love God. Thus far my life has been almost a life of complete disappointment. God has tried me as by fire. Well was I aware that if I contended boldly for his cause, I must suffer. Yet I chose to suffer affliction with his people, than to enjoy the pleasures of sin for a season. And I believe that the glorious declaration was about to be made applicable to me, that was made to God's ancient covenant people by the prophet. Comfort ye, comfort ye, my people: say unto her that her warfare is accomplished, and that her iniquities are pardoned. I believe that a rich award awaits me, if not in this world, in the world to come. O, blessed reflection. The bitterness of my soul has departed from those who endeavored to discourage and hinder me in my Christian progress; and I can now forgive my enemies, bless those who have hated me, and cheerfully pray for those who have despitefully used and persecuted me.

Fare you well, farewell.

Kate Richards O'Hare
Gives the Farewell Address of a Socialist

*"I would not, if I could, have one day different;
one hour unlived; one deed undone; one word
unspoken."*

On July 17, 1917, in Bowman, North Dakota, Kate Richards O'Hare (1876–1948) delivered a lecture she had given more than 130 times. "When I see the downy face of a boy upturned on the battlefield, I see not only the young life wasted, but I see back of that boy the mother who gave him life," she said. The socialist O'Hare vehemently opposed U.S. participation in World War I and traveled the country, assailing the bloodshed from a wife and mother's viewpoint.

When a newspaper report quoted her as saying "that the women of the United States were nothing more or less than brood sows, to raise children to get into the army and be made into fertilizer," a statement she denied, O'Hare was charged with interfering in recruitment, found guilty of sedition under the Espionage Act, and sentenced to five years in prison.

This is the conclusion of O'Hare's farewell address to freedom, delivered in several cities throughout New York in mid-April 1919, a few weeks before she entered the Missouri State Penitentiary. Here, the woman called a "premier barnstorming orator," "second only in popularity to Eugene Debs," is solemn but resolute. Socialist suppression will only lead to "blind, insane, unintelligently directed revolution," she says, and the consequences are streets running "red with the blood spilled in mad revolt."

President Wilson commuted O'Hare's sentence in 1920, and Calvin Coolidge later granted her a full pardon.

F riends! I know and you know, if you have the moral courage to face the facts, that we are on the verge of social revolution. A social revolution that is coming, not because Socialists have preached the gospel of industrial democracy, but because you have turned a deaf ear to it. The streets of this city, and of every other city may run red with the blood spilled in mad revolt—in wild, unrestrained and insane revolution, before the snow falls again—unless there is more breadth of vision, more real statesmanship displayed by our elected officials than has yet been displayed.

And that red revolution will not be stayed by a Supreme Court decision that sends a thousand Socialists to prison by sustaining the "espionage" act. That decision of the United States Supreme Court handed down on the third day of March, 1919, may be but another Dred Scott decision, that decides nothing but the sublime stupidity of the ruling class. Judge Taney and his associates, by that memorable decision in 1857, sent one poor, humble negro back to slavery, but he also sent one million of the pick and flower of American manhood to death on the battlefields of the Civil War, and he sent three million negroes to final freedom.

That red revolution that threatens will not be stayed by passing laws making it a crime to display a red flag. Revolution can come under a pink flag, or a green one, or a blue, or under the Stars and Stripes, or under no flag at all. The want of a biscuit, a beefsteak and a job has caused more revolutions than all the flags that ever waved, and when red revolution comes in this country, it will not be because of the bitter want for bread, meat, labor and love.

Comrades, I am closing now. This may be the last message that I shall ever give you, for in a few short days I, too, will be one of the political prisoners shut behind steel bars.

For myself I have no regrets, and only a deep sense of humility and thankfulness if I may be counted worthy to take my place at the very bottom of that illustrious list of those who have died for the love of their fellow men.

Looking back over twenty years, I am content. I gave to the service of the working class all that I had and all that I was, and no one can do more. I gave my girlhood, my young woman-hood, my wifehood and my motherhood. I have taken babies unborn into the thick of the class war; I have served in the trenches with a nursing baby at my breast; I leave my children now without my care and protection, but I know that I have only done my duty.

I would not, if I could, have one day different; one hour unlived, one deed undone; one word unspoken. I have nothing to regret, nothing to retract, nothing for which to apologize. I am willing to leave my life as I have lived it; and let the future judge between me and my judges.

I want you to know that I am calm, serene and unafraid, and face my ordeal without hate in my heart and without fear for the future. Nothing that I may find behind prison walls can injure me. I can and will rise above it all. And I will not be idle there; my work will not end; there is a bigger and more urgent work for me to do in prison than I ever found outside. I have tried to serve the workers because I felt they needed service, but the thousands of helpless victims of our stupid, outworn penal system need me more. If there is any institution in our social organism which needs the light of intelligent study, rational understanding and sane revolution, it is our criminal laws; their administration and systems of punishment.

When I go to prison, I leave four children outside: a boy of fifteen, a girl of twelve, and twins, boys ten years of age.

And to my children, I know no one can take a mother's place, but they, too, come of good fighting stock, and they will face the loss of their mother with courage worthy of their ancestry. When they are old enough to understand, they will rather have had a mother inside prison walls true to her ideals and principles, than outside, a craven coward who dared not protest when our rights were wrested from us and when grievous wrongs were thrust upon us.

It is not my fate or the fate of my children that I tremble for, it is the fate of my country. It is not a prison cell that I dread, but blind, insane, unintelligently directed revolution. It is not the nightmare of gray stone walls that fills my dreams, but the picture of gutters of our cities running red with the blood of our people.

Princess Diana
Seeks a More Private Life

*"... I will be reducing the extent of the public
life I have led so far."*

The ultimate irony, Earl Charles Spencer said of his sister, was that "a girl given the name of the ancient goddess of hunting was, in the end, the most hunted person of the modern age." The third and youngest daughter of Viscount Althorp, Diana, Princess of Wales (1961–1997) became a global celebrity at age twenty, when she married Prince Charles, heir to the British throne. Nearly 700 million people watched the televised storybook wedding, held at St. Paul's Cathedral in 1981, but by 1996, the union had unraveled, painfully and publicly, in divorce.

On December 3, 1993, one year after the royal couple's separation, Princess Diana announced her withdrawal from public life at a charity event in London. Relentlessly hounded by photographers "the people's princess," revered for her beauty as well as her work on behalf of the homeless, dying, and distressed, was feeling the weight of obsessive media intrusion. The attention had become "hard to bear" and, in this emotional, simply stated appeal, she asks public and press for "time and space."

The press did not yield, however; nearly four years later, in August 1997, the "most photographed woman in the world" lost her life in a car accident in Paris—the crash allegedly triggered by a combination of pursuing paparazzi, high speed, and her driver's insobriety at the wheel. More than two billion people gathered around televisions to watch her funeral, held in Westminster Abbey.

— • —

. . . A year ago, I spoke of my desire to continue with my work unchanged. For the past year I have continued as before. However, life and circumstances alter, and I hope you will forgive me if I use this opportunity to share with you my plans for the future, which now indeed have changed.

When I started public life twelve years ago, I understood that the media might be interested in what I did. I realized then that their attention would inevitably focus on both our private and public lives.

But I was not aware of how overwhelming that attention would become; nor the extent to which it would affect both my public duties and my personal life, in a manner that's been hard to bear.

At the end of this year, when I have completed my diary of official engagements, I will be reducing the extent of the public life I have led so far. Obviously, I attach great importance to my charity work and intend to focus on a smaller range of areas in future.

Over the next few months I will be seeking a more suitable way of combining a meaningful public role with, hopefully, a more private life.

My first priority will continue to be our children, William and Harry, who deserve as much love, care and attention as I am able to give, as well as an appreciation of the tradition into which they were born.

I would like to add that this decision has been reached with

388 | PRINCESS DIANA

the full understanding of The Queen and The Duke of Edinburgh, who have always shown me kindness and support.

I hope you can find it in your hearts to understand and to give me the time and space that has been lacking in recent years.

I couldn't stand here today and make this sort of statement without acknowledging the heartfelt support I've been given by the public in general.

Your kindness and affection have carried me through some of the most difficult periods—and always, your love and care have eased the journey.

I thank you, from the bottom of my heart.

Select Bibliography

Archives

Jane Addams Papers, Library of Congress Manuscript Division, Washington, D.C.

History of Women Collection, Schlesinger Library, Radcliffe, Boston, Mass.

Clare Boothe Luce Papers, Library of Congress Manuscript Division, Washington, D.C.

Eleanor Roosevelt Papers, Franklin D. Roosevelt Library, Hyde Park, N.Y.

Records of the National American Woman Suffrage Association, Library of Congress Rare Book and Special Collections Division, Washington, D.C.

Dorothy Thompson Papers, George Arents Research Library, Syracuse University, Syracuse, N.Y.

Histories and Biographical Reference

Addams, Jane. *The Second Twenty Years at Hull House.* New York: MacMillan, 1930.

Andrews, William L., ed. *Classic American Autobiographies: Mary Rowlandson, Benjamin Franklin, Frederick Douglass, Mark Twain, Zitkala-sä.* New York: Penguin Group, 1992.

Astor, Lady Nancy Langhorne. *My Two Countries.* London: W. Heinemann, 1923.

Blackman, Ann. *Seasons of Her Life: A Biography of Madeleine Korbel Albright.* New York: Scribner, 1998.

Branden, Barbara. *The Passion of Ayn Rand.* Garden City, N.Y.: Doubleday, 1986.

Bradford, Sarah. *Elizabeth: A Biography of Britain's Queen.* New York: Farrar, Straus and Giroux, 1996.

Bush, Barbara. *Barbara Bush: A Memoir.* New York: Scribner's, 1994.

Chisholm, Shirley. *The Good Fight.* New York: Harper & Row, 1973.

Dole Robert, and Elizabeth Dole with Richard Norton Smith. *The Doles: Unlimited Partners.* New York: Simon & Schuster, 1988.

Fields, Bertram. *Royal Blood. Richard III and the Mystery of the Princes.* New York: HarperCollins, 1998.

Fletcher, Sheila. *Maude Royden: A Life.* London: Basil Blackwell, 1989.

Frith, Valerie, ed. *Women and History. Voice of Early Modern England.* Toronto: Coach House Press, 1995.

Goodwin, Doris Kearns. *No Ordinary Time: Franklin and Eleanor Roosevelt.* New York: Simon & Schuster, 1994.

Graham, Katharine. *Personal History.* New York: Knopf, 1997.

Hahn, Emily. *The Soong Sisters.* Garden City, N.Y.: Doubleday, 1941.

Hale, Sarah Josepha Buell, ed. *Woman's Record; or Sketches of All Distinguished Women, from the Creation to A.D. 1868.* New York: Harper & Brothers, 1870.

Ibárruri, Dolores. *They Shall Not Pass: The Autobiography of La Pasionaria.* International Publishers, 1966.

Jordan, Barbara, and Shelby Hearon. *Barbara Jordan: A Self-Portrait.* Garden City, N.Y.: Doubleday, 1979.

Josephson, Hannah. *Jeannette Rankin. First Lady in Congress.* New York: Bobbs-Merrill, 1974.

Kennedy, Patricia Scileppi, and Gloria Hartman O'Shields. *We Shall be Heard: Women Speakers in America.* Dubuque, Iowa: Kendall Hunt, 1983.

Martin, Ralph G. *Golda Meir: The Romantic Years.* New York: Scribners, 1988.

Meir, Golda. *My Life.* London: Weidenfeld and Nicolson, 1975.

Morris, Sylvia Jukes. *Rage for Fame. The Ascent of Clare Boothe Luce.* New York: Random House, 1977.

Neale, J. E. *Elizabeth I and Her Parliaments, 1559–1581.* New York: W. W. Norton, 1958.

———. *Elizabeth I and Her Parliaments, 1584–1601.* New York: W. W. Norton, 1958.

———. *Queen Elizabeth I.* Chicago: Academy Chicago Publishers, 1992.

Painter, Nell Irvin. *Sojourner Truth: A Life, a Symbol.* New York: W. W. Norton, 1996.

Pankhurst, Emmeline. *My Own Story.* New York: Hearst, 1914.

Pantel, Pauline Schmitt, ed. *A History of Women in the West. From Ancient Goddesses to Christian Saints.* Boston: Harvard University Press, 1992.

Partnow, Elaine. *The New Quotable Woman.* New York: Meridian, 1992.

Rand, Ayn. *Philosophy: Who Needs It?* New York: Bobs-Merrill Co., 1982.

Renshon, Stanley A. *High Hopes: The Clinton Presidency and the Politics of Ambition.* New York: New York University Press, 1996.

Sanders, Marion K. *Dorothy Thompson: A Legend in Her Time.* Boston: Houghton Mifflin, 1973.

Scott, Anne Firor, and Andrew MacKay Scott. *One Half the People: The Fight for Woman Suffrage.* Chicago: Unviersity of Illinois Press, 1982.

Sheed, Wilfred. *Clare Boothe Luce: A Life.* New York: E. P. Dutton, 1982.

Stanton, Elizabeth Cady, Susan B. Anthony, et al., eds. *History of Woman Suffrage.* Six volumes, 1881–1922 editions.

Sterling, Dorothy. *Ahead of Her Time: Abby Kelley and the Politics of Antislavery.* New York: W. W. Norton, 1991.

Stern, Sydney Ladensohn. *Gloria Steinem: Her Passions, Politics and Mystique.* Secaucus, N.J.: Birch Lane Press, 1997.

Thatcher, Margaret. *The Downing Street Years.* New York: HarperCollins, 1993.

———. *The Path to Power.* New York: HarperCollins, 1995.

Thomas, Robert David. *With Bloody Footsteps: Mary Baker Eddy's Path to Religious Leadership.* New York: Knopf, 1994.

Wallace, Patricia Ward. *Politics of Conscience: A Biography of Margaret Chase Smith.* Westport, Conn: Praeger, 1995.

Oratory

Campbell, Karlyn Kohrs, ed. *Women Public Speakers in the United States, 1800–1925. A Bio-critical Sourcebook.* Vol. 1 Westport, Conn.: Greenwood Press, 1993. *Women Public Speakers in the United States, 1925–1993. A Bio-critical Sourcebook.* Vol. 2 Westport, Conn.: Greenwood Press, 1994.

Hardwicke, Henry. *History of Oratory and Orators.* New York: Putnam, 1896.

Jamieson, Kathleen Hall. *Eloquence in an Electronic Age.* New York: Oxford University Press, 1988.

Matthews, William. *Oratory and Orators.* Chicago: Griggs, 1879.

O'Connor, Lillian. *Pioneer Women Orators.* New York: Columbia University Press, 1954.

Ringwalt, Ralph Curtis. *Modern American Oratory.* New York: Henry Holt, 1898.

Speech Collections

Copeland, Lewis, ed. *The World's Great Speeches.* Garden City, N.Y.: Garden City Publishing, 1942.

Dubois, Ellen Carol, ed. *The Elizabeth Cady Stanton–Susan B. Anthony Reader. Correspondence, Writings, Speeches. Rev. ed.* Boston, Northeastern University Press, 1992.

Gates, Jr., Henry Louis, and Nellie Y. McKay, eds. *The Norton Anthology of African American Literature.* New York: W. W. Norton, 1997.

Hicks, Frederick C., ed. *Famous Speeches by Eminent American Statesmen.* St. Paul, Minn: West Publishing Co., 1929.

Lerner, Gerda, ed., *Black Women in White America. A Documentary History.* New York: Vintage, 1992.

MacArthur, Brian, ed. *The Penguin Book of Historic Speeches.* London: Penguin, 1995.

———. *The Penguin Book of Twentieth-Century Speeches.* London: Viking, 1992.

Morris, Charles, ed. *The World's Great Orators and Their Orations.* Philadelphia: Winston, 1917.

Peterson, Houston, ed. *A Treasury of the World's Great Speeches.* New York: Simon & Schuster, 1954.

Safire, William, ed. *Lend Me Your Ears: Great Speeches in History.* New York: W. W. Norton, 1992.

Acknowledgments

From the start, I knew this would be an interesting but challenging project. Women have made significant and diverse contributions to oratory, which meant that hundreds of speeches would have to be identified, located, and reviewed. Many friends, archivists, scholars, and contributors helped eased this challenge, and I am especially grateful for their kind assistance.

I owe a special debt to the many women in this book and others who kindly facilitated access to materials and shared both their time and enthusiasm for this project. Among them—Madeleine Albright, Laura Melillo Barnum, Benazir Bhutto, Barbara Bush, Joyce Campbell, David Demarest, Vanna Derosas, Elizabeth Dole, Sean Ferrell, Sheila Fletcher, Katharine Graham, Thomas Hamm, Jeane Kirkpatrick, Chip Knight, Vivian Labaton, Simon Lewis, Diane LeMont, Henry Luce III, Stewart McLaurin, Suzanne McPartland, Leonard Peikoff, Brian Sailer, Evelyn Small, Gloria Steinem, Margaret Thatcher, Barbara Tiplady, Kerry Tymchuk, Anne Wold, Eugene Winnick, and Mark Worthington.

Several institutions and libraries were instrumental to my research. I am particularly indebted to the archivists and research staffs of the Library of Congress, the Hoover Institution, the Smith College Archives, the Schlesinger Library at Radcliffe College, the Franklin D. Roosevelt Library, the International Institute of Social History in Amsterdam, and the Fawcett Library in London.

Finally, my thanks to Andrew Ferguson, Brenda O'Connor, James and Shirley Nix, Ron and Ellen Prater, Shessy Thomas, and many other friends and colleagues, for their advice and encouragement over the long course of this work.

Index

Index entries for speakers are indicated by **bold type.**

Addams, Jane, 87–92
African Americans, 99–105,
    157–59, 287–93, 303–14
Albright, Madeleine,
    329–36
anarchism, 83–86, 204–10
annus horribilis (1992), 93–96
Anthony, Susan Brownell,
    164–66
Astor, Lady Nancy, 254–60

Bhutto, Benazir, 360–64
Boadicea, 11–12
British Empire, 63–66
Britons, 11–12
Bush, Barbara, 324–28
Byzantine Empire, 53–54

celebrity, 386–89
Chisholm, Shirley, 287–93
Christian Science, 339–44
citizenship, 164–66

Civil War, U.S., 19–22
Clinton, Hillary Rodham,
    186–98
coal miners, 124–27
communism, 211–16, 270–75
conscription, 204–10
Conservative party, British,
    282–86

de Cleyre, Voltairine,
    83–86
Democratic party, U.S.,
    294–99
Diana, Princess of Wales,
    386–89
Dickinson, Anna, 19–22
diversity, 324–28
Dole, Elizabeth, 350–59

Eddy, Mary Baker, 339–44
Elizabeth, Queen Consort
    of Edward IV, 367–69

Elizabeth I, Queen of England, 17–18, 55–58, 372–76

Elizabeth II, Queen of England, 63–66, 93–96

emotionalism in politics, 251–53

equal rights, 137–42, 153–56, 157–59, 171–76

Esther, 350–59

Falklands War, 44–49, 67–69

fascism, 33–35

Flynn, Elizabeth Gurley, 211–16

Foster, Abby Kelley, 146–52

free press, 219–25, 238–48

"G.I. Joe and G.I. Jim," 261–69

godliness, 377–81

Goldman, Emma, 204–10

Graham, Katharine, 238–48

Grey, Elizabeth Woodville, 367–69

Grey, Lady Jane, 370–71

Grimké, Angelina, 106–12

Harper, Frances, 113–16

Haymarket Square Riot, 83–86

Hitler, Adolf, 219–25

Holmes, Oliver Wendell, 73–76

Hortensia, 201–3

Howe, Julia Ward, 73–76

Ibárruri, Dolores, 33–35

impeachment, 238–48, 276–81

Independence Day, 59–62

Islam, 360–64

Jones, Mary Harris "Mother," 124–27

Jordan, Barbara, 276–81

Kansas, 77–82

Keller, Helen, 26–32

Kirkpatrick, Jeane, 294–99

Korean War, 36–40, 270–75

labor movement, 124–27

Lease, Mary, 77–82

"Little Princes," 367–69

Lockwood, Belva Ann, 171–76

Luce, Clare Boothe, 226–37, 261–69

McCarthy, Joseph (McCarthyism), 128–33, 211–16

"male element," 160–63

Mary I, Queen of England, 13–16

Meir, Golda, 41–45

militant movement, 177–79

minority voting, 287–93

nationalism, 329–36

Native Americans, 117–23

Nixon, Richard M., 238–48, 276–81

O'Hare, Kate Richards, 382–85

Pankhurst, Emmeline, 23–25, 177–79
Parliament, British, 55–58, 254–60
patriarchy, 303–14
patriotism, 59–62, 87–92
philosophy, 315–23
prejudice, racial, 99–105, 303–14
president's spouse, 324–28
press, 217–48, 386–89
Protestant religion, 370–71

queenship, 372–76

Rand, Ayn, 315–23
Rankin, Jeannette, 180–85
Reagan, Ronald, 294–99
Republican Party, U.S., 261–69, 287–93, 294–99
responsibilities of women, 146–52
Richard III, King of England, 367–69
Roman Empire, 11–12
Roosevelt, Eleanor, 270–75
Roosevelt, Franklin D., 261–69
royal marriage, 13–16, 55–58
Royden, Maude, 345–49

San Francisco Democrats, 294–99
Senate, U.S., 128–33
Seneca Falls Convention (1848), 137–42, 186–98
sensational news, 226–37
Shaw, Anna Howard, 251–53
slavery, 19–22, 106–12, 113–16, 143–45

Smith, Margaret Chase, 128–33
Smith Act, 211–16
Smith College, 303–14
socialism, 26–32, 282–86, 382–85
Soong Ching Ling, 36–40
Spanish Armada, 17–18
Spanish Civil War, 33–35
Stanton, Elizabeth Cady, 137–42, 160–63
Steinem, Gloria, 303–14
Stewart, Maria, 99–105, 377–81
Stone, Lucy, 153–56
suffrage movement, 160–63, 164–66, 167–70, 177–79, 180–85, 251–53, 345–49
Sun Yatsen, Madame, 36–40

taxation of women, 201–3
Thatcher, Margaret, 44–49, 67–69, 282–86
Theodora, Empress, 53–54
Thompson, Dorothy, 219–25
Truth, Sojourner, 143–45, 157–59

United Nations (UN), 270–75

voting rights, 160–63, 164–66, 167–70, 177–79, 180–85, 251–53, 345–49

Washington, George, 87–92
Watergate, 238–48, 276–81
Wellesley College, 324–28
Willard, Frances, 167–70

women in politics, 251–53,
254–60
women's rights, 135–98, 303–14,
345–49, 360–64
World War I, 23–25, 26–32,
180–85, 204–10

World War II, 261–69
**Wright, Frances,
59–62**
Wyatt's Rebellion, 13–16

Zitkala-sä, 117–23